WITHDRAWN
UTSA LIBRARIES

Acknowledgments

I would like to acknowledge the following people who were especially helpful to me in the writing of this report: Matt D'Amico, Matthew Armstrong, AICP, V.E. Baker, Frank Bangs, Eric Bergman, Beth Carroll, Douglas Casarella, Barbara Casey, Frances Chandler, Tom Danahy, Lee Einsweiler, AICP, Robert C. Einsweiler, FAICP, Reid Ewing, Grady Gammage, Josh Gammon, Melinda Gulick, Shelley Hamilton, Bruce Hoben, AICP, William Hyatt, Brian James, AICP, Phyllis Jarrell, AICP, Rex E. Jensen, Douglas A. Jorden, Lane Kendig, Jim Lively, AICP, Mila Limson, Bob Martin, Alec McIntosh, Robert McMurry, Stuart Meck, FAICP, Deborah Miness, AICP, Carmen Moran, AICP, Marya Morris, AICP, Carla M. Moynihan, Ehud Mouchly, Steve Ormiston, James A. Paulmann, AICP, Elizabeth Plater-Zyberk, Todd Pokrywa, Peter Pollock, FAICP, Donald Priest, Paul Reitenbach, Brian Richards, George Rosello, Bill Ruska, AICP, Adrienne Schmitz, Keith Schneider, Dave Schreiner, Doug Sharpe, Benjamin J. Siders, Jack Simoneau, AICP, Debra Stark, AICP, Geoff Stern, Nancy Stroud, AICP, Cecily T. Talbert, Jerry Weitz, AICP, Mark White, AICP, Jackie Zalinka, Mario Zavarella.

Special thanks to Dwight Merriam, FAICP, Harold A. Ellis, David L. Callies, AICP, Patricia Allen, and Carol B. Clark, AICP, for writing sidebars that truly enhance the value of this PAS Report. The Merriam article also appears on the CD-ROM that accompanies this report.

I would also like to thank Dean Kent Syverud of the Washington University School of Law for research assistance that helped support this project.

And thank to Douglas J. Casarella, J.D. candidate 2008, Washington University, for his contributions to Chapter 5 of this report, and Joshua Gammon, J.D. candidate, Washington University 2008, for his contributions to Chapter 6.

The CD-ROM that accompanies this report has a separate page of acknowledgments for the materials on it. Nevertheless, I and the editors want to thank here as well those people who helped compile the wealth of material on that CD-ROM. They are:

- Karen Melby, AICP, for her permission to reprint her article from *Planning* concerning the advantages of developing via PUD regulations rather than traditional zoning, citing the 34 PUD handbooks accepted by Sparks, Nevada. As she documents, the Sparks approach has made it possible for development to meet the community's smart growth objectives. We feature Kiley Ranch in the report and on the CD-ROM, a smart growth project with higher-than-usual densities, a regional trail system, and hundreds of high-paying jobs, which will also result in a reduction in vehicle miles traveled throughout the region. We have also included in full their excellent design manual, which provides the guidance for approving the PUD handbooks.

- Gary M. Vogrin of LandDesign, Nashville, Tennessee, for permission to reprint the Jamison Station Pattern Book it developed, and Jamie Grocie, planner for Franklin, Tennessee, for acting as our liaison to gain permission.

- The Sonoran Institute for permission to reprint the executive summary from their fine report on planned unit developments and master-planned communities, *Growing Smarter at the Edge*. The entire report is available on their web site. It is especially helpful as a discussion of problems in planned unit developments in the western states.

- Carey Hayo, AICP, of the Glatting, Jackson firm, not only for providing an excellent set of plans and photos of planned communities they designed, but for providing much help and guidance in the preparation of this report.

- Bob Jacob of the SWA Group for providing the specific plan River Islands at Lathrop and also for his thoughtful advice.

- David Powell for providing the course outline and PowerPoint presentation for his law school course in planned unit development, and for his extensive comments on his own experience in practice with planned unit developments and master-planned communities.

Planned Unit Developments

Daniel R. Mandelker, FAICP

TABLE OF CONTENTS

Acknowledgments i

Chapter 1. Planned Unit Development as a Zoning Concept 1
   Some History 2
   Early Reports and Model Regulations 3
   What PUD Is today 4
   The Changing Market and Policy Environment for PUDs and
      Master-Planned Communities 5
   New Urbanist and Design Issues 5
   Resource Preservation 6
   Challenges and Changes in the Regulatory Environment 7
   Fitting PUD Into the Surrounding Community 10
   The Role of the Comprehensive Plan 11
   The Advantages of Master-Planned Communities as a
      Development Alternative 11
   How This Report was Done and What it Includes 12
   Conclusion 13

**Chapter 2. A Checklist for Drafting Planned Unit Development and
Master-Planned Community Ordinances** 13
   Development As-Of-Right or by Review? 14
   One Type of PUD or Many? 15
   PUD Categories 18
   Which Ordinance, Which Agency 21
   How Should the Zoning Be Done? 21
   How To Use the Drafting Recommendations in Chapters 3 and 4 25

**Chapter 3. A Review and Approval Process for Planned Unit Developments and
Master-Planned Communities** 27
   Overlay District or New Base District? 28
   Approval of Development Plan at Time of Rezoning 29
   Approval as a Special or Conditional Use 30
   The Zoning Process 30
   Procedures for the Review of Development Plan Applications 40
   Development Agreements 47
   Amendments to Development Plans 50
   Failure To Develop and the Zoning Reverter 52
   Control Following Completion 52
   Subdivision and Resale 53
   Record Keeping 54

Chapter 4. Standards for the Approval of Planned Unit Developments and Master-Planned Communitites 57
    PUD As-of-Right 58
    Purpose Clauses 62
    Definitions 64
    Ownership 65
    Size of Development 65
    Project Approval Standards 66
    Phasing 68
    Adequate Public Facilities 69
    New Urbanist Design Standards and Policies 70
    Infill Development 73
    Jobs/Housing Balance 74
    Traffic Circulation Systems 74
    Connectivity 75
    Internal Traffic Capture 77
    Pedestrian Circulation Systems 78
    Design 79
    Permitted Uses 83
    Master-Planned Communities 85
    Agricultural and Nonurban PUDs 87
    Transfer of Development Rights 88
    Affordable Housing 88
    Density 89
    Site Development, Dimensional, and Bulk Standards 92
    Vested Rights 106

Chapter 5. The Law of Planned Unit Development 109
    Delegation of Legislative Power 110
    Authority To Adopt a PUD Ordinance Under the
        Standard Zoning Enabling Act 110
    Procedures for Regulating PUDs 112
    Judicial Review of Decisions Approving PUDs 113
    Amendments to Development Plans 115

Chapter 6. Planned Unit Development Statutes: A State-By-State Summary 117
    State Summaries of PUD Legislation 118

Partially Annotated List of References 133

CHAPTER 1

Planned Unit Development as a Zoning Concept

As I write, more than 20 percent of all homes in this country are built by the nation's top 10 builders. This is an amazing statistic. It highlights a growing concentration in the home building industry that is changing the shape of land development because large builders build at a large scale. Planned unit developments (PUDs) and master-planned communities now make up the largest share of new development in many suburban areas and contribute to the growing demand for infill development in urban centers. In California alone, one law firm had 204,000 units of housing approved in PUDs and master-planned community projects when interviewed for this report. These trends call for a new look at PUDs and master-planned communities as a zoning strategy.

SOME HISTORY

PUD as a land-use concept began in the 1950s and 1960s. Simply put, a PUD is a development project a municipality considers comprehensively at one time, usually in the zoning process employed to approve a development plan. A PUD proposal will contain a map and the regulations under which the project will be built. PUDs were at first primarily residential. They were a change in style from the standard residential developments common after the Second World War.

This change occurred because the standard subdivision ordinance and the accompanying zoning regulations have serious design flaws when applied to residential land-use projects. Most conventional zoning ordinances do not allow single-family, multifamily, and nonresidential uses in the same zoning district. They also contain site development standards for setbacks, site coverage, and the like that produce dull projects because they apply uniformly throughout each district. Subdivision control deals principally with infrastructure and lot and block layout in new subdivisions. Neither allows the review of a project on a comprehensive basis as an integrated entity, where a jurisdiction can consider its development and design details.

Allowing for effective open space was another problem inherent in standard subdivision ordinances. Building lots at the time subdivision legislation was adopted were small and located in built-up urban areas where parks were provided by the local government. As development moved to the suburbs, lots became bigger, but most of the open space surrounding single-family homes was unusable. Yet there was no way under existing zoning and subdivision regulations to link the approval of new residential development with common open space that would provide recreational and other amenities for project residents.

Developers who had to comply with these zoning and subdivision regulations typically built residential projects with a sameness that led to the nickname "cookie-cutter" development. Residential lots were all the same size. The ranch house style was common, leading to what some called "cheesebox on a raft" development in which look-alike ranch homes were built on oversized lots with private open space that received little use. Nothing in the regulations required attention to design. The song by Malvina Reynolds popular at the time caught the idea:

> Little boxes on the hillside
> Little boxes made of ticky-tacky
> Little boxes, little boxes
> Little boxes all the same

The PUD concept was a response to these failings in residential development. It was implemented by a new set of regulations in the zoning ordinance that applied primarily to residential development and required a discretionary project review followed by the approval of a development plan that displaced zoning regulations in residential zones. In its early stages, PUD was intended to provide a comprehensive development review that could overcome the shortcomings of zoning and subdivision regulation, improve project design, and provide for of common open space in return for "clustering" development elsewhere in the project at increased densities. Open space was either privately held and available only to the residents of the PUD or dedicated to the local government. Total project density was not increased. This form of PUD is usually called "cluster" development.

Planned unit cluster development had other attractions for developers. Project costs would be lower because clustering reduces the length of streets and other linear facilities. This hoped-for saving does not always occur, however, because developers claim that savings in development costs are more than offset by the increased cost of complying with PUD regulations.

PUD regulation did mark a change from the way in which land-use regulations had been applied. Instead of zoning regulations that decided what development was allowed as a matter of right, and subdivision regulations limited to measurable requirements such as street widths, PUD regulations allowed municipalities the discretion to decide what kind of development they would approve.

Changes in development style can be threatening to neighbors, and discretionary review can be unfair to developers, but several factors make limited PUD more acceptable to many communities. One was homogeneity in the residential development and demographics at the time. This was a time when a majority of the country lived as nuclear families with an average of 3.37 children. The father worked, and the mother stayed at home. Single-family housing dominated, and styles were similar. PUD ordinances allowed communities to use their discretion in deciding what developments they would accept, but that discretion was limited because any developments they approved would serve the typical family and would likely be built in the familiar development pattern. In addition, PUD regulations that followed the cluster development model were limited to single-family development and did not allow an increase in density.

EARLY REPORTS AND MODEL REGULATIONS

The standard zoning act adopted by most states does not contain statutory authority to regulate PUD. This was a concern. By the mid-1960s, attention turned to the need for statutory authority. The Urban Land Institute published a model statute and held a conference introducing it about that time (Babock and McBride 1965). It was not widely adopted and proved too rigid, though a number of states have enabling legislation for PUD today that enacts a different statutory model.

There also was a need for model regulations, so the American Society of Planning Officials, later to become the American Planning Association, asked me to prepare a report on PUD that contained recommendations for a model ordinance (Mandelker 1966). Several years later APA published another report on PUD based on a questionnaire, national interviews, and a review of PUD regulations that updated my earlier report (So, 1973). The Urban Land Institute then published a report some years later that discussed how PUD was carried out in practice and included a discussion of regulatory problems and issues (Moore and Siskin 1984).

These reports and recommendations generally assumed the typical PUD would be a cluster development limited to single-family development with no increase in project density. Multifamily uses might be permitted marginally, and commercial development could be allowed if accessory and related to the residential uses. The PUDs studied in the ULI report were also small in size. Only a few were larger than 100 acres. Development at this scale does not raise problems at the regional level, such as the impact on highway facilities and the jobs/housing balance. Cluster development could also be approved under the subdivision ordinance, though the reports recommended including PUDs regulations in the zoning ordinance as a rezoning or conditional use if a change in use or density was required.

These reports were limited in the changes they suggested. As proposed in these reports, PUD was only a marginal change to existing land-use regulation and did not substantially modify the regulatory framework. It filled a gap in existing regulations by allowing a comprehensive review of new development that promised new design opportunities while preserving open space. This expectation was clear in ordinance purpose clauses providing

Changes in development style can be threatening to neighbors, and discretionary review can be unfair to developers, but several factors make limited PUD more acceptable to many communities.

that local governments could not approve a PUD unless they found it would provide a better built environment than what could be accomplished under existing regulations. This type of purpose clause is still common.

Though the type of development contemplated under PUD regulation did not differ much from what had been done before, this kind of regulation did change the basis for development because it required PUDs to obtain approval in a discretionary review process. This was a major change. Zoning ordinances allow uses as-of-right, and subdivision ordinances have set standards. This kind of nondiscretionary regulation can be arbitrary, but it is fair if the review standards in the ordinance are fair and fairly applied.

By comparison, a discretionary approval process can provide opportunities for unfair and arbitrary decision making. The PUD review process can become an invitation to essentially standardless negotiation if the ordinance is not written properly. It can also provide opportunities to developers to overreach and obtain excessive concessions or even default on their promises by failing to provide improvements and infrastructure that were promised (Turque 2006). One feature of my early report was a concern that approval standards provide sufficient guidance and that ordinances contain sufficient protections, so that developers could not take unfair advantage. Strict provisions about development phasing, for example, are necessary so that developers do not build a profitable part of a development first and then not provide promised amenities, such as common open space. Controlling the exercise of discretion in planned development regulation is still a major problem.

WHAT PUD IS TODAY

The origins of PUD regulation explain what PUD is today. It has a dual character. As the Urban Land Institute report stated several years ago, PUD is both a physical plan and a legal concept (Moore and Siskin 1984, 5). This definition highlights the difficulty in defining PUD, as it is both a development type and a legal process for approving a development type. This dual character is reflected in a definition of PUD contained in a Eugene, Oregon, General Information sheet:

> A planned unit development (PUD) is a comprehensive development plan intended to provide flexibility in design and building placement, promote attractive and efficient environments that incorporate a variety of uses, densities and dwelling types, provide for economy of shared services and facilities, and preserve natural resources. (Eugene, Oregon, Planning and Development Department, n.d.)

This definition includes both the process and physical design elements of PUD. It notes the opportunity for flexibility in design and building placement, which can occur through the approval process, but also emphasizes elements in physical design that must be included, such as mixed uses, densities, and the preservation of natural resources. The definition does not expressly state that the design of PUDs must be better than what might be obtained through traditional zoning, but it is implied.

One omission is a size requirement. PUDs can range in size from infill housing development on a few acres in a downtown area to a large master-planned community of 50 square miles in outer suburbia. This variety suggests that different kinds of regulation are required for different types of development and that no single approach to PUD regulation can fit all alternatives. Downtown sites, for example, may not have natural resources to preserve. A definition may not be able to catch all of these alternatives.

A PUD that has a variety of mixed uses is usually called a master-planned community when it is built on a large scale. The development of increasing numbers of these communities is one of the most important changes in the PUD concept in recent years, and this increase has significantly changed the way in which communities draft and apply PUD regulations. We have had master-planned communities for some time, of course—large-scale developments often with thousands of homes and divided into neighborhoods with mixed uses, including retail and employment centers. Now, especially in the west, the south, and other growing areas of the country, the master-planned community is becoming the standard method of development. Their larger scale and mix of uses may require different kinds of regulatory treatment in PUD ordinances.

So how should a PUDs be defined, or is a definition necessary? The Eugene definition can be generalized to better emphasize both the process in which PUDs are approved and the type of development contemplated by the regulations:

> A PUD is a development that has been approved in a process that requires the comprehensive review of project design and that can include a variety of project types, including infill developments, housing developments, and mixed-use developments, such as master-planned communities.

Ordinances may need definitions more specific to the types of PUDs that are allowed.

THE CHANGING MARKET AND POLICY ENVIRONMENT FOR PUDS AND MASTER-PLANNED COMMUNITIES

Changes in market demand, development practices, the scale of development, and community expectations have substantially altered the market and policy environment for PUD regulation. These changes need to be considered.

Housing demand, for instance, has called for major changes in the housing products that PUDs and master-planned communities offer. One observer commented several years ago that a mass market in housing no longer exists; rather, it is breaking into niche markets with different housing needs (Halter 1998, 1). This change has occurred because the homebuyer profile has changed, and the stereotypical nuclear family of the past no longer drives the housing market. The nuclear family is a minority, and the number of children on average in each family has decreased by one-third. Employment has shifted from production to service, and time is a growing amenity as many families need dual incomes, and work demands put pressures on family life. Working at home through telecommuting is increasing and requires a different kind of housing that contains a work environment. Developers may also design and build for different housing preferences, featuring "green," "conservation," and other types of development in their projects based on polling efforts before a spade of earth is turned (McCrummen 2006).

Another important influence on PUD and its regulation was the publication in 1998 by APA and the International City/County Management Association of a best-selling influential book, *Best Development Practices* (Ewing and Holder 1998). The book recommended land-use, transportation, housing, and conservation practices now widely used by developers—practices that have found their way into PUD ordinances. *Best Development Practices* did not deal with design issues, but design issues have also become increasingly important. Some of this is just greater attention to good design, but some of it shows the influence of the development model preferred by the new urbanism movement (Arendt 2004).

NEW URBANIST AND DESIGN ISSUES

The current popularity of new urbanist development is evident by the number of books and articles expounding its advantages over develop-

Changes in market demand, development practices, the scale of development, and community expectations have substantially altered the market and policy environment for PUD regulation. These changes need to be considered.

ment produced by conventional zoning. One of its important concepts is a development model of self-contained, self-sufficient communities in which reliance on the automobile is substantially reduced. This objective is achieved by providing internal employment opportunities, improving pedestrian access, and requiring street connectivity to the adjacent grid, eliminating the isolated cul-de-sac that reduces mobility. New urbanism also has specific design standards for homes and buildings that feature front porches and street adjacency, while mandating details all the way down to facade specifics.

New urbanists have not favored PUDs as a means of implementing their community design philosophy, but several PUDs have included the concepts. A town center, mixed uses, street connectivity, and more are featured in The New Town at St. Charles near St. Louis, Missouri.

Used with permission from The New Town at St. Charles

The new urbanist movement attacks traditional zoning as a barrier to the kind of development it would like to see, but it has not favored PUD as a method of implementing its design ideas. It prefers, instead, a detailed "form-based code" that prescribes the new urbanist criteria for development and that applies as-of-right with no need for approval in a review process. Whether a detailed code of this type is desirable is a matter of debate. Some experience with form-based codes shows they can produce unintended and undesirable results (Mitchell 2002). Another option, which some communities have adopted, is to include new urbanist design standards as requirements for the approval of PUD. It is also possible to adopt standards allowing hybrid developments that include both new urbanist and traditional designs (Ewing 2000).

PUD ordinances, like new urbanist codes, contain design requirements intended to avoid look-alike and "cookie-cutter" developments that jurisdictions want to avoid. Anti-monotony requirements that require variations in exterior treatment are one example (Kendig 2004). Comprehensive design standards can also be included that enact general design principles. Some communities have adopted highly sophisticated and detailed design standards in the PUD ordinance that must be applied in development plans (Melby 2005).

RESOURCE PRESERVATION

Demands for natural resource conservation have also influenced the regulation of PUDs. These regulations from the beginning required usable and adequate open space for residents, but the open space required was usually intended for resident activity, with no extensive attention to the preservation of natural resource areas. The publication of Randall Arendt's book, *Conservation Design for Subdivisions* (Arendt 1996), was an influential event that brought conservation concerns more immediately into land development practice. Arendt argued for specific attention to the preservation of natural resources. He showed how a subdivision planned for the total buildout of a site could be redesigned to preserve natural resources, yet keep its density in a cluster design that increased densities outside preserved areas. Arendt took the concept of cluster housing a step further by making natural preservation a dominant priority. Communities have followed his lead in PUD ordinances by enacting natural resource preservation and requirements for developers to follow. They have also adopted conversation design subdivision regulations that require the application of Arendt's principles.

Vicky Ranney

The publication of Randall Arendt's Conservation Design for Subdivisions *in 1996 was an influential event that brought conservation concerns more immediately into land development practice. Arendt argued for specific attention to the preservation of natural resources. He showed how a subdivision planned for the total buildout of a site could be redesigned to preserve natural resources yet keep its density in a cluster design that increased densities outside preserved areas. This is Prairie Crossing, a conservation subdivision PUD, near Chicago.*

CHALLENGES AND CHANGES IN THE REGULATORY ENVIRONMENT

These changes in development practices, and in the variety and character of PUDs, have challenged the regulatory environment in which communities process these developments.

A threshold question is whether the discretionary approval process common to PUDs ordinances is still necessary; that is, if problems exist in the zoning ordinance, why not fix them? If PUD ordinances are intended to produce "better" development and if a community knows what kind of development it prefers, why not draft ordinances that require the "preferred" development and allow that development as-of-right without the need to go through a discretionary approval process? Such an alternative allows up-front agreement on the preferred type of development, and on standards for that development which can then serve as the basis for drafting ordinance standards. Conservation design subdivision ordinances are such an alternative, as are new urbanist codes.

Other critics fault the costs of discretionary review in PUD ordinances, including the cost of delay, the cost of showing compliance with PUD regulations, and the cost of uncertainty created by not knowing when, whether, or how a PUD application will be approved. They argue a zoning ordinance can be written to accommodate the desirable features of PUD without requiring an expensive and time-consuming review process.

Finally, the NIMBY issue often arises; namely, PUDs offering a different style of housing or higher densities sometimes attract community opposition and challenge in a voters' referendum. Process attracts public participation, which is necessary and can be helpful, except that NIMBY opposition often is unjustified, and securing approval over public opposition is difficult. I have heard of difficulties with NIMBY opposition to PUDs everywhere. Allowing PUDs as-of-right avoids this problem.

ORGANIZING SUPPORT FOR THE PLANNED UNIT DEVELOPMENT PROGRAM

By Dwight H. Merrian, FAICP
Robinson & Cole LLP, Hartford, Connecticut

Planned development projects are similar to many others, except they tend to be larger and more complex. These attributes make them targets for opposition. Following just 10 cardinal principles can help win over the opposition and get approvals.

1. **Don't Think of The Opposition as "Opposition," but as Potential Allies to Be Won Over**

    Many developers go into a project approval process believing there will be opposition they must somehow defeat. The reality is that most future opposition can be avoided. The developer and the public advocates supporting the planned development need to start with a positive attitude.

    The effort should began with the objective of having no opposition at the hearing and getting a unanimous decision. The developer must be committed to do everything that is reasonable and not budget-busting or project-killing to satisfy each and every need and desire (no matter how bizarre) of everyone who may have an interest in the project. Some planned development project advocates may say, or think, that such kowtowing to the "opposition" is demeaning or ridiculous, or not required by law, or costs money, or involves extra time, or sets bad precedent for future projects—and most of developers start out saying that, until they experience positive results from addressing the needs of opponents. Meeting the real and perceived needs of the community leads to projects being approved, gets the project into positive cash flow territory, generates local tax revenues more quickly, and earns planned development advocates a reputation as caring people who listen, respond, and accommodate.

2. **Have a Plan of Action and Keep It Close to the Chest**

    First, there must be a plan of action. It may or may not be written, in whole or in part, depending upon the sensitivity of the strategy. However, there must be a plan of some type. Second, the secret details of the plan must remain secret. The plan should not be widely disclosed because it will ultimately leak out. If the plan includes land acquisition and assembly, developers and planners will need to work through one or more layers of business entities to prevent those whose properties are being acquired as part of a larger assembly from leveraging their positions.

    In military security, a person must have the necessary clearance to receive confidential information, but they also must have a "need to know." No one involved in the development team should know more than they need to know to do their job. Those who think they are being helpful by widely distributing memos and other status reports to a large development team are simply opening the floodgates to disclosure.

    All of the players must be known for the plan to be complete. Part of the action plan, from the market survey through land assembly, should be to identify the key players in the community and address how to approach them.

    These key players are important in the process of "grass-tops" organizing, as distinguished from what is the better known technique of "grassroots" organizing. "Grass-tops" organizing is a method of obtaining the support of community leaders, as opposed to the support of the general public found in "grassroots" campaigns. Don't fall into the populist trap of thinking it is necessary to convince the masses. It isn't. You need to convince the influential leaders.

3. **Know the Community's Agenda**

    Armed with the information about who the real powers are in the community, it is then essential to learn more about the community's agenda(s). Much of it will be as expected. Some of it is often unimaginable.

    One of the most straightforward techniques, which can be part of a grassroots organizing campaign, is to do a telephone survey. Another way to find out more about the community's agenda is to conduct one-on-one interviews and focus groups.

    Finding out what personal agendas might exist can be extremely important. In one project, a portion of the development required the construction of a stormwater drainage line on the developer's property in a location that required the removal of a large tree on the developer's property. A woman who owned a house abutting the project expressed a concern for that tree to which she had considerable attachment because she had looked at it for many, many years from her kitchen window. She thought it was "hers." The developer's response to this concern was a simple one: no problem, he offered to construct an additional manhole in the stormwater system and divert the pipe around the tree.

    Was this crazy? Absolutely not. For the cost of a thousand dollars he turned one of the members of the potential opposition (an abutter with statutory standing to appeal) into a stalwart ally who sang his praises throughout the neighborhood during the time the application was pending before the administrative agencies and ultimately was part of the group that supported the project before the legislative body at its final hearing.

4. **Be Willing to Set Aside Perceptions of What Constitutes the Public's Agenda When There Is Better Information**

    One of the leading causes of aircraft crashes during instrument operations is the pilot's refusal to believe the instruments. If there is good information from the telephone surveys, written surveys, focus groups, individual interviews, and so forth, it is essential to set aside biased perceptions of the public's agenda (even though some will claim they know they are right and the survey data must be wrong) and begin following what is really important to the community.

    In one large planned development, the developer was so certain that traffic was going to be the premiere issue that he spent $80,000 on a computer simulation of traffic flows around the facility. The money was not totally wasted because it was an excellent way to present complex information, but it turned out that the public did not care as much about traffic as it did about their personal safety when parking in the proposed structured parking

    With all of the initial discussion of traffic, the proponents had logically pushed the discussion of personal safety down to number five or six in the list of subjects to be presented during the hearings.

(continued)

> **ORGANIZING SUPPORT FOR THE PLANNED UNIT DEVELOPMENT PROGRAM** *(continued)*
>
> With this new information, the presentation for the hearing was reordered, with the safety issue addressed upfront by credible experts. The public's concerns were largely set aside at the outset and the project was approved.
>
> 5. Follow the Guidance of *Getting To Yes* and Make Sure that Trust Is Never an Issue
>
>   One of the practical suggestions of "principled negotiation" as set forth in the important book, *Getting To Yes*, is that we should never make trust an issue in dealing with potential adversaries. When planners and developers start asking the neighbors to trust them, they are generally not going to get the support they need. Instead, tell those who might be adversaries that trust is not an issue, that the proponents are prepared to step up to the plate, reduce to writing, and guarantee by bilateral, enforceable contract exactly what the developer and its successors will do and exactly what is expected of them.
>
> 6. Hire a Public Relations Professional
>
>   Many planners, lawyers, and experienced developers like to feel they know how to put together the right message and communicate it to others. But the fact is most developers and community advocates never go into a major project anymore without a public relations specialist because they have learned so much from them about how to shape their message to win approvals.
>
>   Also, the public relations person can do a better job generally than the planner, developer, or the lawyer in keeping communications flowing to the community. A dedicated website is a must today.
>
> 7. Do Everything You Can to Keep Members of the Community from "Prematurely" Taking a Public Stance against the Project
>
>   Once somebody has "gone public" with their position, it becomes a "face saving" problem to get them to come off that position.
>
>   If you think you are going to lose someone's support, you need to do everything you can to get them to hold off announcing their position until you have had a chance to resolve any problems they may have. Planners and developers should even delay the commencement of a hearing and perhaps withdraw an application to avoid someone of importance going public against the project.
>
>   Doing that (holding off on a hearing or withdrawing) sends a strong message to the influential person that you really care about their position and you want to work with them.
>
> 8. Show You Care
>
>   If you show you really care about the interests of people in the community, they will almost always (but not always) respond favorably. This means returning phone calls promptly, being accessible 24/7, meeting people face-to-face, driving out of your way on the way home from work at night to drop off packages of information, keeping everybody fully informed with all types of documentation as to what you are doing, and so forth.
>
>   No question about it, it's a big job, but in the long run it takes much less time and much less money to take care of the community's concerns in this way. The most successful planned development proponents are the ones who will take their personal time, especially evenings, to go to the community.
>
> 9. Show Gratitude after the Fact
>
>   Project advocates need to look forward and think of the project they may have next year or next decade where they will need the community's support. There is nothing more powerful at a public hearing than to bring an abutting or near neighbor from a prior, controversial project and have them testify about how wonderful you were in addressing the community's concerns and how great the project has been since it was completed. And there is nothing better than having opponents see the success of prior projects first hand.
>
>   Some surveys of the impact of large-scale projects on single-family residential neighborhoods show no adverse impact on property values. Generally, the most powerful opposition groups to projects come to really like their neighbors when the projects are done.
>
>   So when the planned development breaks ground and when it first opens, make sure to hold a ceremonial event and invite everyone, including the toughest opponents, because they ultimately may be advocates later on.
>
> 10. Give When It Makes Economic Sense to Give; Do Not Fight for a Position Because You Know Your Position Is the Right One or the Legal One, But Fight Only for that which Makes Economic Sense
>
>   If the planned development is in a hot residential market that looks like it may be peaking and there will be a million dollars more profit by getting units constructed and marketed this year rather than next year, it makes sense to spend $100,000 or even $500,000 in getting the community satisfied with the project and getting it approved now instead of a year later.
>
>   But sometimes it is necessary to fight fire with fire. The opposition may be created and funded directly or indirectly by market competitors. Sometimes people will simply be out to extort money. If people are not willing to deal honestly about their alleged concerns, you are bound to look behind them and try to find out who is the cause of the opposition. There are grave anti-trust implications of some types of opposition, conducted in certain ways, and you should not be reluctant to discover that activity and take action against the miscreants.
>
>   It is true that the Noerr-Pennington Doctrine protects much of the opposition, even by market competitors, but sometimes people can go too far, and you need to be able to identify those situations and be prepared to take corrective action.
>
> **CONCLUSIONS**
>
> These 10 principles are not magic. The commonality is that it takes thinking about the needs of the opposition and working hard to meet those needs to get the planned development project through the approval process.

Whether as-of-right ordinances can produce good projects without the opportunity for discretionary review is another matter, and other critics argue that discretionary review is still needed to obtain really good project design. It is also true that even ordinances with as-of-right standards require interpretation to decide what they mean and sometimes end in judicial review to determine that meaning. A compromise is to enact detailed standards in a PUD ordinance to provide a development format but still require discretionary review of individual projects. Some communities take this approach, but other critics believe it is too rigid and open-ended standards are preferable.

FITTING PUD INTO THE SURROUNDING COMMUNITY

PUDs, especially larger projects, have an impact on the surrounding community, and can create jobs, housing, and traffic problems. When a PUD is limited in scale, its external impacts are likely to be minimal, especially if it includes only single-family residential development with no increase in density, as in cluster zoning. These developments should not generate substantial additional traffic, should not make new demands on public facilities, such as schools, and should not notably affect the jobs/housing balance. There should be no question of consistency with the plan if a residential PUD is in a neighborhood previously designated by the plan for residential use.

The impact of a PUD is often a source of contention with surrounding residents. When a PUD is limited in scale, however, that impact is likely to be minimal, especially if the PUD includes only single-family residential development with no increase in density, as can be provided for with cluster zoning. There should be no question of consistency with the plan if a residential PUD is in a neighborhood previously designated by the plan for residential use. This is The Glen PUD near Chicago.

Daniel R. Mandelker

All this changes once a PUD does not comply with existing zoning by changing the authorized housing type, increasing densities, or introducing nonresidential uses. Modest density increases and the introduction of limited nonresidential uses may not have a significant effect on traffic congestion, the adequacy of public facilities, or the character of the surrounding area, but major changes in use and density will. The problem is even more serious in undeveloped outlying areas where a developer proposes a large-scale master-planned community.

PUD ordinances can include requirements to take these problems into account. One is a jobs/housing balance requirement that requires an adequate balance of jobs and housing to reduce effects on the community outside the project. Another is a requirement that a PUD must provide an adequate amount of affordable housing so that housing will be available for persons who cannot afford market-rate housing (Weitz 2003). Ordinances can also address the traffic problem by requiring a development to capture internally the traffic it generates. A number of communities have an adequate public facilities requirement for all new development to ensure the development will not occur unless adequate public facilities are available. PUD ordinances can also include their own adequate public facilities requirement.

THE ROLE OF THE COMPREHENSIVE PLAN

The role of the comprehensive plan in the review of PUDs is closely tied to whether they will have impacts on the community at large. They may then have a major effect on growth and development and the adequacy of public facilities, issues considered in the comprehensive plan. Consistency with the comprehensive plan should then be required. Statutory mandates for a comprehensive plan, and statutory requirements that land-use regulations be consistent with a comprehensive plan, are becoming more common. PUDs must be consistent with the plan in states that require it, and consistency can be required by ordinance even with no statutory mandate. Some PUD regulations require projects to be consistent with a comprehensive plan, but often there is little detail or guidance on what consistency means, and the comprehensive plan may not include policies for PUDs.

This latter situation is not a good one. If a community expects to have PUDs and master-planned communities on a major scale, it needs to plan in advance to integrate them into its development and public facility policies. This can be done by providing a development framework that shows where they should be located and how the necessary public facilities and services will be supplied. The plan can also provide essential design policies, such as a design policy for project development that will ensure the development of communities that implement the plan. Densities, the mix of uses, and other design elements that will shape the character of PUDs can be further identified. The PUD ordinance can then implement the plan with more detailed standards and requirements and can require consistency with the plan.

THE ADVANTAGES OF MASTER-PLANNED COMMUNITIES AS A DEVELOPMENT ALTERNATIVE

Master-planned communities raise smart growth questions. Though smart growth proponents support PUDs as infill in urban centers, they oppose sprawl development at the urban edge, and some consider the master-planned community an unsuitable form of urban sprawl. This objection needs consideration because master-planned communities have many advantages as a development alternative that regulations can support to obtain a more desirable living environment.

One problem with this argument is that infill development in urban centers cannot meet all anticipated development needs; in other words, master-planned communities are needed as development alternative (Priest 2002). And development at the edge will not create urban sprawl if growth management programs limit sprawl through urban growth boundaries and the careful placement of self-contained satellite communities. In this kind of development framework, the scale of master-planned communities provides good opportunities to achieve hoped-for planning objectives. As Donald Priest points out:

> The large scale of sites to be developed gives development planners great flexibility in arranging land uses. This greatly enhances the opportunities to establish compatibility between the needs of man and nature. This is a major advantage, considering the planning constraints that apply to small-scale projects. Planning at a large scale necessitates evaluation of natural systems and environmental impacts at a large scale. It also leads to the evaluation of more alternative development possibilities. Indeed, the assessment of the suitability of land for development is the starting point for planning large-scale projects. These actions provide the basis for plans that ensure that the communities will represent the best expressions of the principles of sustainable development. (Priest 2002, 12)

The scale of master-planned communities provides good opportunities to achieve hoped-for planning objectives.

Priest also argues that large-scale development provides better opportunities to protect natural resources because environmental protection and conservation measures are more easily carried out in large-scale developments. They also have the necessary scale to:

- provide mixed uses and a variety of housing types;
- create a jobs/housing balance;
- reduce trip lengths;
- use infrastructure and transportation facilities efficiently and responsibly; and
- respond to consumer preferences in housing.

These comments underscore the importance of scale in regulating PUDs, and the need to have more than one PUD option when development at dramatically different scales is expected. They also provide a different perspective on whether there should be a minimum size for PUDs. The issue is not whether a minimum size is necessary, but, rather, a community should mandate different minimum sizes for different kinds of PUDs if size is an issue.

HOW THIS REPORT WAS DONE AND WHAT IT INCLUDES

The purpose of this report is to provide recommendations on how PUD ordinances can be drafted and to review the case law and state statutes that authorize the regulation of PUD as a development technique. There is no all-purpose model of PUD regulation. Communities will need to make choices about which review process to use and which substantive standards should apply. This report recommends a number of alternatives for PUD regulation that communities can consider.

In preparing this report, I did a literature search on PUDs as well as telephone and on-site interviews with planners, developers, and local government officials in different parts of the country. I also interviewed planning consultants who have a wide national experience in writing and implementing PUD ordinances. Typical PUD ordinances, graphics, and other materials were collected, and ordinances were extensively searched on the web.

Chapter 2 provides an overview of the issues a community must consider when it decides to adopt a PUD ordinance. Chapter 3 provides recommendations on process, and Chapter 4 provides recommendations on substantive standards. Chapter 5 discusses the case law. Chapter 6 reviews statutory authority. A CD-ROM accompanying this PAS report includes graphic material, such as maps and photographs, development plans and agreements, articles, statutory materials, and electronic files of Chapters 4 and 5 to facilitate the extraction of regulatory language that communities may find suitable for use in their PUD standards. As always, consult with your local land-use attorney to make certain that the language complies with all applicable law in your state and local jurisdiction.

CONCLUSION

PUD has clearly changed from a modest attempt to provide flexibility, better design, and open space in residential development to a major land-use program that can create developments for both small-scale infill spaces and large master-planned communities on the urban fringe. Its content has also changed to place new emphasis on design, natural resource preservation, social objectives, and the implementation of land development policies included in comprehensive plans. It is an exciting change in the way we use our land that requires careful analysis and attention.

CHAPTER 2

A Checklist for Drafting Planned Unit Development and Master-Planned Community Ordinances

Any community considering an ordinance to regulate PUDs or master-planned communities needs to determine what kind of ordinance should be adopted or whether the community wants PUDs at all. Chapter 1 provided an overview on where PUD and master planned community regulations are today, and the different types of development for which a PUD ordinance may be needed. This chapter provides a checklist of issues communities should consider when deciding whether to include provisions for PUD or master planned communities in their land-use regulations. The chapter uses the term PUD throughout, but its guidance applies as well to ordinances that regulate master-planned communities.

DEVELOPMENT AS-OF-RIGHT OR BY REVIEW?

Traditionally, PUDs are authorized only when approved through a review process that requires the submission of development plans and review and approval by the legislative body, planning commission, and administrative staff. As Chapter 1 noted, however, this kind of negotiation process can be disabling. It can be lengthy, taking several years for major developments and imposing delay and financial costs on developers and local governments. Outcomes may be uncertain, and uncertainty makes it difficult for developers to plan and for local governments to implement their planning policies.

Permitting PUD as-of-right has become a popular alternative in many communities. Remember that PUD is both a physical plan and a process. If it is possible to identify and agree on the elements of a PUD in the zoning ordinance, approval should follow without difficulty if ordinance standards are met. PUD as-of-right is especially possible when there is agreement on a development format, such as traditional neighborhood development. PUD as of right is also possible on smaller sites, such as infill sites in downtown areas, where the community can establish design requirements in its land-use regulations. Growth areas where the community has decided on a development pattern, such as growth in dispersed villages, are another example. The conservation design subdivision is another popular development form that has been legislated as an as of right alternative. Some planners recommend PUD approval through a review process only for special situations, such as redevelopment sites where uses differ, for master planned communities where different elements in the project require full scale review, or for special kinds of topography. This report contains examples of ordinances that authorize as-of-right developments that incorporate PUD principles.

Permitting PUD as-of-right has become a popular alternative in many communities. If it is possible to identify and agree on the elements of a PUD in the zoning ordinance, approval should follow without difficulty if ordinance standards are met. PUD as-of-right, for instance, should be possible on smaller sites, such as infill sites like this one, because the community can establish design requirements in its land-use regulations for the area. This is The Boulevard development in St. Louis, Missouri.

In a sense, authorizing as-of-right PUD means "fixing" the zoning ordinance, as some critics have recommended. This alternative is possible when the community agrees about the project elements it wants. It may not be possible in a development environment in which different kinds of development are anticipated at different locations. Nor is it workable when the community wants to retain some form of discretionary review. Providing a fixed development format in the ordinance may avoid negotiation and bargaining over project approvals, but it also prevents flexibility in fitting project design to each development environment. It may also lead to unintended design outcomes, as has happened with some new urbanist ordinances, or may turn out not to be marketable in a changing market environment. An alternative is a mixture, as some communities have done, in which the ordinance contains both discretionary and as of right forms of PUD. Some communities have also adopted hybrid ordinances in which development standards are spelled out clearly, but administrative review is still required. This is a useful alternative if the standards adopted do not bind too tightly

ONE TYPE OF PUD OR MANY?

This discussion suggests that adoption of a single development option for all types of PUD may not be possible. Many communities, especially larger communities with substantial and different development areas, have adopted more than one PUD ordinance. One ordinance might allow residential cluster housing, while another might allow mixed use development or a master planned community. Some PUDs may be allowed as of right, and some may require discretionary review. What types of development will be allowed will depend on the community's planning policies and what kind of development it wants built.

The Detail Issue: Short Form vs. Long Form

A key element in the regulation of PUDs everywhere is the tension between providing detail and authorizing discretion. Should an ordinance confine the decision maker by providing detailed guidance, or should it provide general directions that allow the exercise of a considerable amount of administrative discretion? This problem is most acute in defining the standards that PUDs must meet. Design standards, for example, can be highly detailed or prescriptive, or they can simply provide a general directive. A detailed standard would specify what facades should look like. A general standard might just require housing styles that "are compatible with the old town style" of the community with illustrations of styles that would be considered "compatible." Provisions for procedural requirements are more standardized, but even here choices exist. A provision for a concept plan can simply require a statement of "the objectives and purposes" of the development and the location and type of densities and uses, or it can require more detailed information about the project so the developer understands what must be submitted and what will be reviewed.

There is a trust issue in the drafting of PUD ordinances. Providing discretion to approve development plans with limited detail in the ordinance assumes a trust that the ordinance is specific enough to govern the decision making process, and that local governments will administer the ordinance in a fair manner. Local governments can take advantage of a broadly written ordinance by attempting to make excessive demands on developers or by denying applications for approval arbitrarily.

There is also a trust issue in how PUDs are approved. If a local government approves a PUD based on a sketch or concept plan that does not include all of the development details, it must trust the developer to carry out the

In a sense, authorizing as-of-right PUD means "fixing" the zoning ordinance, as some critics have recommended. This alternative is possible when the community agrees about the project elements it wants.

project as intended. It must also trust the developer to provide promised facilities and infrastructure, a problem only partially remedied by insisting on bonds and sureties. Experience with developers who have defaulted on their original intentions has led many communities to adopt detailed approval standards and to insist on detailed plans as the basis for approval. The conditional zoning technique used in some communities reflects this insistence on certainty.

Figure 2-1. The concept plan for the Kiley Ranch commercial portion of the development in Sparks, Nevada.

For all these reasons, PUD ordinances must walk a fine line between specifying in detail the kind of project that is acceptable, and giving developers an opportunity under more generalized guidance to provide a good development product. This tension has always been present and is difficult to resolve. The assumption in the early ordinances was that the ordinance would be strict on some issues, such as detailing open space requirements, but more open on other issues, such as site development, because changes in use and density were not allowed. The early ordinances were thus more concerned with infrastructure issues and less concerned with design issues that determine what kind of development will be produced. New influences on what is expected in project development have encouraged communities to adopt ordinances more concerned with project design and character.

There are two extremes in dealing with these drafting tensions. At one extreme, a particular development format, such as the new urbanism format, can be adopted in the PUD ordinance as the standard for approving individual PUDs in a review process. This is the hybrid compromise with the as of right option discussed earlier. It provides detailed development standards but still requires discretionary review and an opportunity to apply these standards on a project-by-project basis.

At the other extreme, the ordinance can adopt generalized approval standards that leave considerable discretion to the approving agency. This type of standard is very common. On the design issue, for example, it may require the PUD to have a "better" design than what would be possible by complying with the zoning ordinance, or that the PUD be "compatible" with adjacent areas, or simply that the PUD must have "good" or "innovative" project design. These standards leave considerable room for interpretation. Most, though not all, courts would probably accept them, but they can make the review process an open ended invitation to bargaining and negotiation. More precision is possible if the community can include examples from the community or elsewhere that illustrate good design, though PUD ordinances seldom do this.

An intermediate approach goes beyond generalized standards but does not enact a detailed development format. New urbanism standards, for example, might specify facade and street treatment in detail. An intermediate standard would not do this but would contain a directive standard that can be applied in different ways. It might contain a connectivity standard, for example, specifying how many access points the project might have, but it would not specify how they should be provided. An ordinance could also deal with traffic problems by including an internal capture of traffic requirement but not specify how this is to be carried out. A jobs/housing balance requirement could establish a jobs/housing ratio but not detail how that ratio should be achieved. Generalized design guidelines can be provided without specifying design elements in detail, such as a requirement for a gridiron development pattern of lots and blocks.

When regulating PUD, some communities adopt a short form ordinance with minimal standards that require a substantial exercise of discretion in their application. Other ordinances are substantially longer and more detailed. Which alternative to choose is a matter of preference, though judicial rules about delegation of power may require detailed regulation in some states.

PUD ordinances must walk a fine line between specifying in detail the kind of project that is acceptable, and giving developers an opportunity under more generalized guidance to provide a good development product.

The Detail Issue, Part 2: Entitlements and the Timing of Plan Approval

Resolving the detail issue also requires important decisions about the content, timing, and specificity of development plans and their approval. This issue is linked to what is usually called the "entitlement" question. When does a developer obtain an entitlement to development allowing it to proceed without concern about future changes or modifications that the community might make? This vested rights issue is considered in Chapter 4.

The first issue is to decide what kind of plans the developer must submit and when. My 1966 report suggested the preparation and approval of a concept (or sketch) plan as the first stage in the review process. This plan is sometimes called a "bubble" plan because it contains identified areas of the project where densities and development types are indicated in only a general fashion. Once the concept plan is approved, the developer proceeds to the preparation of a preliminary and then a final development plan. These plans are detailed.

The concept plan has many advantages. Principally, it allows the legislative body to approve the major elements of a PUD that require policy decisions and gives staff and the planning commission the responsibility to approve project details in later plans. This is a clear and desirable separation of function. Developers prefer getting concept plan approval because it gives them a legislative endorsement of the essential elements of their development while giving them the flexibility to plan the details later. Especially with large-scale projects that may take many years to complete, they can avoid the expense of detailed plan preparation at the time of application that may produce a plan that becomes dated and unusable as markets change.

Local governments often have good reasons, however, to oppose reliance on concept plans as the basis for project approval. When a project will have a greater density and more intensive uses than are common in the surrounding area, for instance, adjacent neighbors will almost certainly demand more detail in the plans presented for approval so they will know for certain what will be built. The question is whether requiring a detailed development plan as the first plan submitted for approval creates other equally difficult problems, such as a rigidity in plan details that may require change as markets change—changes that may be difficult and expensive. The solution to this problem can perhaps be linked to the type of development proposed. Detailed development plans can probably be submitted initially for developments like intensive infill on a limited scale where the planning and design objectives are clear, and the time frame for development reasonably short. Large-scale developments with a longer build out time and more uncertainties and risk, like master-planned communities, cannot plan in detail in advance with any certainty.

PUD CATEGORIES

If the community decides to adopt a PUD ordinance, the next question is which ordinance should be used, and which agency should be responsible for its administration. The key to answering this question is to develop a list of categories of expected PUDs and to note that each category may require a different type of ordinance and a different type of administration. Usually, the zoning ordinance is the proper place for PUD regulations, except for very limited single-family cluster developments with no density increases, which can be handled through the subdivision ordinance. When the PUD regulations are in the zoning ordinance, however, a problem of coordination with subdivision review may arise. Concurrent review under the subdivision ordinance may not be possible because PUD plans do not usually include the detailed engineering necessary for subdivision review and approval. In communities with unified development ordinances that combine all of their land development ordinances in one package, the selection of an ordinance "home" for PUD regulation is less difficult.

With this in mind, let's look at the various types of PUDs and master-planned communities. One preliminary issue is that PUDs and master-planned communities are not necessarily built only on greenfield sites in suburban or nonurban areas. The redevelopment of inner city areas was one of the reasons why PUD regulation was originally considered, and PUD on infill sites in downtown and other areas is still quite common and included in PUD regulations.

Another initial point is that differentiation may not be necessary if an ordinance adopts an open and flexible set of standards that apply to a wide variety of development types. Cluster development is usually limited to outer suburban areas where it is considered an alternate form of residential development, for example, but the same ordinance can apply in urban areas. Some ordinances adopt a set of standards that apply to all PUDs and then modify them for particular kinds of development, such as infill development, that may need different approval criteria.

PLANNED UNIT DEVELOPMENT REGULATIONS, ST. CHARLES COUNTY, MOSSOUR

By Harold A. Ellis
Associate County Counselor, St. Charles County, Missouri

St. Charles County is a rapidly growing collar county in the St. Louis metropolitan area. Since 1993, the county has operated under a home rule charter adopted pursuant to Missouri's Constitution. That charter grants the county legislative power with respect to planning and zoning "in the part of the County outside incorporated Cities, Towns, and Villages" (St. Charles County Charter Article II, Section 2.529). Under that provision of its charter, the county has adopted a Unified Development Ordinance (UDO) with chapters on the zoning and subdivision of land, and regulating "land disturbance" activities to control sediment and erosion at sites under development (Ordinances of St. Charles County, Missouri, Chapters 405, 410, and 412).

St. Charles County's zoning regulations have long included provisions that authorize "planned districts" or—more recently—"planned unit development overlay districts" or "PUDs" (see the UDO, Sections 405.185 through 405.240). Although the county's zoning program does not apply to any development within the county's municipalities, the county has had considerable experience in approving planned districts or PUDs and in monitoring their development. This sidebar explains how the county's current provisions on PUDs operate.

To begin, some preliminarily observations are in order. St. Charles County's PUD regulations contemplate flexible multiuse developments (Section 405.195). But because the county's zoning powers apply only to unincorporated areas, it is not surprising that its PUD regulations are aimed principally at the reservation of land (at least 15 percent) for open space (Sections 405.190, 405.200.C, and 405.210), at the application of housing density bonuses for open space (Section 405.205), and—in order to discourage "strip commercial development"—at the inclusion within residential areas of "neighborhood- oriented" or "community-oriented" "nonresidential uses" (Section 405.190). In fact, most planned districts or PUD districts in St. Charles County have been developments, principally, of detached, single-family residences.

Under St. Charles County's current PUD regulations, an owner or developer cannot develop a PUD unless it is on a tract at least 10 acres in area (Section 405.100.A). But if that requirement is met, an owner or developer may apply to rezone the tract to impose an overlay district upon it (Section 405.220). It is often the case that such applications are joined with applications to change a tract's underlying zoning as well. Such dual applications may be used to yield an applicant's desired mix of uses, which under the county's PUD regulations, depends on a tract's underlying zoning (Section 405.195). More often, however, such dual applications are used to yield a higher overall density because most PUDs in St. Charles County have not been mixed-used developments.

Any application for PUD rezoning must be accompanied by a "concept plan" (Section 405.220.2). The plan is an essential part of any such application—and of any rezoning ordinance passed in response to it. In fact, in Missouri, the approvals of a PUD rezoning and of the plan approved with it constitute a single legislative act and are reviewed accordingly by the courts (*State ex rel. Helujon, Ltd. v. Jefferson County*, 964 S.W.2d 531, 536 (Mo. App. 1998)). Such approvals of plans are emphatically distinguished from administrative subdivision approvals. In effect, the plan or—to use St. Charles County's term—the "concept plan" is an integral part of the county's legislatively approved zoning map.

Once St. Charles County approves a PUD rezoning, the PUD's developer must submit a "preliminary plat and final development plan" for the county's approval (Section 405.223). At this point, the county's process approaches the standard subdivision process—except that it is still conjoined with the review of a developer's "final development plan." In fact, "[t]he preliminary plat and final development plan may be provided in one (1) document" (Section 405.223.A). By contrast, the approval of a "final plat" is uncomplicated by the mixture of legislative plan-review elements of the PUD approval process (Section 405.225).

St. Charles County's process for approval of PUDs, therefore, develops along a continuum that ranges from legislative action to approve PUD rezonings (with their concept plans) to administrative approvals of final plats. This staged process—first adopted in 2005—has met with the development community's approval. Already two projects have been submitted for approval under it.

The author thanks Wayne Anthony, St. Charles County Director of Community Development, and Steve Lauer, St. Charles County Director of Planning and Zoning, for reviewing this material and offering corrections and suggestions for improvements. Mistakes, of course, are mine.

Here is a list of the type of developments that qualify as PUDs or master-planned communities:

1. *Single-family residential density transfer, or cluster, developments with no increase in density.* This type of development tries to cure some of the typical problems of conventional residential subdivisions by providing common open space in return for a clustering of dwelling units on the rest of the property and hopefully better design. This type of development is sometimes called "cluster housing" or "cluster zoning." The total number of dwelling units remains the same, but they are clustered on smaller lots in one area of the project. Though it is possible to have a cluster subdivision on a large tract, they are usually built on small tracts up to 30 to 50 acres, though they can be larger in outlying areas. This type of PUD can be approved administratively in the zoning or subdivision ordinance. It is sometimes limited to suburban or agricultural areas.

2. *Single-family residential development with an increase in density.* This type of PUD goes beyond cluster development by increasing project density. The density increase requires action under the zoning ordinance from the legislative body.

3. *Multifamily residential development with or without single-family residential development, and with or without an increase in density.* A development is mixed use if it combines two residential building types. If the multifamily development is in a single-family zone, a rezoning is usually necessary unless the multifamily development is allowed as a special use. Increases in density will also require legislative action.

4. *Single-use nonresidential development, such as office, commercial, or industrial development.* This type of PUD can be done on a limited site in an already developed community or on a greenfield site.

5. *Nonresidential uses combined with residential uses, either single family, multifamily, or both, with or without a change in density.* This is an expanded mixed-use project that will require legislative approval for use and density changes. It can take the form of a town, village, or employment center that can provide a major development node. It is usually limited in acreage and typically forms a single integrated project. There are two forms of this type of PUD:

    a. *Infill development* on a vacant site or site to be redeveloped in an established community. Transit oriented development located at a transit stop or station is an example of this type of infill development. The development or redevelopment of a downtown center is another example.

    b. *New development* on a greenfield suburban or nonurban site.

6. *Master-planned community.* A master-planned community is a PUD, usually on substantial acreage, that combines employment, office, retail, and entertainment centers with associated self-contained neighborhoods. It can include diverse housing types as well as its own retail, entertainment, and office centers. A master-planned community can also be a new town. There is a scale problem here. Master-planned communities are often required to have a minimum size between 600 and 1,000 acres. Their size and scale require a phased planning and development process.

Many communities have different PUD regulations for different types of PUD. Approval standards and review details vary depending on the type of development. Detailed design standards might be adopted for a limited infill development, for example, while no or very limited design standards need to be adopted for a cluster residential PUD. For larger developments, the community may prefer open-ended standards that allow flexibility in planning.

WHICH ORDINANCE, WHICH AGENCY

This discussion of PUD types suggests roles for different ordinances and different agencies. As noted above, the zoning ordinance is the most appropriate place to locate PUD regulations. One exception is a density transfer option for residential development, which can be located in the subdivision ordinance. Many communities have also adopted uniform development codes that combine all of their land development regulations (Meck 2006). This is especially helpful for PUDs because they require approval under the subdivision code as well as the zoning code if platting is to occur, which will happen in any development where individual lots are sold. This PAS Report includes suggestions for integrating PUD review with subdivision review, but integration is much easier when a uniform development code has been adopted.

Which zoning agency to use also creates problems. Basic legislative decisions on use and density are clearly the responsibility of the legislative body. Decisions about plan details once those decisions are made can be left to the planning commission and planning staff. This process is straightforward, and the ordinance recommendations in this report are based on this division in authority. More difficult questions arise in deciding which other requirements in PUD ordinances need legislative approval. There is not much judicial guidance on this issue as yet, but any element of the PUD that requires a policy decision about the character of the development should probably receive legislative approval. An affordable housing requirement is an example.

There is no place for the zoning board of adjustment in PUD ordinance because its function is to decide questions of interpretation under the ordinance and provide administrative relief, which is vastly different from the review of PUD projects. An exception is the use of the board of adjustment to grant special uses in PUD projects when special uses are authorized, either as part of the underlying zoning ordinance or in the PUD ordinance itself. Consideration of a conditional uses within a PUD may also be appropriate for a residential cluster housing development where an increase in density is not contemplated.

> *Decisions about plan details once those decisions are made can be left to the planning commission and planning staff. This process is straightforward, and the ordinance recommendations in this report are based on this division in authority.*

HOW SHOULD THE ZONING BE DONE?

Communities face a number of questions when deciding how to fit a PUD regulation into their zoning ordinance. Initially, a community needs to realize that PUD regulation is not just another add-on, but a major regulatory program requiring careful analysis and study before being included in a zoning code. The following sections discuss the alternatives that a community should consider.

As-of-Right

One alternative is to provide for PUD as-of-right. The conservation subdivision is one example of an as-of-right PUD. New urbanist traditional neighborhood development is another. Form-based codes can provide a development format for traditional neighborhood development as-of-right, which is what many communities have done. Huntersville, North Carolina, is one of several examples. This is an alternative to using PUD regulation to achieve this kind of development.

Overlay Zone or New Base Zone?

If a community decides to adopt a PUD ordinance that provides for project review followed by a rezoning, it must decide how the zoning should be

Figure 2-2. The Site Plan from the Prairie Crossing Development near Chicago.

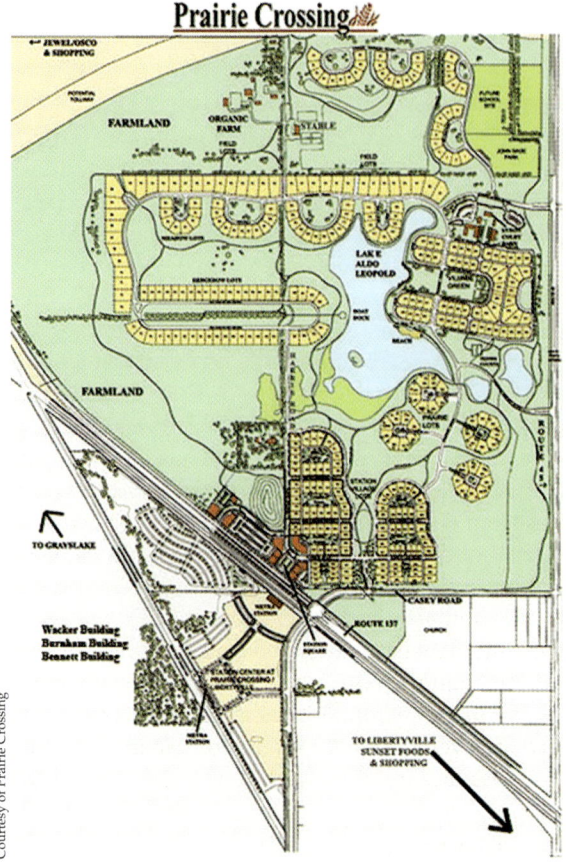

done. It has two choices. It can adopt an ordinance that provides for a PUD overlay zone that supplements the existing, underlying zoning. Alternatively, it can provide for the adoption of a PUD base zone that contains its own set of regulations and displaces the underlying zone. In either case, the decision to adopt the PUD zone is a rezoning decision requiring action by the legislative body. This two step process usually requires a "floating zone" procedure. The community first adopts the PUD zone in the text of the ordinance and then applies the zone to individual tracts on a case by case basis. Another option is to predesignate PUD district zones on the zoning map. It can make the PUD option mandatory or voluntary in these zones if it chooses this option.

Under either alternative, the adoption of the PUD zone is followed by the legislative adoption of a development plan for the PUD, in the form of either a concept plan or a detailed development plan. The ordinance specifies what goes into the plan and the standards under which it is reviewed for approval.

Under some ordinances, the legislative body adopts the development plan at the same time it adopts the rezoning. One advantage of this approach is that plan details are adopted by a legislative rather than an administrative or quasi judicial action that is subject to more demanding judicial review. Legislative actions enjoy a presumption of constitutionality that protects legislative decisions from judicial reversal.

If the community adopts a PUD ordinance as an overlay zone, the effect of the rezoning is that all the regulations in the original zone still apply to the PUD unless modified. Modification can be detailed in the PUD ordinance or authorized on a case by case basis, through exceptions, variances, or the application of customized standards. Often the ordinance will include limitations on what may be changed. It may provide, for example, that use restrictions in the underlying zoning ordinance may not be changed and may limit modifications to site development requirements, such as setbacks and lot sizes.

This kind of overlay ordinance restricts the extent to which a PUD may depart from the requirements contained in the underlying zone. It can give the community and its residents protection against developments that depart too far from existing requirements, but it also substantially limits design and development opportunities. An overlay zone of this type is also cumbersome to administer. Modifications may have to be approved in time consuming procedures with their own requirements that do not match the objectives of the PUD. Numerous modifications may be needed, which can cause delays and unnecessary expense.

If a new base PUD zone is adopted, it displaces the existing zoning for the tract and becomes its own independent zoning district. A notation is then made on the zoning map, and the district is given a designation, such as PUD-1, and additional districts are numbered as they are approved. There are various ways of providing for use, density, and site development requirements in base zones. Many ordinances list the uses allowed, either individually or by indicating which zoning districts apply in the PUD district. Other ordinances provide that uses be determined when the PUD plan is approved under standards provided in the ordinance. The ordinance can also contain site development standards, either as quantified setback, lot size, and other requirements, or as performance standards, such as a "compatibility" requirement for perimeter treatment. The ordinance can also specify the kind of development it contemplates in the purpose clause, such as mixed use development with a town center. An ordinance can be even more specific if it specifies the development format in more detail, such as a new urbanist village center.

ADOPTING PUD ZONES

Drafting Options	Use when
As-of-Right	For established development formats, if local government believes review is unnecessary
By Review	Local government believes discretionary review of project is required
Short-Form Ordinance	Maximum amount of discretion in reviewing applications is wanted and development is not expected to present complex problems
Long-Form Ordinance	Development problems are complex and more than one type of PUD is expected
Concept Plan	Approval of basic elements of PUD by legislative body is desired before detailed plans are drawn
Detailed Development Plan	Approval of project detail is desired as first step in approval process
Legislative Body	Legislative decisions are required on project applications
Planning Commission	Details of project are to be approved in development plans following legislative approval
Board of Zoning Adjustment	PUD is to be approved as conditional use or requires variances or special exceptions
Overlay Zone	Underlying zoning is to control project subject to modifications in the development plan
Base Zone	Planned development zone and plan replace existing zoning
Conditional Zoning	Local government wants detailed conditions governing development

Monitoring and administration are issues with both kinds of districts. Especially as the number of PUD districts increases, methods must be found to record and to make available the development plans and other regulations that apply, and to ensure that compliance occurs as the development progresses.

Conditional Zoning

Some communities use conditional zoning as the technique for approving PUDs; in fact, it is a common practice in some areas of Arizona and California. Under this approach, a development plan is prepared for the project that includes regulatory provisions, and the legislative body adopts the plan at the time of rezoning. In addition, the legislative body adds its own set of stipulations at the time of rezoning that govern the way in which the development will be built. These stipulations can be quite lengthy and detailed, running to 40 or more pages. The difference between approval through conditional zoning and approval through adoption of a development plan is that the stipulations adopted as part of a conditional zoning provide an additional detailed level of regulation to the one contained in the zoning ordinance. If conditional zoning is used, the community will also approve a development plan. The stipulations adopted with the conditional zoning can avoid conflict with the development plan by incorporating the plan as one of the stipulations.

Communities that use the conditional zoning technique seem satisfied with it, and I have not heard of any legal challenges, but it has its problems. One is that detailed specification of project design can create problems during build-out because changes in the stipulations may be necessary if the market changes or if the developer decides on a different development plan. These changes will again require legislative approval and its usual delays and opportunities for opposition.

Another problem is legal. Zoning is a legislative act in most states, and where it is, the legislative body may not do anything that bargains away the legislative power. Opponents of conditional zoning for PUDs can argue it is a bargaining away of the legislative power because the developer agrees to the stipulations in the rezoning ordinance in return for zoning approval. This argument should not hold, however, because no bargaining and no contract between the developer and the municipality really exist. The developer unilaterally agrees to the stipulations, and the municipality makes the decision whether to grant the rezoning. Most courts accept this kind of conditional zoning (Mandelker 2003, Sections 6.62–6.65).

Terminology and court decisions on this issue are mixed and confusing, but the basic distinction is between what is usually called contract zoning, an explicit bargain between a developer and a municipality that is illegal, and conditional zoning, which is zoning in response to developer acceptance of restrictions, a process most courts uphold. In the typical conditional zoning, the developer asks for an upzoning to a more intensive use, such as a commercial use, and records restrictions on the property that limit its use. The legislative body adopts the rezoning once the restrictions are recorded. Conditional zoning for PUDs is similar if it requires the prior recording of easements or other restrictions, such as open space easements. But conditional zoning for PUDs is also different because it includes detailed restrictions governing the development of the property that may not need recording but require developer agreement before the legislative body is willing to adopt the rezoning ordinance. Municipalities considering this rezoning technique for PUDs would be wise to consult their law on conditional zoning before adopting this strategy.

Rezoning With Plan Approval: The Plan as Regulation

In a more typical PUD approval process, the development plan for the PUD is approved at the same time as or after the legislative body approves the rezoning. There is no conditional zoning. What kind of approval process the community provides will depend on what kind of plans it requires. As noted above, the community can employ a three-step process, with a concept or sketch plan followed by a preliminary and final development plan, or a two-step process in which a preliminary and then a final plan is approved. Final plans are approved if they substantially comply with the preliminary plan. If the PUD is built in phases, detailed development plans will be required for each successive phase. Subdivision review may be carried out concurrently with development plan review or separately. Most communities, in fact, adopt a three-step or a two-step approval process.

Specific Plans

A few states, including California and Arizona, have statutory authority for a document known as a specific plan that can be used to provide the development plan for a PUD. Specific plans are intended as subarea plans to implement the community's comprehensive plan, and they can accomplish a number of planning objectives, including the preparation of a development plan for a PUD. The legislative authority is quite general and allows a considerable amount of discretion in the drafting of a specific plan document. This approach to planning for a PUD differs from some other alternatives because it requires the submission of a detailed development plan at the time of the legislative rezoning approval.

The Zoning Format

PUD ordinances are now fairly standardized. Though variations exist, a typical ordinance will have the following elements:

- Purpose clause
- Type or types of PUD authorized
- Zoning procedures
- Standards for approval

The ordinance may contain definitions, which can be helpful but may not be necessary. A definition of what a PUD is may not be necessary, for example. Recall that a PUD is both a physical plan and a process. If the community wants a particular physical plan or type of development, it may be necessary to define what a PUD is. This may not be necessary if the community believes the standards it provides for the approval of a PUD will produce the type of development it wants to see. When there are several types, or "flavors," of PUD, however, the community may want to define what each type of PUD should be like.

HOW TO USE THE DRAFTING RECOMMENDATIONS IN CHAPTERS 3 AND 4

Chapters 3 and 4 contain recommendations for PUD and master-planned community ordinances. Some ordinance provisions, such as those authorizing the development review process and the provision of common open space, have been substantially standardized. As noted above, however, the considerable variety in PUDs makes it impossible to propose a single model ordinance for every kind of development and every kind of purpose. This is especially true for ordinance provisions that provide substantive requirements.

Chapters 3 and 4 contain recommendations for PUD and master-planned community ordinances. . . . The considerable variety in PUDs makes it impossible to propose a single model ordinance for every kind of development and every kind of purpose.

The sections in the following two chapters are therefore arranged by procedural and substantive problems, such as what should be the contents of a concept plan, or what should be the requirements for the approval of a PUD. Alternative drafting recommendations are sometimes presented. The source for recommended ordinance provisions is given when one or more ordinances are used as models. In many cases, the language of the original ordinance has been adapted, and this is indicated.

The length and content of PUD ordinances varies considerably. For this reason, long and short forms for particular problems are often presented. If anything, however, the recommendations err on the side of presenting less, rather than more, detail. The CD ROM accompnaying this PAS Report contains a list of the ordinances consulted in preparing this report, along with the links to the ordinances on the Internet. Ordinances mentioned or referenced in the recommended provisions can thus be consulted for more detail and additional, useful provisions. Other ordinances can easily be searched through their Internet addresses. The ordinances reviewed were ordinances recommended to me as containing good PUD regulations. Additional ordinances were selected at random around the country from a sampling of cities and counties that could be expected to have experience with PUDs or whose ordinance had a good reputation for excellence.

CHAPTER 3

A Review and Approval Process for Planned Unit Developments and Master-Planned Communities

A local government must adopt a process to approve PUDs and master-planned communities. Some states, such as Nevada, have proscribed procedures for PUD approval (see Nevada Revised Statutes, Section 278A.430). Procedures for PUD review and approval are now fairly standardized and resemble procedures for other land-use approvals, such as subdivision approvals. The critical step is the approval of the development plan, which contains a map and text that govern project development. The PUD ordinance contains approval standards the legislative body must apply when it decides whether to approve a development plan. Depending on how the ordinance is written, the development plan can supplement an underlying zoning ordinance, or it can provide an independent set of regulations for the PUD.

Local governments use three different procedures for approving development plans:

- A three-step procedure beginning with the submission and approval of a generalized concept or sketch plan, followed by the successive submission and approval of a detailed preliminary and final development plan. A development plan may be adopted for the entire project, or it may be adopted in phases. The final development plan is simply the confirmation of what was in the preliminary plan.

- A two-step procedure that omits the concept or sketch plan and requires only the approval of a detailed preliminary and final development plan. For phased developments, the approval of a detailed development plan for the entire project is followed by more detailed site plans for each phase.

- The submission of a final development plan without the submission and approval of a preliminary development plan.

This chapter reviews each of the steps in the rezoning process for PUDs and recommends ordinance provisions that can enact them. The approval of a development plan requires decisions by the legislative body and the planning commission. I have attempted to draw the correct line between decisions that are legislative and those that are not, but case law must be checked in each jurisdiction to determine whether the allocation of authority is correct.

Many of the recommended ordinance provisions in this and the next chapter contain bracketed language. This has several functions. It can indicate where the name of the approving body or an applicable section of the ordinance should be inserted. It can include optional language that does not have to be included. It can also provide alternative textual suggestions.

The local government should choose between designating the PUD district as an overlay district with regulations supplementary to the underlying zoning district or as a base district.

OVERLAY DISTRICT OR NEW BASE DISTRICT?

The local government should choose between designating the PUD district as an overlay district with regulations supplementary to the underlying zoning district, or as a new base district displacing the zoning in the underlying district. In either case, the municipality will approve a development plan that contains maps and text with the regulations that apply to the PUD. The second approach is preferable, though overlay zoning may be appropriate if only marginal changes from the underlying zoning regulations are contemplated.

The following provision establishes a PUD district as an overlay district where the provisions of the underlying district apply:

> A PUD district may overlay any base district or contiguous districts. Base district regulations shall apply except to the extent modified by an overlay district. The Official Zoning Map shall identify the area covered by each PUD district. (Adapted from Gilbert, Arizona)

As an alternative, this problem can be handled in the section on permitted land uses. The ordinance can state that the uses, densities, and intensities allowed by the underlying zoning ordinance apply, perhaps authorizing variances from the district regulations and any special uses authorized in the underlying district.

The following provision authorizes the approval of a PUD district as a new base district:

> When approved by the [legislative body], a PUD district shall be a new zoning district that replaces the existing zoning district or districts that apply to the PUD. The development standards and land uses in an approved development plan are the zoning regulations, standards, and land uses for a PUD in the PUD district. The Official Zoning Map shall identify the area covered by each PUD district.

It is important to distinguish between the PUD district, which is a zoning district in the zoning regulations, and the PUD to be built within the zoning district. The ordinance can make it clear that the PUD district is a floating zone first adopted in the text of the ordinance and later established by amendment for each PUD district:

> The PUD district is a floating zone designated in the zoning ordinance and not pre designated on the zoning map. It is designated on the zoning map by the [legislative body's] approval of an application for a PUD district zoning map amendment. (Adapted from Carroll County, Georgia)

APPROVAL OF DEVELOPMENT PLAN AT TIME OF REZONING

In the examples so far, the approval of a development plan for a PUD occurs following the adoption of a PUD district. A community may prefer to require the approval of a development plan at the same time it approves the PUD district (i.e., the time it rezones to accommodate the PUD) so it will know at that time what kind of development it has allowed. The following provision illustrates this alternative:

> The [legislative body] shall review and approve the development plan for the PUD concurrently with its review and approval of the application for a rezoning to a PUD district. A PUD district is an amendment to the zoning map and is controlled by the approved development plan for that district. (Adapted from Apex, North Carolina, and San Antonio, Texas)

In some jurisdictions, a rezoning for a PUD district is accompanied by conditions (or stipulations) adopted by the legislative body. These conditions can be quite extensive. Because they are negotiated on a case by case basis, they are not specified in the ordinance and can cover any issue affecting the PUD. The relationship between the rezoning conditions and the development plan is important. The rezoning conditions can provide that the development plan is incorporated into the rezoning ordinance as a condition. Other rezoning conditions would then supplement the plan or at least not contradict it.

An ordinance can also specify the conditions that a community can include in a rezoning, as in the Gilbert, Arizona, ordinance. It includes a list of 10 conditions the legislative body can impose, though the list is specifically not exclusive. The conditions are:

1. timing and phasing of development;
2. offsite and onsite improvements;
3. development standards;
4. design guidelines;
5. conditions of use;
6. dedication of land for public purposes;
7. granting of utility easements;
8. granting of easements for public use of trails and open space areas;
9. requirements for the establishment of a homeowners' or property owners' association or other mechanism to ensure continued maintenance of commonly owned land and facilities; and
10. reservation of land for future public acquisition.

These conditions are illustrative, and other communities may have other conditions they want to include, such as the preservation of natural resource areas. This approach is advantageous because it provides notice of the type of conditions that may be included but does not specify their content. The

It is important to distinguish between the PUD district, which is a zoning district in the zoning regulations, and the PUD to be built within the zoning district.

inclusion of conditions in the ordinance does not necessarily cure any constitutional problems that may arise, however, such as those that might be presented by land dedications or reservations for public uses.

APPROVAL AS A SPECIAL OR CONDITIONAL USE

Another option for the approval of a PUD is to authorize its approval as a special or conditional use. This is one of the options provided by APA's *Growing Smart*℠ *Legislative Guidebook* (Meck 2002, Section 8–103(12)(b)). Approval as a special or conditional use is practicable, however, only for a PUD on a limited scale that does not require substantial changes in land use and intensities. An example would be a residential cluster-housing PUD that does not require an increase in density or change in use. The board of zoning appeals, which usually approves conditional uses, does not have the authority or expertise to approve large-scale developments that require major planning and land-use decisions.

The following provision authorizes PUD as a special use:

> The [board of zoning appeals] may approve a PUD as a [conditional use] in [any or designated] zoning district[s] that complies with the requirements for [conditional uses or PUDs] in [the zoning or PUD] ordinance.

This provision authorizes either the conditional use requirements in the zoning ordinance or in the PUD ordinance as the requirements that apply to the review and approval of conditional uses. This is possible because zoning enabling acts authorize the local government to provide the criteria under which special uses will be approved.

APPROVAL AS A SUBDIVISION

Approval of a PUD as a subdivision is also possible in limited circumstances in which there is no change in use or density. A cluster residential development is an example, and provisions for the approval of cluster developments as subdivisions are discussed below. The APA *Growing Smart*℠ *Legislative Guidebook* also includes a general provision for the approval of PUDs as subdivisions (Meck 2002, Section 8–103(12)(a)). Coordination with development approval under the terms of the subdivision ordinance is required if PUDs are approved under the zoning ordinance. This is an important issue and is discussed below.

THE ZONING PROCESS

The Preapplication Conference

Many communities begin the PUD review process with a preapplication conference. It can be mandatory or optional. Using a preapplication conference is desirable and standard practice in any land-use procedure. It can be especially helpful in PUD review when a major project is contemplated that requires complex planning and design decisions. PUD ordinances contain a variety of preapplication conference requirements. Some simply require a conference with planning staff, and some are more elaborate and require comments by planning staff the applicant must take into account. An informal meeting with the legislative body may also be required and can be helpful, especially for a master-planned community.

A requirement for a preapplication conference can be brief:

> Pre-submittal Meeting: Prior to submitting a PUD application, the applicant shall meet with the Planning Department to review the zoning classification of the site, review the regulatory ordinances and materials, review the procedures and examine the proposed use and development of the property. The planning staff shall aid and advise the applicant in preparing the application and supportive documents as necessary. (Bloomington, Indiana)

Using a preapplication conference is desirable and standard practice in any land-use procedure. It can be especially helpful in PUD review when a major project is contemplated that requires complex planning and design decisions.

An ordinance can also state the purpose of the conference in more detail:

> (1) The purpose of the Pre-Application Conference shall be to familiarize both the developer and the Planning Board with each other's intentions with respect to the PUD. Although a Pre-Application Conference is not required, this preliminary meeting between the Planning Board and the developer is desirable since it should help clarify many procedural and policy issues.
>
> (2) At the Pre-Application Conference, the Planning Board shall familiarize the developer with the process for obtaining a rezoning for a PUD and explain to him issues that should be considered in planning the project. The developer may discuss his range of options concerning development and inform the Planning Board of his development concept. Any statement made by either the Planning Board or the developer concerning a potential decision on a rezoning application of the final form of the development shall not be legally binding.
>
> (3) The developer shall not be required to present any written or graphic materials at the Pre-Application Conference. The Planning Board shall make available to the developer at this time any forms required for the application. (Adapted from Cambridge, Massachusetts)

The ordinance can also make the preapplication conference mandatory and can require the applicant to submit detailed plans and sketches similar to what would be required for a concept or sketch plan. The Salem, Oregon, ordinance contains this requirement.

Some ordinances require planning staff to make detailed comments on the PUD proposal if they find it unsatisfactory:

> The Department of Planning staff shall provide comments in writing to the applicant stating whether the application meets the criteria contained in the ordinance for forwarding the application for [consideration as a rezoning to a PUD district or consideration of the development plan]. Planning staff shall point out any areas of noncompliance with the PUD ordinance, if any, and include comments from referral agencies. They shall also provide written recommendations to inform and assist the applicant in submitting another application if this is required. (Adapted from So, Mosena, and Bangs (1973), and Weld County, Colorado)

Other ordinances require meetings with neighbors. Involving neighbors and neighborhood organizations is an important and often necessary part of an effort to secure approval of a PUD:

> No application for a rezoning to a PUD district shall be accepted, and no PUD shall be approved by the [legislative body] until a neighborhood work session has been completed pursuant to this section. The applicant shall conduct at least one open meeting with interested individuals residing or owning property, and with any neighborhood organization, within [1,000] feet of the boundaries of the proposed PUD. The purpose of the meeting is to provide information concerning the PUD to adjacent property owners and citizens and to neighborhood organizations [and to make a good faith effort to resolve potential conflicts prior to hearings on the application.] The applicant shall notify all land owners within [1,000] feet of the boundaries of the proposed PUD that an application for the approval of the PUD has been filed. (Adapted from Queen Creek, Arizona)

The language in brackets, which is contained in the Queen Creek ordinance, imposes a good faith duty to resolve differences. This is a substantive requirement that makes neighborhood consultation part of the basis on which a PUD is considered. Failure to consult in good faith could presumably result in a denial of the application.

The Concept or Sketch Plan

Many PUD ordinances authorize or require the submission of a concept, sketch, or outline plan to begin the application review process. This kind of plan is sometimes called a "bubble" plan because it identifies uses and densities in circles, or "bubbles," on the plan map without additional detail. The purpose of requiring a concept plan is to give the legislative body an opportunity to approve the critical elements of a PUD that require legislative approval. It usually is not possible to vest a right to develop at the concept plan stage, however, because the plan does not contain enough detail to allow vesting. A concept plan will be processed like a normal zoning amendment, with reference to the planning commission for comment if this is the locally established procedure. The concept plan is especially useful for large master-planned communities that will be built in phases over a substantial period of time.

Figure 3-1. The Kiley Ranch Concept Plan.

A provision for a concept plan can be general:

> The applicant shall submit a preliminary concept plan to convey the overall concept and to guide and coordinate any phased development. (Adapted from Carroll County, Georgia)

The following provision requires a more detailed concept plan:

Concept Plan

An applicant who submits an application for a rezoning to a PUD district shall also submit a concept plan that includes:

(1) An accurate map of the project area including its relationship to surrounding areas, existing topography and key features.

(2) A plan of development and presentation of the development concept. The plan shall at least contain sufficient detail to make possible the evaluation of approval criteria contained in Section [xxx] of this ordinance. The plan of development and presentation shall include the following:

   (a) The planning objectives and the character of the development to be achieved through the PUD, and the approximate phases in which the development will be built, if any.

   (b) The approximate location of distinct development areas, such as neighborhoods, village and town centers, and mixed use development [and information necessary to calculate the jobs/housing balance].

   (c) The number and type of dwelling units proposed, including [affordable housing and] the density and intensity calculations required by this ordinance, and the approximate location, arrangement, and intensity of use and bulk of any nonresidential buildings and structures and their parking facilities.

   (d) The approximate proposed traffic and pedestrian circulation plan, including major streets, pedestrian and bike paths, and trails.

   (e) The approximate location of any proposed major common open space and any proposed community and public facilities, and any floodplain, wetlands or other natural resource areas designated for preservation.

   (f) A statement explaining how the proposed PUD complies with the policies and objectives of the comprehensive plan.

   (g) A statement or visual presentation of how the PUD will relate to and be compatible with adjacent and neighboring areas.

(3) Such other information as the planning commission shall require, including any additional information necessary to determine compliance with the standards for the approval of a PUD contained in this ordinance. (Based in part on Madison, Wisconsin)

The term "presentation" is purposely left open and can include text, photos, drawings, and other visual presentations. This concept plan provision is really a checklist. It is drafted broadly enough to include all the elements a PUD is likely to include, but elements that may not be relevant, such as village and town centers, can be omitted. The language in brackets in subparagraphs (2)(a) and (2)(b) can be omitted if these requirements are not included in the ordinance, for example.

This provision most easily applies to PUDs in suburban areas, but it can also apply to infill developments in urban areas. Infill projects include the "distinct development areas" cited in subparagraph (b), for example, and a reference to the "policies and objectives" of the comprehensive plan includes any reference to redevelopment or infill policies that apply.

Approval and Effect of Concept Plan

Provision must also be made for the approval and effect of the concept plan:

(1) The planning commission shall forward a recommendation to the [legislative body] that the concept plan be approved as submitted, approved with modifications, referred for further consideration, or disapproved. Upon receipt of the recommendation of the planning commission, the [legislative body] shall determine whether or not to [adopt a proposed zoning change to establish the proposed PUD district and] approve the concept plan.

Figure 3-2. Concept Plan Application, Rockville, Maryland.

City of Rockville
Dept. of Community Planning & Development Services
Planning Division
111 Maryland Ave. • Rockville, MD 20850-2364 • 240-314-8200
www.rockvillemd.gov

APPLICATION FOR
COMPREHENSIVE PLANNED DEVELOPMENT (CPD) CONCEPT PLAN APPROVAL

PROJECT IDENTIFICATION: _____

Application is hereby made with the Mayor and Council of Rockville for approval of a Comprehensive Planned Development Concept Plan Approval for the property described below:

[Form fields: Property Address (Number, Street & Zip; Subdivision; Lot; Block; Zoning; Tax Account No.; Property Size in square feet); Applicant (First, Last); Property Owner (First, Last); Architect Registration # (Company, Last, First); Engineer/Other Registration # (Company, Last, First); Attorney (Company, Last, First); Gross Floor Area & Site Size (Total Gross Floor Area, Office Gross Floor Area, Retail Gross Floor Area, Hotel Gross Floor Area, Number of Dwelling Units: MF TH SFD, Number of Parking Spaces, Site Size)]

* A letter of authorization from the owner must be submitted if this application is filed by anyone other than the owner.
Description of what this application is for _____

I hereby certify that I have the authority to make this application, that the application is complete and correct and that I have read and understand all procedures for filing this application.

TO BE COMPLETED BY THE PLANNING DIVISION
Application #: _____
Staff Reviewer: _____
Target Planning Commission
Review Date: _____

Signature of Applicant _____
Received by: _____
Date: _____
Total fee: $ _____

City of Rockville, Maryland

(2) Approval of the rezoning and related concept plan shall establish the basic uses, densities and intensities for the PUD in conformity with the plan as approved, which shall be recorded by the Zoning Administrator as an integral component of the PUD district regulations, but the concept plan shall be conditioned upon approval of a final development plan, and shall not make permissible any of the uses, densities or intensities as proposed until a final development plan is submitted and approved for all or a portion of the area covered by the concept plan. (Adapted from Madison, Wisconsin)

This provision includes two alternatives. If the bracketed language is included, the rezoning and concept plan are approved at the same time. If the bracketed language is omitted, a rezoning for a PUD district will have already been done and only the approval of the concept plan will be necessary at this stage. This provision also makes it clear that the concept plan adoption establishes the basic uses, densities, and intensities, but that a final development plan must be approved before the development can go forward.

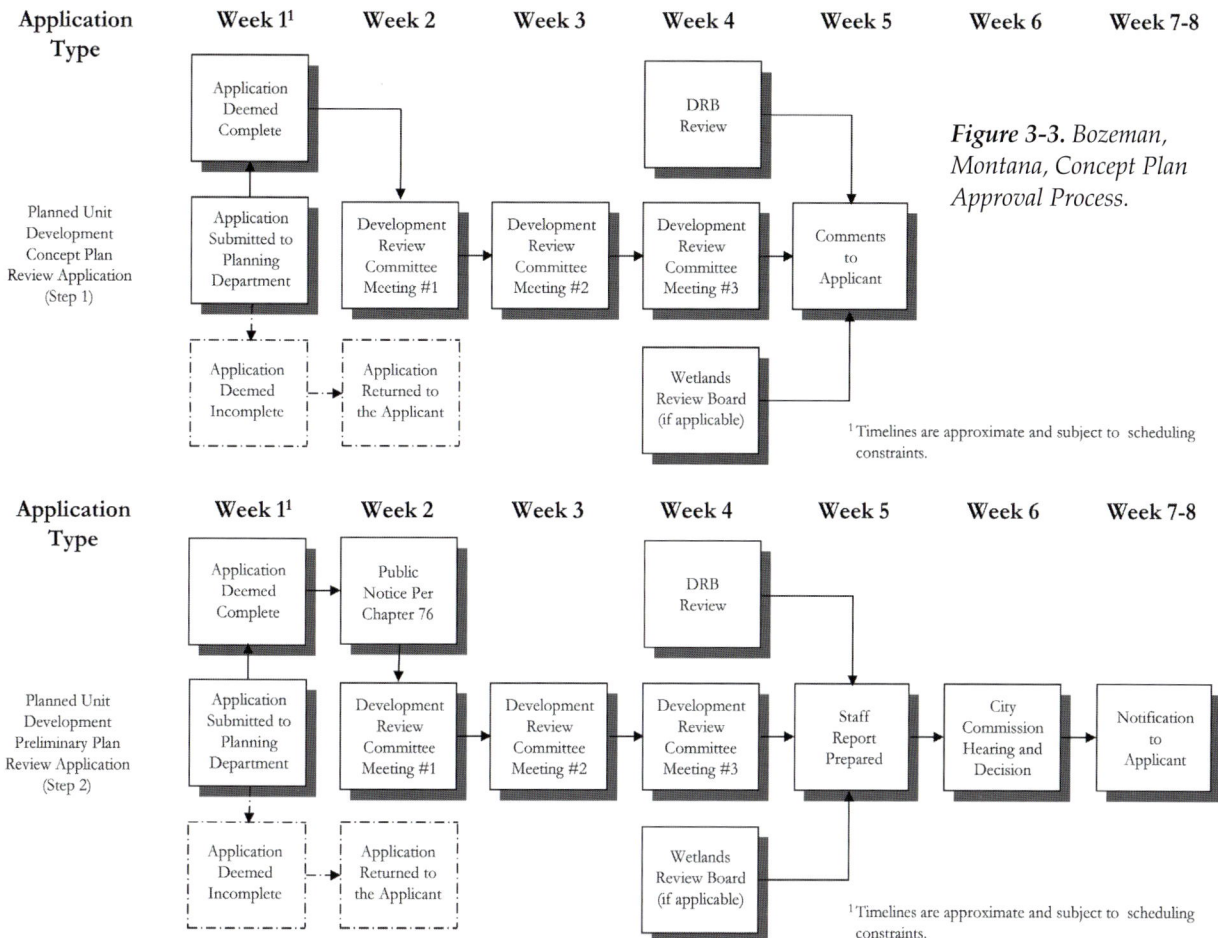

Figure 3-3. Bozeman, Montana, Concept Plan Approval Process.

Source: Bozeman, Montana, Department of Community Development

Preliminary Development Plan

The development plan is a detailed plan of development equivalent to a site plan and must have enough detail to serve as the regulations that apply to the PUD. In some jurisdictions, this is known as a regulating plan. If the PUD district is an overlay district, the jurisdiction must carefully correlate the text and map of the development plan with the provisions of the underlying district. The detail in the development plan must also be specific enough to provide what is known as an "entitlement," which is a vesting of the uses, densities, and other elements of the project in the plan. Vesting can be handled through a development agreement or a vesting statute or ordinance, and is discussed below.

The preliminary development plan is preliminary only in that it is the first step in the approval of a plan for the PUD. If a concept plan has been approved, the planning commission usually has the responsibility of approving the preliminary development plan. If not, the legislative body approves the preliminary development plan and may approve it at the same time it approves the rezoning for the PUD.

The second step is the approval of the final development plan, which the planning commission approves if it conforms substantially to the approved preliminary development plan. This two-step procedure is borrowed from the subdivision ordinance. If the PUD, like a master-planned community, is to be developed in phases, it may be necessary to adopt a development plan for each phase of the development that implements the project development plan in more detail.

The preliminary development plan is a critical document. It must include information on all of the requirements in the PUD ordinance in detail.

Integration with the subdivision ordinance is another critical issue in the review of the preliminary plan. Subdivision approval requires detailed platting and engineering for streets and other public facilities that may not be possible or desirable at the development plan stage, especially when the development will be built in phases. For this reason, most ordinances do not require PUD plans to have this information, and coordination with subdivision approval is necessary.

For all these reasons, the preliminary development plan is a critical document. It must include information on all of the requirements in the PUD ordinance in detail. It must also include information about related requirements from other ordinances, such as a landscaping ordinance if this ordinance is the basis for landscaping in PUDs. Once approved, the preliminary development plan becomes the regulatory plan for the development.

The requirements for preliminary development plans vary considerably. The following provision is written expansively to include all or most of the requirements a PUD ordinance might contain. It repeats some information, such as a statement of objectives, that can be transferred from the concept plan document and that should probably also be included in the final development plan.

Preliminary Development Plan

An applicant shall submit a preliminary development plan for the PUD within [nine] months of the approval of a concept plan. The preliminary development plan shall include:

A. Written Documents.

1. A legal description of the total site proposed for development.

2. The planning objectives and the character of the development to be achieved through the PUD.

3. If the development is to be built in phases, a development schedule indicating (a) the approximate date when construction of the project can be expected to begin; (b) the stages in which the project will be built and the approximate date when construction of each stage can be expected to begin; (c) the anticipated rate of development; (d) the approximate date when the development of each of the stages will be completed; and (e) the area and location open space, community and public facilities, and preserved floodplains, wetlands, and other natural resource areas that will be provided at each stage.

4. Documents, including but not limited to easements and land dedications, for community and public facilities and for the preservation and management of common open spaces and the preservation of floodplains, wetlands, and other natural resources areas.

5. A statement explaining how the PUD complies with the policies and objectives of the comprehensive plan.

Commentary: *Paragraphs 1 and 2 call for elements also included in a concept plan and may not be needed if a concept plan has been approved.*

B. Development Plan and Graphics with Supporting Maps. The development plan and graphics with supporting maps shall show the major details of the proposed PUD and shall include the following information.

1. Existing site conditions including contours at [five] foot intervals.

2. The location and size of floodplains, wetlands, and other natural resources areas, for which preservation measures have been adopted, and the location and size of these and any other areas to be conveyed, dedicated, or reserved for common open spaces, public parks, public parks, recreational areas, school sites, and similar public and semi-public uses.

3. Proposed lot lines.

4. The location, types, and density or intensity of [mixed-use neighborhoods, commercial and other] proposed uses, common open space, and natural resource areas. The plan shall also show the floor area and height of all dwelling units and nonresidential buildings and structures, and architectural drawings and sketches that illustrate the design and character of proposed buildings and structures.

Commentary: The bracketed language in the first sentence of section B.4 can be omitted if the project does not have mixed-use neighborhoods or commercial uses. A requirement for architectural drawings and sketches is necessary if the ordinance contains design standards. As an alternative, the ordinance can require the preliminary development plan to include a design plan. Some communities, such as Sparks, Nevada, have adopted design manuals, which the ordnance can incorporate by reference: "A design plan in compliance with the Design Standards Manual adopted by the [legislative body]." Design issues are discussed below.

5. A traffic circulation system, including arterial, collector, and local streets; off-street parking areas and facilities; service areas; loading areas; and points of access to adjacent public rights-of-way.

6. A pedestrian and bike path circulation system, including trails, and its interrelationship and proposed treatment of points of conflict with the traffic circulation system.

7. A utility system, including sanitary sewers, stormwater sewers, and water, electric, gas and telephone lines, and any facilities required for stormwater treatment.

8. A landscape plan showing the materials to be used and their treatment for private and common open space.

9. Signage and lighting plans.

Commentary: Subsections B.5 through B.9 assume the PUD ordinance contains parking, access, landscaping, signage, and lighting requirements. If the PUD ordinance instead requires compliance with ordinances that have these requirements, language should be substituted requiring compliance with these ordinances. There may also be separate ordinances that have buffering and other requirements. If so, the development plan should show compliance with these ordinances as well and should include any necessary plans to show compliance.

10. Enough information on land areas adjacent to the proposed PUD to show the relationships between the proposed development and adjacent areas, including land uses, zoning classifications, densities and intensities, circulation systems, public facilities, and floodplains, wetlands, and other natural resource areas.

11. The proposed treatment of the perimeter of the PUD, including land-use restrictions, setbacks, landscaping, and other measures, such as screens, fences and walls.

C. Additional Information. Such other information as the planning commission shall require, including any information necessary to determine compliance with the standards for the approval of a PUD contained in this ordinance. (Adapted from Mandelker 1966, and So, Mosena, and Bangs 1973).

The ordinance may include other requirements, such as an affordable housing requirement or a jobs/housing balance requirement, for which information should be included in the preliminary development plan. Other programs may also apply to PUDs, such as a transfer of development rights program for natural resource areas or an adequate public facilities requirement. These may be handled by separate ordinances or may be specified in the PUD ordinance. In either case, the preliminary development plan should contain information about these programs if they apply.

It should be noted that Florida has a state-mandated procedure, including review at the state level, for what are known as developments of regional impact (DRI) (Florida Statutes Annotated, Section 380.06). These are large scale developments, and some PUDs in that state may constitute DRIs. The statute requires plans for DRI review that are as extensive as those required for zoning review, but the DRI plan and review supplement the zoning ordinance, and DRI applications are reviewed under different criteria contained in the state statute.

Master Development Plan Followed by Development Area Plans

The preliminary development plan, once approved, is followed by a final development plan that is approved if it is in substantial compliance with the preliminary development plan. For large developments, such as master planned communities developed in phases, it is necessary to provide for a master development plan followed by more detailed development plans for each stage. This technique substitutes the master development plan for a concept plan and splits project details between the master development plan and the development area plans. They are approved if they are in substantial compliance with the master development plan. The following provisions are adapted from the Santa Clara, California, ordinance and provided the basis for the award-winning Rivermark planned community:

> **Master Development Plan**
>
> The master development plan shall include the following information:
>
> 1. A master development plan summary providing, in narrative form:
>
>   a. A general description of the proposed development, including a legal description of the property.
>
>   b. Definitions of the land-use designations, including density ranges and product types for residential development shown on the master development plan graphics required by this section.
>
>   c. A table setting the minimum and maximum total dwelling units and nonresidential square footage, and the minimum acreage for common open space, natural resource areas, public uses, and any other planned uses.
>
>   d. A description of residential and mixed-use neighborhoods; commercial, office, and research and development uses; common open space and natural resource areas, public buildings, schools, and other public uses; and any other proposed uses.
>
> 2. Master development plan graphics showing generally:
>
>   a. Land-use designations for each distinct use in the master planned community and in adjacent areas.
>
>   b. A public circulation system, including street classifications and cross-sections, pedestrian paths, and bikeways.
>
>   c. Common open space and natural resource areas.
>
>   d. Public buildings, schools, and other public uses.
>
>   e. A preliminary public infrastructure plan, including drainage, sewerage, water, power, and telecommunication utilities
>
> 3. A map showing the existing topography of the district at [one]-foot intervals.
>
> 4. Design guidelines and development standards. (Adapted from Santa Clara, California)

The ordinance details the project features for which the community provides design guidelines and development standards. It also requires

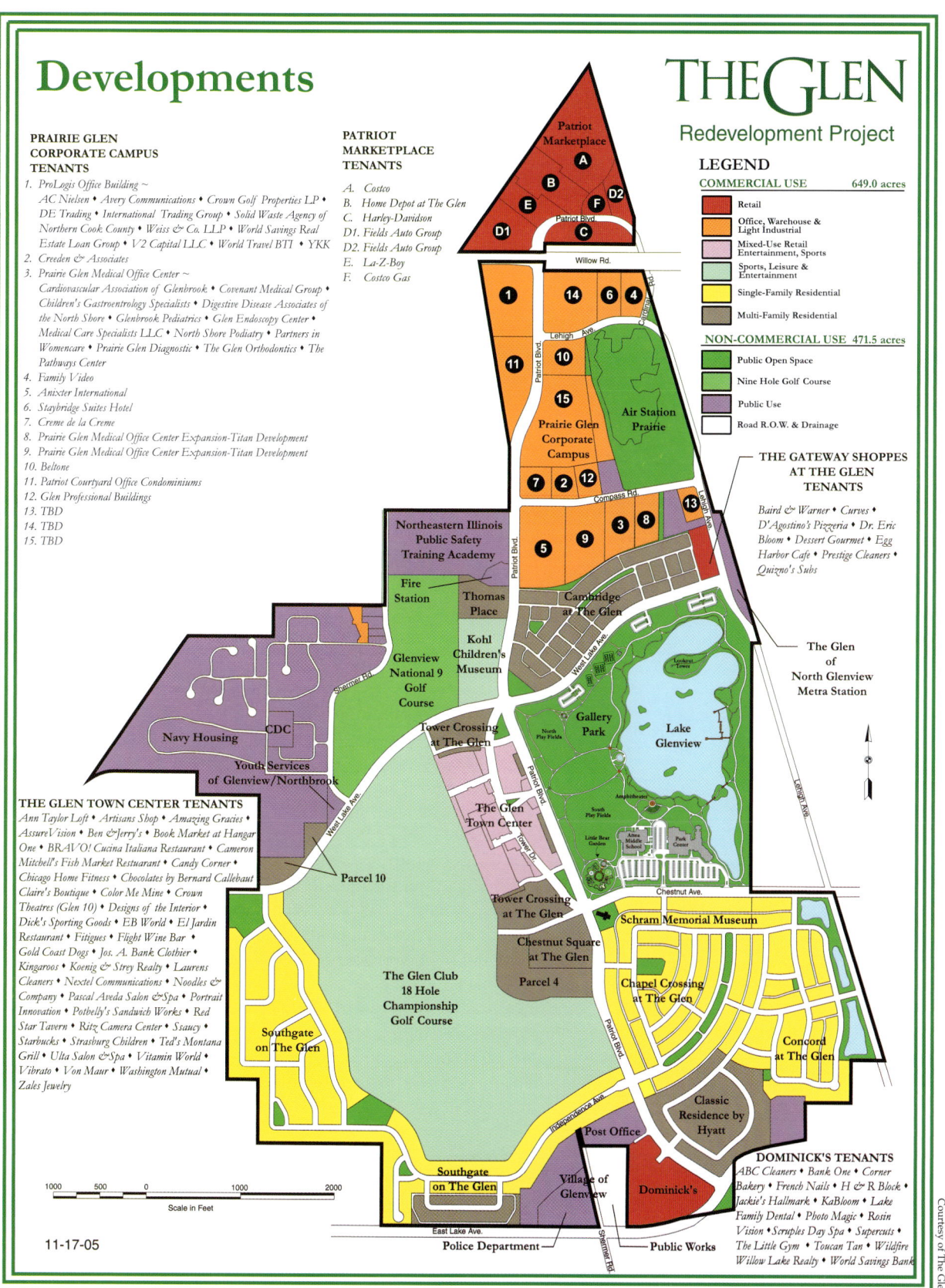

Figure 3-4. Map of the Master Development Plan for The Glen, North Glenview, Illinois.

a financing plan for on-site and off-site infrastructure. Development area plans must be submitted for each phase of the development after the master plan has been approved and must show project features in more detail. The development area plan should provide enough detail to govern the development of the PUD once it is approved:

> **Development Area Plan**
> Development area plans shall include the following information:
> 1. A summary showing how the development area plan conforms to the master community plan, the total dwelling units in the plan by type, the square footage of nonresidential uses, and a parking calculation of required and provided spaces by use.
> 2. Development area plan graphics showing:
>   a. Areas of proposed land use, including common open space and natural resource areas.
>   b. Streets, pedestrian paths, and bikeways.
>   c. A preliminary infrastructure plan.
>   d. A proposed plot plan for each building site in the plan. A typical plot plan can be included for single family dwellings. Plot plans shall show existing and proposed buildings indicating maximum and minimum distances between buildings, between building and property or building site boundaries, percentage of building coverage, percentage of landscaping if any, and paving and other areas to be landscaped.
>   e. A parking and loading plan drawn to scale.
>   f. Preliminary elevations of all proposed structures drawn to scale. They shall indicate building heights, materials, fenestrations, colors, and the general appearance of existing and proposed structures.
>   g. Preliminary floor plans for the proposed structures.
>   h. A preliminary landscaping plan.
>   i. Fencing, trash disposal and recycling storage areas.
> 3. A map showing the existing topography of the district at [one] foot intervals. (Adapted from Santa Clara, California)

The Specific Plan

Arizona and California authorize by statute the adoption of a "specific plan" that many communities use as a substitute for a development plan (Fulton and Shigley 2005, 215–16; see sidebar for provisions). In California, the specific plan and other zoning actions for PUDs must also go through the environmental review procedures required by the California Environmental Quality Act.

Some municipalities where specific plans are authorized have regulations providing for the preparation and adoption of a specific plan for PUDs (e.g., Rohnert Park, California). Since the specific plan is the equivalent of the development plan, the ordinance can specify that uses, site development requirements, and densities are governed by the specific plan, as is the case in Santa Clarita, California.

PROCEDURES FOR THE REVIEW OF DEVELOPMENT PLAN APPLICATIONS

Under some ordinances, the legislative body adopts a rezoning for a PUD district and also approves the development plan, either at the time of rezoning or later. Alternatively, the decision whether to approve the development plan is usually given to the planning commission. This decision is made in a quasi judicial process that requires a noticed public hearing, findings of fact, and a written decision. Because a review process of this type is needed for all development applications, its inclusion elsewhere in the zoning ordinance is preferable, and the PUD ordinance can reference it. If the local government has a unified development code that includes a provision for PUDs, the review process will be part of that code. Some PUD ordinances contain their own review procedures for development plan applications, and this section discusses the elements that should be part of those procedures.

The APA Growing Smart℠ Legislative Guidebook contains a model law in Chapter 10 that authorizes a quasi-judicial review process in land-use decision making for applications for development permits (Meck 2002). The model law can be found at www.planning.org, and Chapter 10 of the model law can be found at www.law.wustl.edu/landuselaw in the Statutes section through the Model Legislation link. The intent of the model is to provide a fair and disciplined decision-making process from start to finish that defines the issues the reviewers must decide and limits the decision making process to those issues. A "development permit" is broadly defined to include permission for all land-use approvals that require quasi-judicial decisions, including a permit for a PUD. The provisions recommended here are modified to apply to preliminary development plans. Final development plans require less formal procedures. Chapter 10 also authorizes a consolidated permit review procedure.

The model law includes sections about determining the completeness of an application, requirements for notice and hearing and for a final decision, and time limits on decision making. It is largely based on existing statutory provisions in a number of states. The model law can be adapted for inclusion in a local ordinance, and the sections that follow are adaptations suitable for use in a zoning or PUD ordinance. Not all detail from the model law is included, and it should be consulted for additional requirements. Some commentary is provided here, and additional commentary appears in the model.

PROVISIONS FOR SPECIFIC PLANS

Arizona Revised Statutes, Section 9–461.08, provides in part:

A. The planning agency may, or if so directed by the legislative body shall, prepare specific plans based on the general plan and drafts of such regulations, programs and legislation as may in the judgment of the agency be required for the systematic execution of the general plan. The planning agency may recommend such plans and measures to the legislative body for adoption.

B. Specific plans may, in addition to recommended zoning ordinances and subdivision regulations, include:
   1. Regulations determining the location of buildings and other improvements with respect to existing rights-of-way, floodplains, and public facilities.
   2. Regulations of the use of land, buildings, and structures, the height and bulk of buildings and structures, and the open spaces around buildings and structures.

California Government Code, Section 65450, authorizes the preparation of specific plans. The statute provides that:

a) A specific plan shall include a text and a diagram or diagrams which specify all of the following in detail:
   (1) The distribution, location, and extent of the uses of land, including open space, within the area covered by the plan.
   (2) The proposed distribution, location, and extent and intensity of major components of public and private transportation, sewage, water, drainage, solid waste disposal, energy, and other essential facilities proposed to be located within the area covered by the plan and needed to support the land uses described in the plan.
   (3) Standards and criteria by which development will proceed, and standards for the conservation, development, and utilization of natural resources, where applicable.
   (4) A program of implementation measures, including regulations, programs, public works projects, and financing measures necessary to carry out paragraphs (1), (2), and (3).

b) The specific plan shall include a statement of the relationship of the specific plan to the general plan.

The specific plan may also include any other subjects necessary to implement the general plan. (See Section 65452, and Sections 65453–65456.)

A completeness requirement is especially important for PUDs, which may need to meet complex regulatory requirements.

The Completeness Determination

The ordinance should contain a requirement for a completeness determination so that the local government at some point must accept an application as complete, and so the applicant will be given direction about what is required if the application is rejected as incomplete. A completeness requirement is especially important for PUDs, which may need to meet complex regulatory requirements. The section that follows is a standard completeness requirement. It mandates that the planning commission clearly specify what is needed if an application is incomplete and make its completeness decision in a reasonable time. It is written specifically for applications for development plan approval:

(1) Within [28] days after receiving an application for the approval of a preliminary development plan, the [planning commission] shall mail or provide in person a written determination to the applicant, stating either that the application is complete or that the application is incomplete and what is necessary to make the application complete.

(2) If the [planning commission] determines that the application is incomplete, it shall identify in its determination the parts of the application that are incomplete and shall indicate the manner in which they can be made complete, including a list and specific description of the additional information needed to complete the application. The applicant shall then submit this additional information to the [planning commission] within [28] days of the determination pursuant to paragraph (1), unless the [planning commission] agrees in writing to a longer period.

(3) The [planning commission] shall determine in writing whether an application is complete within [28] days after receipt of the additional information indicated in the list and description provided to the applicant under paragraph (2).

(4) An application for the approval of a preliminary development plan is deemed complete under this Section if the [planning commission] does not provide a written determination to the applicant that the application is incomplete within [28] days of the receipt of an application under paragraph (1) or within [28] days of the receipt of any additional information submitted under paragraph (2).

(5) An application for the approval of a preliminary development plan is complete for purposes of this Section when it meets the completeness requirements of, or is deemed complete under, this Section, even though additional information may be required. The completeness determination does not preclude the [planning commission] from requesting additional information or studies either at the time of the notice of completeness or subsequently if new information is required.

Paragraph (5) is included to give the planning commission the opportunity to request additional information about the development plan subsequent to the completeness decision. It may have to request additional information if it is needed as a basis for making a decision on the development plan application.

Notice and Hearing

A decision on a PUD application is made following a record hearing held after published notice. The model law requires a statement in the notice that a record hearing will be held, for example. It also requires the hearing notice to do the following:

- List the land development regulations and any goals, policies, and guidelines of the local comprehensive plan that apply to the application.

- State that a failure to raise an issue at a record hearing, in person or by letter, or the failure to provide statements or evidence sufficient to afford the local government an opportunity to respond to the issue precludes an appeal to the appeals board based on that issue, unless the issue could not have been reasonably known by any party to the record hearing at the time of the record hearing.

- State that a copy of any staff reports on the application will be available for inspection at no cost at least [seven] days prior to the record hearing and will be provided at actual cost.

The model law also includes requirements for holding record hearings that can be adapted for local use.

Findings and Decision

Adequate findings are very important, especially for a development that can be as complex as PUD. The following section modifies the model law for local adoption:

(1) The [planning commission] shall approve or deny an application for the approval of a preliminary development plan, or shall approve an application subject to conditions. Any approval, denial, or conditions attached to a development permit approval shall be based on and implement the [land development or zoning or PUD regulations], and the goals, policies, and guidelines of the comprehensive plan.

(2) Any decision on an application for the approval of a preliminary development plan shall be based upon and accompanied by a written statement that:

   a. states the [land development or zoning or PUD] regulations and the goals, policies, and guidelines of the comprehensive plan relevant to the decision;

   b. states the facts relied upon in making the decision;

   c. explains how the decision is based on the [land development or zoning or PUD] regulations, the goals, policies, and guidelines of the local comprehensive plan (including the future land use plan map), and the facts set forth in the written statement of the comprehensive plan;

   d. responds to all relevant issues raised by documents and materials submitted to the administrative review; and

   e. states the conditions that apply to the development permit.

(3) Within [30] days of a request for a clarification of findings and decisions specifically included in the written notice of decision, the [planning commission] shall issue a written clarification concerning those specific findings and decisions.

The purpose of Section 3 is to give the applicant an opportunity to request additional information concerning the basis of the decision to help the applicant respond to the decision if the application is denied or approved subject to conditions. The model law also provides that notice of the decision shall be given to the applicant and other interested parties.

The PUD ordinance can also state what action an applicant must take if an application for a PUD permit is conditionally approved:

If an application for the approval of a preliminary development plan is conditionally approved, the applicant shall have 90 days from the date of planning commission action granting conditional approval to submit a revised application to the planning staff. If the planning staff determines that the revised application complies with the conditional approval, it shall forward it to the planning commission for a public hearing.

Time Limits

A final requirement in the model law, adopted by a number of states, is a requirement for timely decisions. This, as well as the requirement for a completeness decision, should minimize the delays that can occur in decision making and that can create difficulties in the approval process for PUDs. This section also provides for appropriate notice to the parties and for fees. It is somewhat modified for adoption as a local ordinance:

> (1) If [the planning commission] fails to approve, conditionally approve, or disapprove an application for the approval of a preliminary development plan within [90] days from the time it makes a written determination that the application is complete or from the time the application is deemed complete, the failure to act shall be deemed an approval.
>
> *Commentary:* This provision means the application is deemed approved if the planning commission does not act within the required time period. The model law contains an alternate provision that allows an action in court to compel the agency required to make the decision to take action, but it is doubtful whether a local government can adopt an ordinance that creates a judicial cause of action of this kind.
>
> (2) The [planning commission] and the applicant for a development permit may mutually agree to an extension of the time limits for a decision specified in paragraph (1) for a period not in excess of [90] days.
>
> (3) The time limits for decision specified in this Section do not run during any period:
>
> > a. not to exceed [30] days in which a local government requests additional studies or information concerning a development permit application; or
> >
> > b. in which the local government is unable to act on applications due to circumstances beyond the local government's control, including a reasonable period for resubmission of applications and related materials destroyed, damaged, or otherwise rendered unusable.

The purpose of reviewing the final plan is to ensure that it includes all the approved elements of the preliminary development plan and that no substantial changes have been made.

Final Development Plan

Once the preliminary development plan is approved, the applicant will submit a final development plan to the planning commission for approval. The purpose of reviewing the final plan is to ensure that it includes all the approved elements of the preliminary development plan and that no substantial changes have been made. Approval can be by the planning commission unless there have been substantial changes, which the ordinance can spell out. A public hearing is required concerning the approval of the final plan and is also required if a revised final development plan is submitted after disapproval. The "substantial compliance" provision of this section can be adapted to authorize the approval of development area plans for phased developments to determine whether they are in compliance with the master development plan:

> **Final Development Plan**
>
> (1) The applicant shall submit a final development plan to the planning commission for review within [one] year of the approval of the preliminary development plan. The planning commission shall hold a public hearing on the final development plan at one of its scheduled meetings to review its compliance with the preliminary development plan.
>
> (2) The planning commission shall approve the final development plan if it is substantially in compliance with the preliminary development plan. A final development is in substantial compliance with the preliminary development plan if it does not:
>
> > a. increase the proposed floor area for nonresidential use by more than [5] percent, or

b. increase the total building coverage by more than [5] percent, or

c. increase the total number of dwelling units by more than [5] percent, or

d. decrease by more than [5] percent the areas proposed for landscaping and for the designation of common open space and natural resource areas, or

e. increase the height of any structure by more than [5] percent, or decrease the spacing between structures by more than [5] percent, or

f. contain any other changes that substantially depart from the preliminary development plan, including but not limited to substantial changes in [here name the plan elements to be included, such as pedestrian and traffic circulation systems, and design plans].

Commentary: The provision first lists changes in the preliminary development plan that can be quantified. Requirements can also be included for less common elements, such as an internal traffic capture or a jobs/housing balance requirement, and can define "substantial change" in those requirements. An example is a 5 percent decrease in the jobs/housing ratio. Other changes in the plan, such as changes in the traffic and circulation systems and changes in a design plan, are more difficult to quantify. Subparagraph f is a catchall provision providing that substantial changes in these systems or plans are also a reason for disapproval. The ordinance should list the plans or plan elements to be considered in making this decision.

(3) If the planning commission finds that the final development plan is not in compliance with the preliminary development plan, it shall return the plan to the applicant, who may revise the plan to make it comply with the preliminary development plan and resubmit it to the planning commission for a decision after a public hearing as provided in Section (1).

Building Permits, Certificate of Occupancy, and Site Plan Review

The jurisdiction can issue building permits and a certificate of occupancy once it approves the final development plan:

The [zoning administrator] shall authorize the issuance of building permits for buildings and structures in the area covered by an approved final development plan if they are in substantial conformity with the approved final development plan. The [zoning administrator] shall authorize the issuance of a certificate of occupancy for any completed building, structure, or use located in the area covered by the PUD if it conforms to the requirements of the approved final development plan and all other applicable regulations.

Whether the jurisdiction also decides to use site plan review procedures, as detailed in its zoning ordinance, for projects within the PUD will depend on how much detail is contained in the approved final development plan. The jurisdiction should conduct a site plan review if it believes the additional control gained through use of these procedures is necessary.

Coordination with Subdivision Regulations

If a PUD requires the subdivision of land, which is likely in many instances, it will also require review under the subdivision ordinance. Coordinating these reviews can be difficult. Coordination at the concept plan stage is not possible because the concept plan does not include enough detail to allow a review of compliance with the subdivision ordinance. Coordination is also difficult even at the preliminary development plan stage because this plan does not usually include the engineering details the subdivision ordinance requires for streets and other facilities. Many developers prefer not to provide these details at this stage, instead preferring to deal with subdivision issues at a later stage under the subdivision ordinance. Engineering plans of this kind are expensive to produce, and there may not be enough commitment to the project even at the preliminary development plan approval stage to justify their preparation.

Figure 3-5. The Process Followed by Sparks, Nevada, for the Approval of the Kiley Ranch Development Subsequent to Approval of the Development Plans.

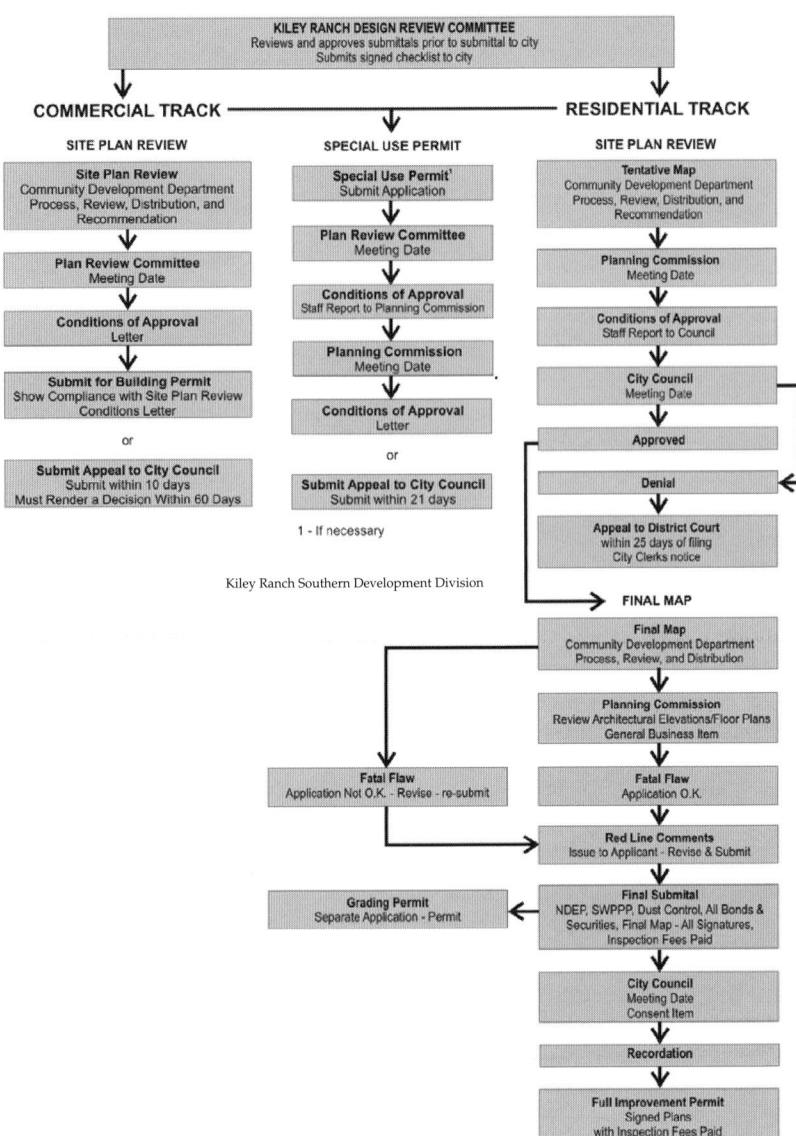

It is possible to require enough detail in a development plan to comply with the subdivision ordinance, however. Review under the subdivision ordinance is then carried out concurrently with review under the PUD ordinance:

> The preliminary development plan shall contain all the information necessary, and be submitted in a form that complies with, the provisions of the subdivision ordinance for preliminary plats required to be approved under that ordinance. The planning commission shall review the preliminary development plan concurrently under both the PUD and the subdivision ordinance.

Another alternative is to separate the subdivision plat and the preliminary development plan but provide for concurrent review:

> The planning commission shall review the preliminary development plan concurrently with its review of the preliminary subdivision plat under the subdivision ordinance.

The ordinance can also make concurrent review voluntary at the option of the applicant, who can be authorized to request a concurrent review. A major issue is to prevent delays, which concurrent review can help avoid. Some ordinances and Chapter 10 of APA's *Growing Smart^{SM} Legislative Guidebook* authorize a consolidated permit review of all permits needed for a development project. This approach provides another alternative for the coordination of subdivision review and any other required reviews with review under the PUD ordinance.

DEVELOPMENT AGREEMENTS

It is common in many areas for local governments to execute development agreements with developers of PUDs, especially for master-planned communities. There are a number of reasons for doing this. One of the most important is that, unlike a rezoning ordinance or a development plan, a development agreement establishes obligations that cannot be modified unless the agreement authorizes this. Another is that the agreement can give the developer an entitlement, or a vested right, to complete the development under the land use regulations in effect at the time the development plan was approved. Subsequent changes in the regulations would not apply. The agreement can also establish other obligations, including developer exactions, allowable uses, and other project elements, the formation of special districts to finance infrastructure, and the preservation of natural resources. A development agreement can be long, reaching as many as 60 to 70 pages or more. Coordination with provisions in the development plan and with conditions attached to the rezoning, if any, is necessary.

The development agreement was initially conceived as a way to provide a commitment or entitlement to developers that gives them vested rights in their approved development plans. This kind of commitment is especially necessary in states, like California, where vested rights are difficult to obtain under the majority rule unless the developer relies on a permit granted by the local government by carrying out substantial physical development (Mandelker 2003, Section 6.15). This is likely to be difficult for many areas of a PUD.

The vested rights problem is especially serious for master planned communities that have a long build-out time and that apply for the approval of development plans for individual phases as the project progresses. It is probable that courts will not find a vested right in subsequent phases based on the approval of an initial concept or master development plan, although some authority exists to the contrary (see, for example, *Village of Palatine v. LaSalle Nat'l Bank*, 445 N.E.2d 1277, 1283 (Ill. App. 1983), in which the court said, "We regard Palatine's approval of the original site plan, the issuance of building permits for Phase I, and the continuing treatment of [the project] as a PUD 'in fact' as the type of affirmative acts of public officials upon which a landowner is entitled to rely"). This lack of vested right puts the completion of the project at risk if the local government makes changes in its land-use regulations that essentially void the completion of the project as proposed in the approved concept or master development plan. As a typical development agreement might state, "The benefit to the developer under this agreement consists of the assurance that the developer will preserve the right to develop the property as provided in the approved concept plan and this agreement."

The two major legal problems presented by development agreements are the need for statutory authority and their constitutionality (Callies, Curtin, and Tappendorf 2003). A number of states now have statutes authorizing development agreements that apply to all kinds of development, including PUDs. They contain a provision freezing the regulations in place at the time of the agreement but authorize the application of land use regulations adopted after the agreement is executed if this is in the public interest. A public hearing is required prior to the approval of an agreement or subsequent modifications. It is important to require a public hearing at this stage and also important to make negotiations prior to the adoption of a development agreement open to the public.

DEVELOPMENT AGREEMENTS FOR PLANNED UNIT DEVELOPMENTS ND MASTER-PLANNED COMMUNITIES

By David Callies
Benjamin A. Kudo, Professor of Law, University of Hawaii

Developer and local government face two difficult problems in the land development approval process. First, local governments are unable to exact dedications of land or fees of the "impact" or "in-lieu" variety without establishing a clear and proportional connection or nexus between the proposed development and the dedication or fee. Thus, for example, a local government could require the developer of a shopping center to provide adequate water, sewer, and roads to serve the project, but under the rules laid down by the U.S. Supreme Court in *Nollan v. California Coastal Commission*, 483 U.S. 825 (1987) and *Dollan v. City of Tigard*, 512 U.S. 374 (1994), it could not require the developer to provide schools or parks since both lack nexus or proportionality.

Second, the developer is unable to "vest" or guarantee a right to proceed with a project until that project is commenced.

The development agreement offers a solution to both landowner/developer and local government. It is especially helpful for planned unit developments and master-planned communities developed in phases, often over a substantial period of time. It can establish the developer's obligations for exactions, and it can vest development rights.

Development Agreements are essentially statutorily authorized agreements between local governments and landowners for the guidance of a multiphase land development. Authorized by statute in 13 states (most prominently, California), the development agreement is designed to accomplish several purposes:

1. Permit local government to require public facilities and improvements beyond those which it may legally require as generated by a proposed land development project.

2. Permit local government greater flexibility in regulating large, multiphase projects extending over many years.

3. Strengthen the public planning process and encourage public and private participation in comprehensive planning.

4. Reduce the economic cost of development and allow for the orderly planning of public facilities and services and the allocation of costs.

In 1980, California passed a landmark development agreements statute in response to its own state supreme court case holding a landowner lacked vested rights even after spending millions of dollars in land improvements (*Avco Community Developers Inc. v. South Coast Regulatory Commission*, 533 P.2d 546 (Cal.1976). So popular is the development agreement as a vehicle for guiding planning and development, particularly of multistage projects, that by the early 1990s over half the local governments in California have negotiated and executed hundreds of such agreements (Curtin and Edelstein 1993, 766). Moreover, not a single reported case has found fault with a development agreement.

Indeed, it was not until 2000 that California courts were confronted with a direct challenge to such statutorily authorized development agreements and then the court of appeals soundly upheld them (*Santa Margarita Area Residents Together (SMART) v. San Luis Obispo County*, 100 Cal. Rptr. 2d 740 (Cal. App. 2000)). The court squarely upheld a development agreement that was challenged directly on "surrender of police power" grounds, holding that a "zoning freeze in the Agreement is not . . . a surrender or abnegation [of the police power]" (at 748). In *SMART*, an area residents association contended that, because San Luis Obispo County had entered into a development agreement for a project before the project was ready for construction and, consequently, freezing zoning for a five-year period, the county improperly contracted away its zoning authority. In holding for the county, the court noted that land-use regulation is an established function of local government, providing the authority for a local government to enter into contracts to carry out the function. The county's development agreement required that the project be developed in accordance with the county's general plan, did not permit construction until the county had approved detailed building plans, retained the county's discretionary authority in the future, and allowed a zoning freeze of limited duration only. The court found that the zoning freeze in the county's development agreement was not a surrender of the police power but instead "advance[d] the public interest by preserving future options."

Virtually all commentary on the development agreement is uniformly positive, from its early inception (Porter and Marsh 1989; Wegner 1987; Griffith 1990) to the present (Callies, Curtin, and Tappendorf 2003).

The statutes also require periodic review of the development agreement, and allow the governing body to modify or terminate the agreement if the developer is unable to comply with its terms. A few statutes also contain provisions describing what kinds of developments can be covered by an agreement. Otherwise, the content of an agreement is not specified. In states without authorizing statutes, a community intending to use development agreements for PUDs must consider whether it has the implied statutory authority to do so. On the constitutional issue, the cases so far have held development agreements are not unconstitutional as a bargaining away of the police power, but this issue is not fully settled.

A section in the PUD ordinance on development agreements may not be necessary because the local government can make the decision to enter into an agreement and determine its contents. Some PUD ordinances have provisions governing the use of development agreements, however. They specify when a development agreement can be used and what the agreement can contain. Queen Creek, Arizona, for example, authorizes a development agreement establishing permitted uses "when it is found by the Town Council that the development represents exemplary quality and value to the community and area for which it is proposed." This decision is made under criteria requiring the PUD to "exceed" existing standards and general plan policies. It includes a requirement that the application for the PUD "proposes substantial land use planning standards and principles over and beyond the minimum standards required in this ordinance or any development ordinance adopted by the Town."

Manatee County, Florida, has an extensive provision for development agreements, including requirements for a hearing and periodic review. (Florida has a statute authorizing development agreements.) In addition to standard clauses, such as a legal description, the names of the parties and duration, the ordinance describes the contents of an agreement, which may include the following:

> The development uses permitted on the land, including population and unit densities, and building intensities and height
>
> A description of the public facilities that will service the development, including who shall provide such facilities
>
> The date any new facilities, if needed, will be constructed
>
> A schedule to ensure that public facilities are available concurrent with the impacts of the development
>
> A description of any reservation or dedication of land for public purposes
>
> A description of all local development permits approved or needed to be approved for the development of land
>
> A finding that the development, permitted or proposed, is consistent with the Comprehensive Plan and this Code
>
> A description of any conditions, terms, restriction, or any other requirements determined to be necessary by local government for the public health, safety, or welfare of its citizens

Manatee County, Florida, has an extensive provision for development agreements, including requirements for a hearing and periodic review.

This is a typical list. Note that the ordinance includes an adequate public facilities requirement, which is required by state statute. Note also that it overlaps with the contents of the development plan as some of these elements, such as uses and intensities, are also included in the plan. The reason for including them in the development agreement is to give them a more binding form, as modification requires the consent of both parties. Other provisions can be included in an agreement, such as a provision for the cost-sharing of facilities and an agreement for the maintenance of open space.

AMENDMENTS TO DEVELOPMENT PLANS

Change is inevitable, and one of the most important issues in the drafting of ordinances for PUDs is to provide authority for the amendment of development plans. Changes in the market or changes in the developer's objectives for the development can require changes in an approved plan. Change can also occur because neighbors or residents who move in early in the project may object to nonresidential development that was in the plan from the beginning but which they believe is not compatible with their residential living environment.

A restrictive approach to amendments would limit them only to unforeseen circumstances:

> The [planning commission or planning director] may approve minor amendments to the final development plan. A minor amendment is an amendment required by technical or engineering considerations first discovered during development that could not reasonably have been anticipated during the approval process. (Adapted from Mandelker 1966)

This type of provision does not allow for changes required by proposals to modify the development. The usual approach for an ordinance that authorizes this kind of change is to distinguish between major changes that require new legislative action and minor changes that do not require legislative action. An ordinance can simply state that a change is major if it is "substantial," or it can provide a list of changes and indicate which are substantial and which are not. A detailed listing is preferable because it removes the need to exercise discretion on what is and what is not "substantial," and provides predictability about what can and cannot be changed and how such determinations will be made.

Minor changes can be approved administratively by the planning director, staff, or planning commission. If approval is by the planning commission, an application should be required, but the completeness, notice, hearing, and decision procedures need not apply. Chapter 10 of the *Growing Smart*^{SM} *Legislative Guidebook* has a provision in Section 10–204 for administrative review without a record hearing that can be used to govern these decisions. If a major change is required, it should be processed as an amendment to the development plan in the same manner as a rezoning. Manatee County, Florida, has a three-tier process in which: (1) listed minor changes are approved administratively; (2) more substantial changes are approved by the legislative body at public hearings after public notice; and (3) substantial modifications extensive enough to be considered a new development plan require approval by both the planning commission and legislative body.

Changes in permitted uses and in the density and intensity of use are obvious candidates for inclusion in a list of changes considered "major," though any element in the development plan essential to the character of the PUD should be included, such as open space, traffic and pedestrian circulation systems, design elements, and the jobs/housing ratio, if one is included. Major changes can be defined qualitatively:

1. An additional use, a more intensive use, or an increase in the parking requirement.
2. Changes in [design,] bulk, mass or orientation.
3. A reduction in the effectiveness of approved transitional screening, buffering, or landscaping, and any reduction in common open space or areas subject to preservation.
4. Substantial changes in the location or type of pedestrian or vehicular access or circulation.
5. Changes in the phasing schedule that change the timing, amount, or completion of common open space, public facilities, or other improvements. (Adapted from Fairfax County, Virginia, and Manatee County, Florida)

Major changes can also be defined quantitatively:

An increase or decrease in density, intensity, height, lot size, setbacks, parking requirements, [jobs/housing ratio, connectivity index,] and common open space of more than [10] percent.

Notice that a decrease as well as in increase in these project elements is included. Most ordinances only include increases in the listed project elements as major changes, except for open space, where a specified decrease in open space is considered major.

Many ordinances define minor changes that do not require legislative approval. Bellevue, Washington, has a useful procedure in which some changes can be approved as an exemption by the planning director without a hearing, while some require approval in a notice and hearing procedure.

Many ordinances define minor changes that do not require legislative approval.

A. Modifications to Development Plans Exempt from Further Review

The Planning Director may determine that a modification to a previously approved development plan is exempt from further review under the administrative amendment process or as a new application, provided the following criteria are met:

1. The change is necessary because of natural features of the subject property not foreseen by the applicant or the city prior to the approval of the development plan; and

2. The change will not have the effect of significantly reducing any area of landscaping, open space, natural area or parking; and

3. The change will not have the effect of increasing the density of the development plan; and

4. The change will not add square footage that is more than [20] percent of the existing gross square footage of the development plan; and

5. If an addition or expansion has been approved within the preceding 24 month period, the combined additions will not add square footage that exceeds [20] percent of existing gross square footage of the development plan; and

6. The change will not result in any structure, circulation, or parking area being moved significantly in any direction; and

7. The change will not reduce any approved setback by more than [10] percent; and

8. The change will not result in a significant increase in the height of any structure; and

9. The change does not result in any significant adverse impacts beyond the site.

B. Administrative Amendment of Development Plans

The Planning Director may approve modifications to an approved development plan as an administrative amendment, subject to the notice, hearing, and decision-making procedures in this ordinance for the approval of preliminary development plans if the following criteria are met:

1. The amendment maintains the design intent or purpose of the original approved development plan; and

2. The amendment maintains the quality of design or product established by the original approved development plan; and

3. The amendment is not materially detrimental to uses or property in the immediate vicinity of the development plan.

C. The Director may impose conditions upon any administrative amendment to ensure the proposal complies with the decision criteria and the purpose and intent of the original approval. (Adapted from Bellevue, Washington)

This provision ensures that the development plan for the entire PUD controls any part of the PUD that is severed, so that no development can occur in the severed part that violates the provisions of the development plan. Development in the severed part must meet the density requirements for this part, for example, and uses cannot be changed. If the severed part contains open space that must be dedicated or preserved, that must also be done, even though the amount of open space is not proportionate to the density allowed in that part. Any change in the development plan will require an amendment:

> If a PUD is subdivided, sold, or leased, all of the owners of the subdivided, sold, or leased PUD may jointly apply for an amendment to the final development plan, which shall be governed by the procedures and requirements contained in this ordinance for the approval of the final development plan.

Provisions in the ordinance governing formation of a homeowners association, if one is required, can provide that its authority and existence are not affected by subdivision, sale, or lease of the project.

RECORD KEEPING

The approval of numerous PUDs and master-planned communities in a community can create serious record-keeping problems, making the monitoring of PUDs and enforcement of the PUD ordinance difficult. A PUD can produce a large number of documents, depending on how it is approved. These can include the following:

- Approved concept and development plans
- A design handbook or plan in addition to the final development plan
- Building permits and certificates of compliance with the final development plan
- Enforcement actions, if any
- Resubdivisions, resales, and leases of all or a part of the project
- Dedications of land, easements, or other documents created to preserve and manage common open space and natural resource areas. This can include documents associated with a transfer of development rights program, if there is one.
- Exactions or impact fees for public facilities
- Agreements concerning the provision of public services, such as a water supply and sewerage, highways and highway access, and other public facilities
- The rezoning ordinance
- Conditions attached to the rezoning ordinance
- A development agreement
- Private restrictions and covenants that apply to the PUD
- Documents associated with approval under the subdivision ordinance
- Documents concerning the creation of special development or other district to provide public services and facilities

This is a formidable list. Only some of these documents are produced under the PUD ordinance and are under the supervision and control of the land-use agency. Even fewer, such as dedications of land, are recorded in the public records office. This can be changed by statute, and the Nevada PUD law (Nevada Revised Statutes, Section 278A.570) requires the recording of approved development plans in the county recorder's office.

In addition to the recording of development plans, all PUD districts should be recorded on the zoning map, and all documents associated with the PUD, including the development plan, should by filed with a record-keeping office in the land-use agency. These documents should include agreements with other public agencies, such as the highway agency, which may not be part of the public record for the PUD. Computer and Geographic Information Systems can be installed that can organize and maintain these documents. Staff is necessary, however, to provide needed overview and supervision if this system of monitoring is to be effective.

The following is an outline of a possible record-keeping and monitoring program:

1. Assign each PUD a planning case number, create a project file, and place any documents relating to the development in that file.

2. Record all PUD districts on the zoning map.

3. File all documents associated with the PUD in a public record keeping office in the land-use agency.

4. To the extent possible, record the final development plan and any associated documents, such as subdivision plat and common open space documents, in the recorders office so they will show up in the chain of title.

5. Consider site plan review for developments within the PUD as they occur.

6. Monitor development of the project and do inspections through building, grading, and other permits for compliance with the development plan and other requirements.

7. Install a computer program to keep track of project development and relate it to building permits.

CHAPTER 4

Standards for the Approval of Planned Unit Developments and Master-Planned Communitites

This chapter contains recommendations for standards that should be included in ordinances to govern the review of PUDs. Differences in the scale and character of PUDs make it difficult to suggest a single model ordinance that can apply to all types of projects. The chapter discusses the issues jurisdictions must consider in drafting standards and recommends alternatives for dealing with each issue. It also discusses drafting problems presented by different types of PUDs and by master-planned communities.

PUD AS-OF-RIGHT

If the objective of PUD regulation is to create better-designed projects, one alternative for accomplishing this objective is to take the design principles that PUD ordinances include as the basis for discretionary review and enact them through an ordinance that allows development as-of-right. In other words, if the requirements in the ordinance are satisfied, the jurisdiction does no review and the development is permitted.

Residential subdivisions present an opportunity for applying the as-of-right approach. Cabarrus County, North Carolina, has adopted an as-of-right subdivision ordinance that authorizes three types of subdivisions. The second and third types described below illustrate the as-of-right approach by incorporating design principles usually included in PUD ordinances for cluster housing:

> **A. Conventional Subdivision**
> Conventional subdivision is a pattern of residential development that provides a majority of property owners with substantial yards on their own property.
>
> **B. Open Space Subdivision**
> Open space subdivisions trade smaller lot sizes (with smaller yards) for additional common open space. An open space subdivision shall be a minimum size to ensure sufficient common open space can be incorporated into the subdivision design.
>
> **C. Amenity Subdivision**
> Amenity subdivisions trade even smaller lot sizes (with smaller yards) for additional common open space. An amenity subdivision allows additional density provided certain enhancements are incorporated into the design of the subdivision. (Cabarrus County, North Carolina)

The ordinance includes a statement of intent and purpose for each type of subdivision. The statement of intent for the amenity subdivision, for example, provides:

> The intent of an open space subdivision is to provide a development alternative to a conventional subdivision. An open space subdivision involves placing a cluster of home-sites within a portion of the development site, allowing housing units on smaller lots than those permitted in a conventional subdivision to promote environmentally sensitive, more efficient use of the land and provide additional common open space.

The ordinance also lists additional purposes:

- To preserve in perpetuity unique or sensitive natural resources such as groundwater, floodplains, wetlands, streams, steep slopes, woodlands, and wildlife habitat;
- To preserve important historic and archaeological sites;
- To permit clustering of houses and structures in a manner that will reduce the amount of infrastructure, including paved surfaces and utility easements, necessary for residential development;
- To reduce erosion and sedimentation by minimizing land disturbance and removal of vegetation in residential development;
- To promote interconnected greenways and corridors throughout the community;
- To create contiguous greenspace within and adjacent to the development site;
- To protect scenic views;
- To protect prime agricultural land and retain farming as an economic activity.

Each subdivision type is assigned to different development tiers in the county. Amenity subdivisions, for example, are assigned to the suburban tier. The ordinance also includes a number of housing types, with illustrations. For each subdivision in each tier, the ordinance specifies the amount of open space required and includes site development standards for each housing type in each zone. These standards include maximum number of dwelling units allowed, minimum acreage, lot dimensions, site dimensions for buildings and units, yard and height requirements, and impermeable surface and structural coverage requirements. Detailed design elements are prescribed for amenity subdivisions, such as block elements and site and building requirements, which include roof overhang, side wall articulation, and front yard trees. There are also stream buffer and perimeter requirements, and the ordinance contains detailed standards for the location, character, and management of open space.

This ordinance mirrors the requirements commonly found in PUD ordinances for cluster housing, except a development plan is not subject to discretionary review. A developer can design a project so long as it complies with ordinance requirements. The ordinance does require a management plan for open space and other common facilities, and includes anti-monotony design standards that require review at the permit stage.

Conservation Subdivisions

Conservation subdivisions are another type of as-of-right housing development that includes design ideas usually found in PUD ordinances. The conservation subdivision carries out principles advocated in Randall Arendt's *Design by Nature* and elaborated in other works (see, e.g., PAS Report No. 523/524). A conservation subdivision is a residential subdivision approved through the subdivision ordinance—similar to the amenity subdivision in Carrabus County—except it is more specifically concerned with the preservation of open space and natural resource area.

The San Antonio, Texas, conservation subdivision ordinance is an example. It has no minimum or maximum size requirements, though its availability is limited by its open space demands. Use and density provisions of the zoning district apply. Lot size, lot width, and minimum frontage requirements do not apply, and the ordinance provides a number of illustrated housing development styles that developers can use to design a project's housing.

The key feature of the San Antonio conservation subdivision ordinance is a requirement for the conservation of designated primary and secondary conservation areas. Thirty-five percent of a subdivision must be designated as primary conservation areas, and an additional minimum of 15 percent must be designated as secondary conservation areas. Wetlands, steep slopes, and floodplains are examples of primary conservation areas. Prime farmland and scenic views are examples of secondary conservation areas. Natural resource protection standards in the ordinance apply to these areas.

By requiring the preservation of a significant amount of open space and authorizing a variety of clustered housing types, the conservation subdivision ordinance achieves the objectives of a cluster zoning project approved under PUD ordinances through discretionary review. Densities are limited in the San Antonio ordinance, but homes are clustered as shown as one example in Figure 4-1 in order to preserve designated conservation areas. Because no site development restrictions exist, a developer has the design freedom to use the available housing configurations to create a residential subdivision limited only by the density ceiling. Approval under the subdivision ordinance is based on compliance with the ordinance standards. The Duluth, Georgia, Conservation Subdivision Overlay District provides another example of this approach.

> *By requiring the preservation of a significant amount of open space and authorizing a variety of clustered housing types, the conservation subdivision ordinance achieves the objectives of a cluster zoning project approved under PUD ordinances through discretionary review.*

Cluster Zoning/Density Transfer PUDs

One of the earliest and most common forms of PUD was the cluster housing or density transfer development, in which project density remains the same, but density is increased in part of the project in return for the inclusion of common open space elsewhere on the site. Early PUD ordinances authorized a discretionary review process for the approval of this kind of development, and an early New York law (N.Y. Town Law, Section 278) authorizes the approval of "cluster developments" as part of the subdivision review process. This term is defined as follows:

> "Cluster development" shall mean a subdivision plat or plats, approved pursuant to this article, in which the applicable zoning ordinance or local law is modified to provide an alternative permitted method for the layout, configuration and design of lots, buildings and structures, roads, utility lines and other infrastructure, parks, and landscaping in order to preserve the natural and scenic qualities of open lands.

This definition captures the purpose of a cluster housing development. A purpose clause in a PUD ordinance can elaborate by noting the reasons for a cluster development, such as improving project design, protecting common open space and natural resource areas, and reducing infrastructure costs:

It is the purpose of this ordinance to permit residential cluster development in order to:

> (1) encourage creative and flexible site design that is sensitive to the land's natural features and adapts to the natural topography; and
>
> (2) protect environmentally sensitive areas of a development site and preserve on a permanent basis common open space, natural features, and prime agricultural lands; and
>
> (3) improve stormwater management by requiring best management practices for the control of nonpoint source pollution, and by reducing the amount of impervious surfaces in site development. (Adapted from Meck 2006)

The usual procedures for the approval of a PUD can apply. A concept plan may not be needed. Cluster housing developments can usually begin with a detailed development plan because densities and housing types are known and do not require a preliminary review through a concept plan.

Density is another important issue. The requirements for lot size determine the density in traditional subdivisions. The following provision changes the calculation for density from the usual lot size measure to number of dwelling units for a PUD using cluster development, which will result in smaller lot sizes and more open space, so as to ensure the same development density:

> The maximum number of dwelling units proposed for a residential cluster PUD shall not exceed the number of dwelling units permitted for the residential zoning district in which the development is located. (Adapted from Meck 2006).

The usual formula is to divide the project area by the lot size required in the existing zoning. Project area must be net, not gross, and the ordinance must indicate what must be excluded from gross project area. One is an exclusion for streets, which is also required to determine net project area for density calculations in traditional subdivisions. Determining the street deduction in a cluster development is more difficult because a cluster development will require less linear footage of streets than it would as a conventional development. One way to handle this problem is to provide a schedule with approximate calculations for street deductions based on lot sizes in the underlying zoning ordinance.

Land set aside for common open space to be available to residents of the development should not be excluded. Because the common open space offsets the density increase that will occur in part of the project, it can be included in net project area to determine how many dwelling units can be built.

It is also possible that some land in the project will be unbuildable because it is on a hillside or in a floodplain or other natural resource area, or because it is a lake or other body of water. These areas would not be buildable in a traditional residential subdivision, so allowing these areas to be included in net project area will increase the number of units allowable in a cluster development to more than would have been allowed under the existing zoning. Some part of these areas can be included in net project area, however, because water areas may contribute to the development and because some natural resource areas may be buildable. Some development is allowed in floodplains, for example, and hillsides on slopes that are not too steep are buildable if development is done properly.

The following provision gives the approving agency the authority to exclude areas it considers not suitable for development or not buildable. It gives the agency the discretion to decide on areas not suitable for development, and it must also exclude areas in which development is prohibited under other regulations. A hillside ordinance, for example, may prohibit development on hillsides with steep slopes. Other hillside areas will be included in net project area for purposes of determining density, but development in these areas will be regulated by the hillside ordinance. This seems a fair solution and should also be applied to wetlands and other natural resource areas subject to regulation:

> The [planning commission] shall calculate the number of dwelling units allowed in a cluster development. To make this calculation the planning commission shall exclude from net project area all stream areas and bodies of water. It shall also exclude from net project area all wetlands, floodplains, hillsides or other natural resource areas in which development is prohibited under [name ordinances]. It shall also exclude an acreage for streets under the following formula:
>
> | Lot Size Under Existing Zoning | Deductible Percentage of Project Area |
> | --- | --- |
> | One Acre | 12 |
> | One-Half Acre | 17 |
> | One-Quarter Acre | 22 |
>
> The acreage available after making these exclusions is the "net project area." The planning commission shall calculate the number of dwelling units available by dividing the net project area by the lot size required by the underlying zoning that applies to the project. Lots within the cluster development may vary in size, but the total number of lots may not exceed those allowed as calculated under this section.

This process provides a fair calculation for streets and will provide some flexibility if the variable lot size language is included. It defers to other ordinances, such as the floodplain ordinance, to determine which areas are unbuildable. As an alternative, the planning commission can be given the discretion to decide which areas to exclude. The ordinance can authorize it to exclude areas which, in its judgment, are "unsuitable for building for topographic reasons or because the area requires preservation as a natural resource." The ordinance can also limit how small a lot can be if minimum size is a concern. It may be helpful to use the residential styles included in the San Antonio, Texas, conservation subdivision ordinance as examples of the types of housing that can be included.

A jurisdiction may decide that "unbuildable" or "unsuitable" areas should not entirely be excluded from net project area. The ordinance can also provide some flexibility, for example, on the exclusion of stream areas and bodies of water:

> The [planning commission] may determine that all or part of stream areas or bodies of water may be included in net project area if they contribute to the quality, livability and amenity of the PUD. [Adapted from Mosena, So, and Bangs 1973))

As an alternative, the ordinance can provide that a specified percentage of bodies of water or natural resource areas may be included in the net project area:

> [Fifteen] percent of [name bodies of water and natural resource areas] shall be included in net project area.

Density bonuses may also be allowed in cluster housing developments. Bonuses are often made available under ordinance provisions that award higher densities for the provision of open space and other amenities. Density bonuses are discussed below.

PURPOSE CLAUSES

A purpose clause is an essential part of a PUD ordinance. It provides the basis for implementing and interpreting the ordinance, and can help avoid objections that the ordinance has improperly delegated legislative power. The purpose clause reproduced above for cluster development is a typical and comprehensive purpose clause that emphasizes the opportunity in PUDs for flexibility, common open space and natural resource protection, and cost reductions in infrastructure.

A purpose clause in a PUD ordinance can emphasize things like reductions in the cost of infrastructure. The canal in this PUD is used as part of a "green infrastructure" system that achieves that purpose as well as preserving natural features.

The opportunity for exceptional project design in PUDs is often emphasized in purpose clauses:

> In return for greater flexibility in site design requirements, planned developments are expected to deliver exceptional quality community designs that preserve critical environmental resources, provide above-average open space amenities, incorporate creative design in the layout of buildings, open space and circulation; assure compatibility with surrounding land uses and neighborhood character; and provide greater efficiency in the layout and provision of roads, utilities, and other infrastructure. (Cary, North Carolina)

It is also common in some ordinances to emphasize the opportunity for "better" design:

> PUDs authorized under this ordinance shall provide a better and more desirable living and physical environment than what would be possible under the zoning regulations that apply to the development.

There may be nothing wrong with this approach, and the interest in requiring "better" qualify is apparent considering the use of PUD as a remedy for the often dull development in conventional projects, but a definition for what is "better" does not seem obvious. The Cary, North Carolina, purpose clause may be preferable as emphasizing "exceptional" rather than "better" quality and can be reinforced by design and other approval criteria in the ordinance.

The purpose clause should also recognize that one of the purposes of the PUD ordinance is "to implement the policies and objectives of the comprehensive plan," where consistency with the plan is required. This purpose can be made more specific for urbanizing areas if the comprehensive plan includes growth management policies:

> To implement the growth management policies and objectives of the comprehensive plan, including the establishment of urban growth boundaries, the location and development of village centers, the provision of adequate public facilities, and the preservation of natural resource areas.

It is also possible to include a more detailed statement of purpose for large-scale, mixed-use developments, such as master-planned communities, which can provide opportunities for good design and mixed-use development.

Purpose clauses can be modified depending on the ordinance's objectives. Here are some examples of purpose clauses for PUDs in urbanized areas:

> To authorize developments suitable for high-density residential or mixed-use development, and to provide a detailed review of how these developments address issues such as affordable housing opportunities, an adequate balance between jobs and housing, connectivity between the circulation system of the development and adjacent streets and highways, mass transit links with employment centers, proximity to adequate recreational facilities, and the provision of adequate public services. (Adapted from Arapahoe County, Colorado)

> The preservation of buildings that are architecturally or historically significant or contribute the character of the [city]. (Adapted from Clayton, Missouri)

> The elimination of blighted areas, deteriorated structures or incompatible uses through redevelopment or rehabilitation. (Adapted from Clayton, Missouri)

> Encouraging quality urban design and environmentally sensitive development by allowing increases in base densities when such increases can be justified by superior design or the provision of additional amenities such as public or private open space. (Cary, North Carolina)

It is also possible to include a more detailed statement of purpose for large-scale, mixed-use developments, such as master-planned communities, which can provide opportunities for good design and mixed-use development:

> PUD is highly appropriate for large-scale mixed-use development and is strongly encouraged. Its purpose is to provide for a mixture of land uses at designated locations at a greater variety, density, and intensity than would normally be allowed. It is a well-integrated development that is allowed greater design flexibility so that large-scale site and master planning may protect natural features and consider most fully the surrounding land use and development context. Development can be more highly concentrated on one portion of a site than would otherwise be the case, with a resulting lower intensity of development elsewhere. (Adapted from Somerville, Massachusetts)

Purpose clauses can also be drafted for a nonresidential, single-use PUD:

> It is the intent of these regulations to provide for the development of commercial centers in scale with surrounding market areas at appropriate locations, and in compliance with the goals, objectives, policies and location criteria of the comprehensive plan and the standards included in this ordinance. The [legislative body] shall approve such developments only where planned development with carefully located buildings, parking and service areas, and landscaped open space will:
>
> (1) Provide for internal convenience and ease of use and is compatible with adjacent and surrounding land uses; and
>
> (2) Have adequate transportation systems and other public services; and
>
> (3) Be compatible with surrounding land uses; and
>
> (4) Not encourage the expansion of office or commercial strip development along adjacent streets; and
>
> (5) Have a project intensity that is consistent with the use that it provides.
>
> (Adapted from Manatee County, Florida)

The Manatee County ordinance has similar statements of purpose for other PUD districts, such as industrial, research park, and waterfront districts.

Some PUD ordinances require a development to comply with the objectives of the purpose clause as a basis for approval. Adding the purpose clause as an approval criterion may not be desirable, however, especially if it is stated in general terms that are difficult to interpret and that may create delegation of legislative power problems. A jurisdiction can draft the specific approval criteria in the ordinance to provide it all the guidance it needs to review PUD applications.

DEFINITIONS

Zoning ordinances define a variety of terms relevant to PUDs, such as lot, block, height, and other dimensional terms. The question is whether a PUD ordinance should contain a separate set of definitions. Some PUD ordinances do contain their own definitions, but some rely on the definitions in the zoning ordinance. (For a set of definitions included in a model residential cluster development ordinance, some of which are usually contained in zoning ordinances, see Meck, Morris, Bishop, and Kelly (2006).)

One important definition issue is whether to define "PUD." This depends on whether a PUD is a physical plan providing for a specific type of development, or a process. If it is a process, the approval standards in the ordinance can control the physical elements of a PUD without the need for a definition. If the ordinance does include a definition, it should be correlated with the list of purposes in the purpose clause.

If PUD is defined, one possibility is to emphasize the need for development as a single entity in compliance with a development plan and to identify the issues a development plan should consider without specifying what kind of development should occur:

> PUD means one or more lots, tracts, or parcels of land to be developed as a single entity, the plan for which may propose density or intensity transfers, density or intensity increases, mixing of land uses, or any combination thereof, and which may not correspond in lot size, bulk, or type of dwelling or building, use, density, intensity, lot coverage, parking, required common open space, or other standards to zoning use district requirements that are otherwise applicable to the area in which it is located. (Meck, Morris, Bishop, and Kelly 2006, Section 8-303(3))

The following definitions go further and define the type of development expected:

> "PUD" means an area of land to be developed as a single entity for one or more planned unit residential developments, one or more public, quasi-public, commercial or industrial areas, or a combination of any or all of these uses. (Adapted from Sparks, Nevada)

> "PUD" means a form of development characterized by unified site design for a variety of housing types and densities, clustering of buildings, common open space, and a mix of building types and land uses in which project planning and density calculation are performed for the entire development rather than on an individual lot basis. (Virginia Statutes, Section 15.2–2201)

Additional definitions can be included, such as definitions of common open space and design regulations. The Sparks, Nevada, PUD ordinance contains some of these definitions, but approval criteria in the ordinance can specify requirements for these elements of the development plan as an alternative.

Remember that definitions will have a substantive effect. If an ordinance defines PUD, for example, objectors to the approval of a project can claim it is unauthorized because it does not comply with the definition in the ordinance. For this reason, definitions must be carefully drawn, and they should not contain substantive requirements. A definition of common open space, for example, should not state how much open space is required and how it should be managed. These issues should be covered by the project approval standards. In general, definitions should never contain standards.

OWNERSHIP

Many PUD ordinances limit the submission of an application to a single owner, but some communities permit a joint application by multiple owners. The advantage of allowing a joint submission by multiple owners is that it authorizes comprehensive planning for multiple parcels by bringing adjacent parcels under a single development plan without an ownership transfer, which may be difficult. There is a risk that one or more of the owners may decide not to proceed, but the advantage of combining multiple ownerships in one application outweighs this risk. Combining multiple ownerships should especially be useful in urbanized or redevelopment areas where divided ownership in small parcels is common:

> An application for the approval of a PUD may be submitted by one or more owners of the property to be included in the PUD. If there is more than one owner of the property, the application shall show that the property is under unified control through the use of enforceable covenants or other commitments that run to the benefit of the local government. (Adapted from Bloomington, Indiana)

The requirement for enforceable covenants provides the community with some assurance that the multiple owners will proceed with the development.

SIZE OF DEVELOPMENT

PUD ordinances often require a minimum project size. One reason for this requirement is the view that PUDs are major projects that require more than just one or two lots. Other reasons for a minimum project size are that, without this requirement:

- the PUD procedures could become a substitute for a conditional use or a variance;
- the PUD process could be used to bypass the rezoning process, which may be more difficult; and
- the PUD review process would be overloaded with too many applications (So, Mosena, and Bangs 1973, 29).

Many PUDs have been built on small sites, however, so that setting a low minimum size may not be advisable. Substantial minimum project sizes are necessary for large master-planned communities, however, and a minimum size between 750 and 1,000 acres is appropriate for these projects. Otherwise, a minimum size is not needed. The authors of APA's 1973 report correctly concluded:

> [A]uthors of [PUD] ordinances should not attempt to control the character of the final product through a minimum parcel size requirement. There are other design standards to control that. The abuses feared by proponents of large parcels should be corrected through better administration and review. (So, Mosena, and Bangs, 1973, 29)

If a minimum size requirement is included, it may be useful to include a waiver provision:

> A PUD may have a lot size of less than [six] acres if the planning commission finds:
>
> (1) That an unusual physical or topographic feature of importance to the area as a whole, such as wetlands, exists on the site or in the surrounding neighborhood that will contribute to and be protected by the PUD; or
>
> (2) That the property or the surrounding area has an historic character of importance to the community that will be protected by the PUD; or
>
> (3) That the proposed PUD is adjacent to an approved PUD that has been completed and will contribute to the amenities and values of the neighboring PUD; or
>
> (4) That the PUD is located in an area that is being redeveloped and will implement the policies of the redevelopment plan. (Adapted from Clark County, Washington)

PROJECT APPROVAL STANDARDS

In addition to specific standards for uses, densities, and site treatment, many PUD ordinances contain project approval standards that a jurisdiction can use to evaluate the design and character of the project as a whole. If the ordinance includes detailed and acceptable standards on project details, such as common open space, circulation systems, design and the like, a requirement that a PUD will be approved only if it complies with these detailed standards may be adequate. If more general project approval standards are included, however, the ordinance must specifically make compliance with these standards a condition for approval.

Project approval standards in some ordinances include a requirement that a PUD will produce a better development as a condition of approval:

> The PUD shall accomplish, by the use of permitted flexibility and variation in design, a development that is better than that resulting from traditional development. (Baltimore, Maryland)

The following set of approval standards captures a number of the elements that will help produce an acceptable and attractive PUD:

> The council shall approve the PUD only if it finds that it satisfies all of the following standards:
>
> (1) It is consistent with the comprehensive plan and meets all the requirements of this ordinance; and
>
> (2) It is an effective and unified treatment of the development possibilities on the project site, [and the development plan makes appropriate provision for the preservation of floodplains, wetlands, streams and stream banks, hillsides, and other natural resource areas]; and
>
> (3) It is planned to harmonize with any existing or proposed development in the area surrounding the project site. (Adapted from Mandelker 1966)

In addition to specific standards for uses, densities, and site treatment, many PUD ordinances contain project approval standards that a jurisdiction can use to evaluate the design and character of the project as a whole.

SUCCESS IN PLANNED DEVELOPMENT REVIEW IN MANATEE COUNTY, FLORIDA

By Patricia Allen, Planner,
and Carol B. Clark, AICP, Planning Director, Manatee County

Manatee County, on the west coast of Florida has implemented a highly successful Planned Development (PD) review process incorporating a number of unique features. In part because county applications for PDs require rezoning, more than 75 percent of rezone applications go before the planning commission and board of county commissioners as PD applications. The county's PD review process, developed and refined over a number of years, benefits residents, developers, and the county.

The County's Land Development Code provides for 14 types of PDs. These range from residential, industrial, and commercial to mixed-use, waterfront, and public interest PDs. Development standards outlined in these sections of the code, include the intent of each district, along with the range of permitted uses. While some design standards are prescriptive, others are negotiable, with the code providing both flexibility and minimum standards. The result is that the county generally secures higher development standards in PDs than in standard zoning districts.

Proposed PDs are evaluated against 24 review criteria specific to PDs. The code is very clear in its requirement that no PD be approved if it is inconsistent with the county's comprehensive plan. The other criteria range from the physical characteristics of the site and its relationship and compatibility with surrounding property and public utilities, facilities, and services to pedestrian and vehicular circulation and access. Design quality, screening, setbacks, signage, and landscaping are all evaluated as well as potential impacts on various natural resources and historic features.

The code's most extensive chapter addresses "Development Standards of General Applicability" and includes requirements for bulk and dimensional standards; accessory, conditional, and temporary uses, and numerous specific sections. Standards not addressed by the PD criteria in such areas as parking, landscaping, and signage, are outlined in this chapter while providing staff and elected officials with the authority to negotiate final results in PDs.

A key to Manatee County's PD process is early public involvement and continuity of staff. The county sends postcards to all property owners within 500 feet of a proposed project. This notification includes a short project description and the contact information for the managing planner. Additionally, notice is sent to participants of the Neighborhood Registry program. County residents can request notification of development proposals within any part of the county. More than 300 individuals and homeowner associations regularly receive these notifications. These notices are sent immediately upon filing of an application. Early participation by the public leads to both better projects and less contentious public hearings. Formal notification is done through posting of signs, legal advertising, and mailed notices to adjacent property owners when hearings are scheduled.

To bolster the upfront guidance provided through preapplication conferences and application completeness and to provide for continuity, we try to have a planner handle the project from preapplication through development. This minimizes problems associated with "handing off" the case from the public hearing process to the development phase and provides citizens with an established contact point.

In 2006, the board of county commissioners began a "project preview" process. During a meeting subject to public notice requirements, the board considers a proposed project early in the review phase. This step enables the board to voice concerns and to identify potential issues, frequently leading to reassessment, redesign, and minimization of county and applicant resource investment. This has been a very positive addition to our review process.

This standard can be supplemented by adding more specific requirements, such as a requirement that the development be served by adequate public facilities, though requirements of this type can also be included elsewhere in the ordinance.

PHASING

The phasing of a PUD is an important issue. If a development is to be built in phases, it is quite likely that each phase will not have the average density approved for the project. A high-density phase may be built first, for example. Density will be exceeded if the entire project is not completed. Phasing problems arise in master-planned communities if some parts of the development, such as a residential area, are built first while nonresidential development, such as a town center, is postponed while residential areas are built. Phasing problems can also occur with common open space because it is also not likely that each phase will have exactly the proportion of common open space required to balance density in that phase; it is even possible there may not be any common open space in some phases at all.

One way of dealing with the density and phasing problem is to require that project density must be maintained during the entire development:

> All PUD projects shall be phased so that the density of any phase, when combined with previously constructed phases, does not exceed the approved overall project density. (Suffolk, Virginia)

This is an extremely rigid requirement. It can be met in single-family residential projects where each phase of the development has the same density as the entire development, but it can cause difficult planning and design problems if density varies in different phases.

The Nevada PUD law allows variation by phases if excess density is made up by lower density later in the project. This law can be adapted for enactment as a local ordinance:

> If a PUD will be developed over a period of years, the development plan, to encourage the flexibility of density, design, and type intended by this ordinance, may authorize a departure from the density or intensity of use established for the entire PUD for each phase to be developed. The development plan may allow for a greater concentration of density or intensity of land use within a phase of development whether it is earlier or later in the development than the other phases, but shall provide that a greater concentration of density or intensity of land use for any phase to be developed must be offset:
>
> (1) by a smaller concentration in any completed prior phase, or
>
> (2) by an appropriate reservation of common open space on the remaining land by a grant of easement or by covenant in favor of the city or county, but the reservation must, as far as practicable, defer the precise location of the common open space until an application for final approval is filed so that flexibility of development, which is a principal objective of this chapter, can be maintained. (Adapted from Nevada Revised Statutes, Section 278.110(3))

This provision will ensure the maintenance of project density if the project is completed. It takes common open space into account because that space will offset density in any phase that is higher than the project average. If the preservation of natural resource areas is provided for in the project, the reservation requirement can be applied to this land as well. The open space provision of the ordinance can also contain a schedule that coordinates the provision of preserved and common open space with development.

A problem arises if the project is abandoned because then average project density may be too high if the phases developed first exceed average project density. Abandonment has been a serious problem in some communities. To protect against this contingency, some communities require completion assurances through agreements and sureties:

> The applicant shall provide agreements, contracts, covenants, deed restrictions, and sureties acceptable to an attorney designated by the [legislative body] for the completion of the development according to the approved development plan and any other documents of record, and for the maintenance of such areas, functions, and facilities as are not to be provided, operated, or maintained at public expense, and shall place covenants on the property to bind any successors in title to any commitments made under this section. (Adapted from Pasco County, Florida, and Sarasota County, Florida)

Notice that the required sureties will cover all elements of the development plan, including elements such as a jobs/housing balance or an affordable housing requirement, if they are included.

ADEQUATE PUBLIC FACILITIES

The availability of adequate public facilities can be an important issue for PUDs. Projects that exceed a certain size may need new or expanded facilities, and the question of how they will be provided is a major one. A residential PUD without an increase in density will probably not affect the adequacy of public services, but at a certain point, an increase in residential density or the inclusion of nonresidential uses in a development will have that effect.

Many communities see the PUD process as an opportunity to ask for exactions from developers to help provide and pay for needed facilities. An exaction can be a requirement to dedicate land for streets, schools, or parks, or an impact fee the local government can use to provide these and other facilities. Agreement on developer exactions and impact fees is usually reached after negotiation outside the review and approval process, and sometimes through bargaining for a development agreement. The provision of common open space in a PUD could be another example of an exaction if it is not offset by the relocation of development to another part of the site to maintain project density or by a density bonus.

Any agreement on exactions for public facilities and infrastructure must satisfy the requirements of Supreme Court decisions that adopted a "nexus" test for these exactions (Mandelker 2003, Sections 2.11, 2.12). Under this test, there must be a connection or nexus between a development, such as a PUD, and any public facility or infrastructure problems the development creates, such as an overload on adjacent streets and highways. Some states have also adopted statutes that control when exactions may be demanded, and any exactions required for a PUD under an exaction ordinance must comply with these statutes if a state has one. The statutes enact the equivalent of the nexus test.

There is a possibility an impact fee or exaction agreed on in a development agreement is exempt from the constitutional nexus test (Callies, Curtin, and Tappendorf 2003, 111–14). The argument is that the nexus test does not apply because a negotiated exaction is voluntary. This is still an undecided question.

Adequate public facilities are an issue for all development in a community, not just PUDs. A number of communities have dealt with this problem by adopting ordinances requiring all new subdivisions to be served by adequate public facilities. The APA *Growing Smart*[SM] *Legislative Guidebook* includes commentary on adequate public facility ordinances and model state legislation that authorizes these ordinances at the local level (Meck 2002, 8–166). State growth management programs in Florida and Washington have a statutory concurrency program for public facilities, especially transportation facilities, that is similar and that requires facilities to be available concurrently with development or planned to be available (White 1996).

Adequate public facilities are an issue for all development in a community, not just PUDs. A number of communities have dealt with this problem by adopting ordinances requiring all new subdivisions to be served by adequate public facilities.

Requiring adequate public facilities for new developments, such as PUDs, can be a complex problem better handled outside a PUD ordinance. Some PUD ordinances require the availability of adequate public facilities as the basis for project approval, however. Some simply state that the development plan must show that the PUD will have adequate public facilities. Another alternative is to require a study of the impact of the project on public facilities:

> To provide information on the capacity of streets and other facilities serving a PUD, the applicant shall conduct a traffic impact study or other infrastructure capacity studies to provide information on the development's expected impacts on existing and planned facilities. (Adapted from Wichita, Kansas)

The powerful influence of the new urbanism movement on urban planning has had its effect on PUDs, and PUD ordinances are beginning to include new urbanism standards.

This information can provide the basis for approving a PUD if it creates an adequate public facilities problem. Nashville, Tennessee, has an adequate public facilities requirement in its ordinance that relates the adequacy requirement to the intensity of the PUD and mirrors the constitutional requirement that exactions demanded from developers must have a nexus to the impact the development creates:

> **Adequate Streets, Utilities, and Drainage**
> Approval of a PUD shall be based upon a finding that streets, utilities, and drainage features have an adequate capacity to serve the proposed development. As part of a development plan proposal, an applicant may offer to upgrade or otherwise provide adequate facilities to support the proposed intensity of development. Public facilities already included in an adopted capital improvements budget may be considered a demonstration of adequate capacity if properly timed with the anticipated construction of the development. (Adapted from Nashville, Tennessee)

This provision can be extended to include parks and schools. It may be necessary to define adequacy, which is done in adequate public facilities ordinances. The adequacy of public streets and highways, for example is usually defined by levels of service.

NEW URBANIST DESIGN STANDARDS AND POLICIES

The powerful influence of the new urbanism movement on urban planning has had its effect on PUDs, and PUD ordinances are beginning to include new urbanism standards. New urbanists have published ordinances, such as traditional (or neotraditional) neighborhood ordinances, that provide detailed standards for new urbanism development and that allow this development as-of-right if it complies with these ordinance standards. One option for PUD ordinances, then, is simply to provide that compliance with the standards in an adopted traditional neighborhood development or similar ordinance is required or that compliance is mandatory for certain kinds of PUDs.

Another alternative is to include new urbanism standards in the PUD ordinance, as several communities have done, where the development will be subject to discretionary review. Placing new urbanism standards in the PUD ordinance may be preferred because it gives the community some control over project design and how new urbanism standards are applied in project planning. This requirement can be quite brief:

> New developments shall be based on traditional forms in terms of placement, design, and quality of materials, so that they share a common identity and express their common heritage with [name of community]. (Traverse City, Michigan)

This type of ordinance leaves the details of a development to the development plan.

The model PUD legislation in APA's *Growing Smart*^{SM} *Legislative Guidebook* includes detailed standards for neotraditional development that can be adapted for inclusion in a PUD ordinance. They identify the essential elements of neotraditional neighborhoods:

> A PUD approved under this ordinance shall [may] provide for:
>
> (a) the creation of compact neighborhoods oriented toward pedestrian activity and including an identifiable neighborhood center, commons, or square;
>
> (b) a variety of housing types, jobs, shopping, services, and public facilities;
>
> (c) residences, shops, workplaces, and public buildings interwoven within the neighborhood, all within close proximity;
>
> (d) a pattern of interconnecting streets and blocks, preferably in a rectilinear or grid pattern, that encourages multiple routes from origins to destinations;
>
> (e) a coordinated transportation system with a hierarchy of appropriately designed facilities for pedestrians, bicycles, public transit, and automotive vehicles;
>
> (f) natural features and undisturbed areas that are incorporated into the open space of the neighborhood;
>
> (g) well-configured squares, greens, landscaped streets, and parks woven into the pattern of the neighborhood;
>
> (h) public buildings, open spaces, and other visual features that act as landmarks, symbols, and focal points for community identity;
>
> (i) compatibility of buildings and other improvements as determined by their arrangement, bulk, form, character, and landscaping to establish a livable, harmonious, and diverse environment; and
>
> (j) public and private buildings that form a consistent, distinct edge, are oriented toward streets, and define the border between the public street space and the private block interior. (Meck 2002, Section 8-303)

Apex, North Carolina, has a Traditional Neighborhood District that can be approved as a PUD district. The statement of purpose and intent for this district states:

> The purpose and intent of the planned development districts is to encourage the design of a more complete and sustainable environment consistent with the Town's small-town character through the application of imaginative approaches to community design that allows and encourages mixed uses, design flexibility, pedestrian-oriented development, and interconnectivity among uses, sensitivity to the natural environment and natural features, and the coordination of development with the adequacy of public facilities. (Apex, North Carolina)

The district includes a set of performance standards which, while not nearly as detailed as the standards contained in neotraditional ordinances, specify in more precise detail than the APA model the design specifics for this type of neighborhood:

> The purpose and intent of the TND Traditional Neighborhood District is to encourage the development of a vibrant mix of residential, retail, and offices uses that adhere to neotraditional neighborhood principles. This is done by allowing design flexibility and a mix of residential, retail, office, and recreational uses, with schools and churches, that are reviewed as a plan for development subject to the application of performance standards that:
>
> 1) *Neotraditional design principles.* Generally require the use of a grid pattern for the majority of development, along with back alleyways and garages and parking at the rear of buildings;
>
> 2) *Town center.* Require the development of a town center that is memorable—a square, green, and/or transit stop, with retail and offices uses connected to the mix of residential uses in a practical way;
>
> 3) *Variety of residential types in neighborhood.* Encourage a variety of dwelling types within a neighborhood;

Sarastota County, Florida, has adopted an elaborate system of development policies in its comprehensive plan that encourages compact development and mirrors new urbanism principles. . . . The plan also requires a greenbelt around each village.

4) *Shops and offices at edge of neighborhood.* Encourage shops and offices to be located at the edge of neighborhoods;

5) *Schools and churches.* Encourage the location of schools and churches within neighborhoods;

6) *Narrow streets.* Require streets to be relatively narrow, with street trees and sidewalks on both sides;

7) *Passive and active recreational opportunities.* Encourage the provision of both passive and active recreational opportunities. Small playgrounds and parks should be scattered throughout the neighborhood within walking distance to most of the homes;

8) *Residential uses mixed with offices.* Encourage the location of residential uses as accessory uses on the upper floors of retail and office uses;

9) *Prominent sites.* Encourage prominent sites to be reserved for civic or important buildings;

10) *Interconnectivity.* Require interconnectivity between uses;

11) *Small-town character.* Require the design of development at a scale that is consistent with [name of community's] small-town character;

12) *Expand opportunities for public transportation.* Establish land-use patterns that promote and expand opportunities for public transportation and for efficient, compact networks of streets and utilities;

13) *Encourage preservation of natural features.* Encourage the preservation of natural features and the natural environment on the site;

14) *Encourage integration of open space into plan for development.* Encourage the integration of open space into the plan for development; and1

15) *Public facilities available.* Ensure that public facilities are available to serve the proposed development. (Apex, North Carolina)

The Apex ordinance is somewhat different from a traditional neighborhood development ordinance because it requires consideration of open space preservation and adequate public facilities, issues not usually considered in traditional neighborhood development ordinances. York Township, Pennsylvania, also has a highly detailed traditional neighborhood development district approved in a process similar to a PUD approval process. The ordinance contains density bonuses for using selected traditional neighborhood development features in a project.

Sarastota County, Florida, has adopted an elaborate system of development policies in its comprehensive plan that encourages compact development and mirrors new urbanism principles. Consider, for example, this policy in the Resource Management Area element:

> To prevent Urban Sprawl by guiding the development of lands outside the Urban Service Area into compact, mixed-use, pedestrian-friendly Villages within a system of large areas of permanent Open Space. (Sarasota County, Florida)

The plan contains detailed requirements for village development, such as minimum size, affordable housing, density, open space preservation, transportation, adequate public facilities, and other requirements, and the following philosophy for village development:

> Neighborhoods form the basic building block for development within the Village/Open Space Resource Management Area and are characterized by a mix of residential housing types that are distributed on a connected street system so that the majority of housing is within a walking distance or one-quarter-mile radius of a Neighborhood Center. Neighborhood Centers have a Public/Civic focal point, which may be a combination of parks, schools, public type facilities, such as churches or community centers, and may include small-scale Neighborhood Oriented Commercial Uses that are no greater than 20,000 square feet of gross floor area and internally designed to specifically serve the needs of that Neighborhood. (Sarasota County, Florida)

The validity of space limits on commercial uses is not fully established, but they may be more easily supported if adopted to maintain the scale of a small-scale neighborhood.

The plan then states:

> The County shall adopt amendments to the Zoning Ordinance and Land Development Regulations to establish the specific requirements for developments within the Village/Open Space Resource Management Area to ensure consistency with the Village/Open Space Resource Management Area. The Zoning Ordinance will include the development of a new PUD-type zoning district that will implement the Village and Hamlet future land-use designations. (Sarasota County, Florida)

The plan also requires a greenbelt around each village.

The zoning ordinance implements these planning policies with several PUD districts that include detailed design standards typical of a traditional neighborhood development ordinance. The statement of purpose for the Planned Economic Development District is an example:

> The purpose of the Sarasota County Planned Economic Development district (PED) is to provide neotraditional design standards for both greenfield and redevelopment sites that will provide an efficient urban land-use form and cost-effective delivery services. The PED district is based on the key principles of urban-type development, which are connectivity, unity, mixed-use, balance, and pedestrian orientation. Connectivity within both newly formed development areas as well as infill sites demand that each site plan be formed and shaped by the context of that site—one size does not fit all. Each project shall be designed so that it offers alternative to the surrounding suburban development, where applicable, while it also connects with that suburban development. (Sarasota County, Florida)

The key to this district is the recognition that a one-size-fits-all format cannot be adopted for this kind of development, and that design must be sensitive to context. This perception provides the basis for including neotraditional development designs in a PUD ordinance, where project review can provide the necessary site-sensitive design, rather than in an as-of-right ordinance where this kind of review does not occur.

INFILL DEVELOPMENT

Infill PUDs can occur as individual buildings on single lots or as larger developments that cover several blocks in an urban area, such as a downtown core area. The ordinance may need a statement of purpose for infill developments:

> The [legislative body] finds that planned unit infill developments, when undertaken on unused land or land in need of redevelopment, at density levels that approximate, or in some instances exceed, historic density patterns can prevent sprawl, conserve open space, achieve a sense of neighborhood, enhance amenities, and reduce public and private costs. They should locate in close proximity to existing religious institutions, schools, and retail, entertainment, and employment centers as much as practicable. (Adapted from Delogu, Merrill, and Saucier 2004).

The design elements of a PUD ordinance, such as allowable uses and densities, can be adjusted for infill sites, and other elements, such as traffic and circulation systems, can include criteria that apply to these sites. Infill development may require special treatment in the ordinance, however. Compatibility with adjacent areas is one issue:

> Architecture and building materials must be consistent with the design of the development and compatible with the adjacent neighborhood. (Clayton, Missouri)

> *Madison, Wisconsin, adopted four design zones for its downtown area, accompanied by specific site development standards for each zone that include detailed design guidelines for developments expected to be more intensive than existing development.*

Another approach is to identify areas in which infill development is expected to occur and adopt design guidelines for these areas. This approach is especially helpful when infill development will have a higher density or intensity than development that surrounds it. To deal with this problem, Madison, Wisconsin, adopted four design zones for its downtown area, accompanied by specific site development standards for each zone that include detailed design guidelines for developments expected to be more intensive than existing development. The guidelines have the following statement of purpose:

> The design criteria serve to articulate community design principles, guidelines, and standards for PUDs in the near-campus design zones with the goal of enhancing the community's overall value and appearance. These criteria reflect the fact that the general development density and intensity of occupancy are expected to be relatively high in these design zones compared to other locations in the city. PUD districts that have residential components may be considered that are significantly larger, taller, and more massive than would be allowed in the underlying zoning districts. (Madison, Wisconsin)

JOBS/HOUSING BALANCE

An important issue addressed in PUD ordinances, especially those that include new urbanism principles, is the balance between jobs and housing within the development. Large PUDs will measurably affect the jobs/housing balance in any community. An imbalance will increase commuting, traffic congestion, and pollution because residents of a PUD will have to commute outside for employment. A jobs/housing balance can help avoid these problems. Implementing this policy requires a number of strategies, such as creating mixed-use developments, locating residential developments near employment centers, revising and modernizing home occupation provisions, and providing for dwelling units that include a workplace.

A number of communities have adopted programs to ensure an adequate jobs/housing ratio in development throughout the community and not only in PUDs. The usual procedure is to select a criterion for selecting the ratio and then quantifying the ratio (Weitz 2003, 20–21). Many PUD ordinances use the ratio of jobs to housing units as the basis for measuring jobs/housing balance. This is an easily applied ratio, though, as Weitz points out, it is accurate only if the number of housing units accurately reflects the work force. Communities that use this measure must be careful to determine the number of workers in each dwelling unit so they can set the jobs/housing balance ratio accurately. If the average number of workers in each dwelling unit is 1.5, for example, the jobs/housing balance ratio can be set at 1.5. The ordinance can then simply require "A jobs/housing ratio of 1.5," which must be reflected in development plans. This can be determined as development plans are presented for approval by examining the ratio of jobs to housing in each plan. There are also phasing problems. These are discussed above and in the section below on internal traffic capture.

TRAFFIC CIRCULATION SYSTEMS

The traffic circulation system is an important element in a PUD, and the ordinance should provide standards for its design. A general directive may be sufficient:

> Special attention in the design of vehicular and pedestrian circulation and parking shall be given to the location and number of access points to public streets; width of interior drives and access points; general interior circulation; separation of pedestrian and vehicular traffic; and the arrangement of parking areas that are safe and convenient and, insofar as practicable, do not detract from the design of proposed structures and neighboring properties. (Adapted from San Antonio, Texas)

This provision does not contain detailed guidelines, and a community may want to provide more specific guidance. The following provision adapted from Sarasota County, Florida, includes new urbanist concepts for street design:

> The visual and functional characteristics of streets are important in the design of the community and shall be guided by the following design principles:
>
> - Streets should be designed to create a sense of place, with attention to maintaining the visual integrity of the community;
>
> - Streets should be designed to accommodate a mix of travel modes including vehicles, bikes, transit and pedestrians;
>
> - Streets should be designed holistically considering the pavement, curbing, bikeways, pedestrian-ways, lighting, signs, front yard setback areas and building facades; and
>
> - Neighborhood streets should be designed to address two specific goals—connectivity and protection of the Neighborhood. This should be accomplished by providing connections to adjacent activities and neighborhood-serving businesses with streets that do not encourage cut-through traffic.

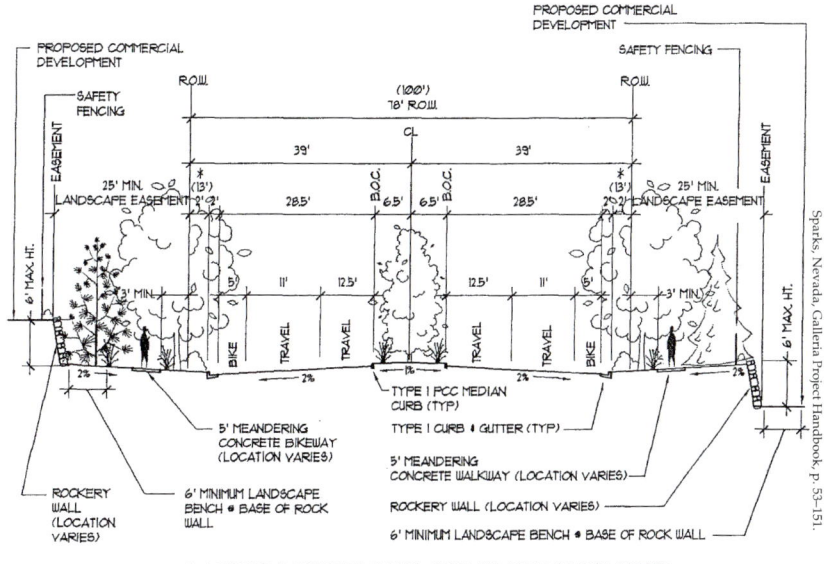

Figure 4-1. Sample Commercial Street Section.

CONNECTIVITY

Connectivity has become an important feature in traffic circulation systems, especially in developments that follow new urbanist principles. APA's Planning Advisory Service (PAS) has published a valuable report on street connectivity that reviews the arguments for street connectivity and provides ordinance examples and case studies of 11 jurisdictions that have dealt with street connectivity problems (Handy, Peterson, and Butler 2003). One point to remember is that connectivity can be an issue for all development, not just PUD, and that a community can adopt a street connectivity program that applies to all development in the community. A PUD ordinance can then require compliance with the ordinance standards in that program.

There is no universal agreement that street connectivity is preferable as a traffic circulation measure. Proponents argue that street connectivity:

- decreases traffic on arterial streets,

- provides for continuous and more direct routes for nonmotorized modes of travel,

- provides better vehicle access and reduced response time for emergency vehicles,
- provides multiple emergency evacuation routes, and
- improves utility connection and maintenance and other transport-based community services.

Opponents argue that connectivity raises levels of through traffic on residential streets, increases infrastructure costs and impervious cover, require more land for the project, decreases housing affordability and threatens profitability (Handy, Peterson, and Butler 2003, 13–14). The PAS Report indicates that, indeed, the evidence supporting some of the claims for connectivity is mixed.

The most common measures for requiring connectivity are regulating block lengths and a connectivity index. The connectivity index is calculated by dividing the number of street links, which are street sections between intersections and cul-de-sacs, by the number of nodes (intersections or cul-de-sacs), or link ends. The higher the number of links is relative to nodes, the greater the connectivity. An index between 1.2 and 1.8 is considered acceptable, while an index of 2.5 is considered optimal. The connectivity index number will depend on how links and nodes are defined, and this varies among communities. Communities also ensure connectivity by prohibiting or limiting cul-de-sacs and private streets and requiring street stubs for future connections. A connectivity index does not prescribe a particular development format and gives developers the flexibility to respond to site-specific issues, such as topography, so long as the connective index is satisfied.

The following provision from Durham, North Carolina, is a good example of a connectivity index:

> A. An interconnected street system is necessary in order to promote orderly and safe development by ensuring that streets function in an interdependent manner, provide adequate access for emergency and service vehicles, enhance access by ensuring connected transportation routes, and provide continuous and comprehensible traffic routes.
> 1. Connectivity Defined
>   (a) Connectivity is defined by the ratio of links to nodes in any subdivision.
>   (b) Connectivity ratio is the number of street links divided by the number of nodes or end links, including cul-de-sac heads.
>   (c) A link is any portion of a street defined by a node at each end or at one end. Stubs to adjacent property shall be considered links. Alleys shall not be considered links.
>   (d) A node is the terminus of a street or the intersection of two or more streets.
>   (e) Any location where a street name changes shall be considered a node.
>   (f) Any curve or bend of a street that exceeds 75 degrees shall receive credit as a node. Any curve or bend of a street that does not exceed 75 degrees shall not be considered a node.
> 2. Required Ratio
>   (a) The street network for any subdivision with internal roads or access to any public road shall achieve a connectivity ratio of not less than [1.40] measured within the PUD.
>   (b) A higher connectivity ratio in a surrounding area shall not provide justification to reduce the required connectivity of a proposed PUD.

3. Sample Calculation
   The following sample calculation shows how the street connectivity ratio for a subdivision shall be calculated.

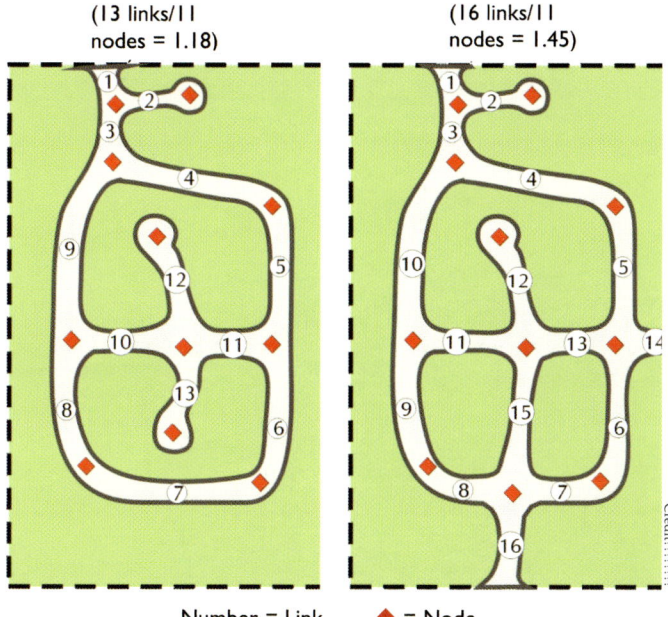

Durham, North Carolina: (Left) does not meet ratio; (right) modified to meet ratio.

INTERNAL TRAFFIC CAPTURE

Internal traffic capture has become another important issue in PUDs because, at a certain scale, the generation of new traffic by a PUD can have an impact on the adequacy of transportation facilities in the surrounding area. To minimize this impact, PUD ordinances can include a requirement that a certain percentage of the traffic generated by the development must be captured by the development internally. This can be achieved through various measures, such as creating an adequate jobs/housing balance, providing office and retail development and locating residential uses near them, improving walkability and pedestrian access, and implementing a traffic management program. An ordinance can deal with this problem by requiring PUDs to "capture internally an adequate [or a stated] percentage of the traffic generated by the development." The development plan will then have to contain measures for achieving the internal traffic capture requirement.

A more specific standard can identify how this should be done:

> The development plan shall implement trip reduction strategies to reduce vehicular trip generation and minimize the number of vehicle trips outside the community. (Ada County, Idaho)

Suffolk County, Virginia, adopted a schedule for phasing nonresidential with retail development to maximize internal traffic capture:

> Because the proximity of jobs and retail uses to housing in a PUD can achieve significant trip reductions produced by the internal capture of homework and home-retail trips, and because nonresidential uses should be established prior to residential uses in order to ensure that employment is created jobs-housing balance is maintained, the development plan shall include the following phasing schedule:
>
> A. Zoning permits for [20] percent of all residential dwelling units may be issued concurrent or prior to the establishment of any non-residential uses.
>
> B. Zoning permits for the next [50] percent of dwelling units shall not be issued prior to the substantial construction of not less than [30] percent of the nonresidential floor area.

C. Zoning permits for the remainder of all residential dwelling units shall not be issued prior to the substantial construction of not less than [75] percent of the nonresidential floor area. (Adapted from Suffolk County, Virginia)

A phasing schedule of this type can also deal with phasing problems created by jobs/housing balance and affordable housing requirements.

PEDESTRIAN CIRCULATION SYSTEMS

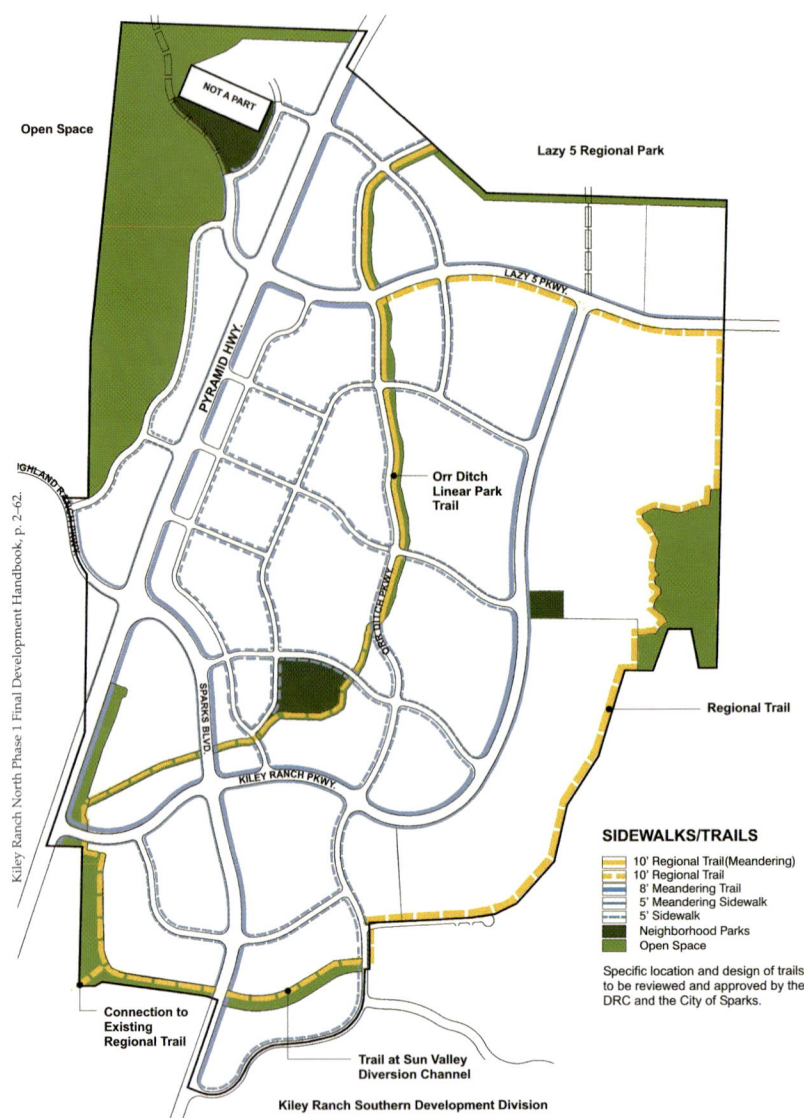

Figure 4-2. Sketch of Pedestrian/Walkway System.

Design standards need to be provided for pedestrian systems, which may not be covered by other ordinances. The system needs to provide a safe and convenient mode of travel and connect with areas outside the project. The following ordinance from Manatee County, Florida, describes the essential elements of a pedestrian network:

Pedestrian Systems

All residential Planned Development districts and other Planned Development districts, shall provide internal or external walkways where pedestrian circulation requires them.

The development plan shall provide for safe, efficient, convenient and harmonious groupings of structures, uses, facilities and open spaces in a manner facilitating pedestrian movement between major origins and destinations, within and adjacent, to the district, with a minimum of conflicts with vehicular traffic.

Pedestrian systems through buildings shall be related to a network of exterior open spaces reserved for pedestrian use and enjoyment, consistent with the handicap accessibility standards. Interior and exterior pedestrian ways shall be scaled for anticipated traffic and form a convenient pattern connecting major concentrations of uses within the district, and shall connect to principal access points within and outside the district.

Access for pedestrians and cyclists entering or leaving the PUD shall be by safe and convenient routes. Where there are crossings of pedestrian ways and vehicular routes at edges of planned developments, such crossings shall be safely located, marked, and controlled, and where such ways are exposed to substantial vehicular traffic at edges of districts, safeguards shall be required to prevent crossings, except at designated points. Bicycle or pedestrian paths, if provided, shall be so related to the vehicular system that street crossings are combined. (Manatee County, Florida)

Criteria for pedestrian systems can also designate destination points the system must connect:

(a) Within the Developed Area, the following standards shall apply:

(1) The pedestrian network shall provide direct pedestrian and bicycle pathways between and among the Village Centers, all Neighborhood Centers, public and private schools, and Recreational Spaces greater than or equal to five acres in size within a Village or Settlement Area.

(2) The pedestrian network shall be in a connected block pattern throughout the Developed Area. Intersections of pedestrian facilities shall occur on every pedestrian facility every 500 feet at a minimum. (Sarasota County, Florida)

Connectivity can also be an issue:

Pedestrian connectivity within the site and to the surrounding pedestrian network is critical. Shorter block lengths and blocks with sidewalks provide the structure for pedestrian connectivity. Block lengths greater than [500] feet require mid-block crossings. (Sarasota County, Florida)

DESIGN

Design review is an important component of many zoning regulations, not only for PUDs but for other types of development as well. Design issues in residential development have especially received considerable attention (Kendig 2004). New urbanist principles, which are discussed above, are an example of a comprehensive design solution.

A community may have adopted a design review ordinance that includes design principles and a design review process, and this ordinance can be applied to PUDs. A separate design review requirement can also be made a part of the PUD ordinance. Design review can be defined narrowly as dealing only with appearance, character, style, and building placement, or can be defined more broadly as including all the critical elements of project design. It can include a requirement for comprehensive design plans or design review standards for elements of the project, such as housing.

Comprehensive Design Review Programs

Some communities have adopted comprehensive design review programs that include extensive guidelines for PUDs. The downtown design standards for Madison, Wisconsin, discussed above are an example of a specialized set of design standards for a limited area. The Design Standards Manual adopted by Sparks, Nevada, is an example of a comprehensive set of design standards. The standards include site planning, such as building placement and land-use buffering, parking and circulation standards, landscape standards, and "Architectural Standards for Compatibility and Context." The manual also includes a separate chapter about basic slope-grading design standards, which are sometimes included in a separate ordinance. The following principles for the design review of nonresidential development provide an example of the Sparks design standards:

> The City's review of nonresidential development will consider the following criteria:
> a. Preservation and/or treatment of natural features;
> b. Compatibility with surrounding uses;
> c. Relationship to transit corridors;
> d. Proportional size, mix and arrangement of buildings;
> e. Placement and orientation of parking;
> f. Provisions of amenities (landscaping, plazas, pedestrian friendly environment, etc.); and
> g. Overall site circulation of vehicles and pedestrians. (Sparks, Nevada)

A city may require detailed design review of amenities offered by the developer, including such things as fountains.

Detailed guidelines for each of these elements are included in the manual. Development plans for PUDs must include a design element that implements these guidelines.

Franklin, Tennessee, has included design guidelines in its comprehensive plan; design and location are the two keystone elements. Design concepts in the plan are clustered in nine large geographic areas called "character areas." Each character area has "a distinctive vision and community identity." The combination of design concepts and land uses in each character area guides the "future quality and identity of the community." A separate section contains design concepts, and a separate map indicates where the design concepts apply, such as mixed-use centers and traditional neighborhood developments. The plan states how the design concepts are to be used:

> The following Design Concepts establish a series of design templates that guide the way different land uses can be developed and mixed relative to each other. The Concepts establish a series of guidelines that will allow the city to evaluate the quality and character of new growth. These guidelines are intended to supplement the city's Design Standards, which focus on more detailed aspects of individual site design. These Design Concepts are intended to link the details of design and the larger-scale issues of integrating and mixing land uses to create quality and livable neighborhoods and districts. (Franklin, Tennessee 2004, 29)

Developers of PUDs in Franklin must prepare a pattern book that accompanies a request for a rezoning. An example of such a pattern book is included on the CD-ROM accompanying this PAS Report. Pattern books have a long history as a way of providing design guidelines. They contain design elements such as lot types, building types, street types, setbacks, and cross-sections, and provide the design guidelines for a development. As one source put it:

> The central message of the modern pattern book is that the character and quality of urban spaces is created through careful attention to detail at three scales: the overall plan for the development; the image of typical urban spaces within that plan; and the individual buildings with their architectural details.... Pattern books provide criteria and patterns that ensure a degree of harmony among elements at all three scales. (Urban Design Associations 2004, 47)

Figure 4-3. Sample from *Jamison Station Pattern Book*, Franklin, Tennessee.

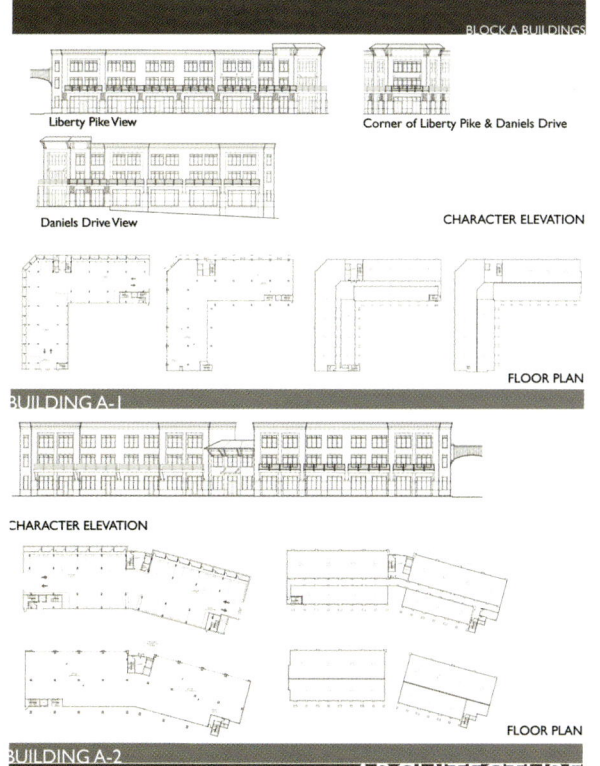

The Franklin ordinance specifically provides:

> A rezoning request for any PUD shall provide a pattern book that includes, but is not limited to, illustrations of elevations and floor plans for dwelling units, nonresidential buildings, and amenities structures, building materials, square footages of structures, street lighting details, and typical streetscapes.

Other communities are experimenting with the pattern book concept.

As an alternative to pattern books or a design manual, a PUD ordinance can include its own set of design standards.

Design Standards in the Ordinance

As an alternative to pattern books or a design manual, a PUD ordinance can include its own set of design standards. Apex, North Carolina, includes design standards for building aesthetics and architectural character. The purpose of each is indicated:

> Building aesthetics establish a base criteria related to the appearance of specific structures. These regulations strike a balance between creativity and innovation on one hand, while avoiding obtrusive, incongruous structures on the other. The Town strongly discourages architectural styles that do not build upon and promote the existing character of the Town. The Town supports the view that inspiring, well-maintained, and harmonious development is in the best economic development interests of all residents and businesses. (Apex, North Carolina)

Architectural character focuses on the micro-level details that greatly affect the overall appearance of a particular development. These architectural character regulations provide direction in aspects of color, facade materials, rooflines, and the enhancement of entryways. The primary goal is to define the "finishing touches" that provide the development with a sense of permanence, style, and compatibility. The town actively discourages proposals that have not taken these matters into account. The town wants all development treated as a lasting contributor to the community and as a "good neighbor" to its surroundings.

Guidelines are provided for each element. The building aesthetics section, for example, contains this directive on massing:

> A single, large, dominant building mass shall be avoided. Where large structures are required, mass should be broken up through the use of setbacks, projecting and recessed elements, and similar design techniques. Changes in mass shall be related to entrances, the integral structure, and/or the organization of interior spaces and activities and not merely for cosmetic effect. (Apex, North Carolina)

And, on anti-monotony:

> Monotony of design in single or multiple building projects shall be avoided by varying detail, form, and siting to the maximum extent practicable, within the standards set forth in this article, to provide visual interest. (Apex, North Carolina)

These are qualitative standards, but some are more specific, such as this standard for recesses and projections on facades:

> Facades greater than 100 feet in length, measured horizontally, must incorporate recesses and projections along at least 20 percent of the length of the façade. Windows, awnings, and arcades should total at least 60 percent of the façade length abutting a public street. (Apex, North Carolina)

Another method for achieving variety in housing design is to specify a number of different housing types in the ordinance, such as different types of single-family and multifamily housing, and then to require that a specified number of these housing types be used in the project or in each area of the project. The following provision for village development in Sarasota County, Florida, is typical:

> Each Village shall contain at least six of the nine Housing Types as defined above. To provide a range of Housing Types within Neighborhoods, each Neighborhood shall contain at least five different Housing Types as described above, and no more than 60 percent of the housing structures within a Neighborhood shall be of one Housing Type. (Sarasota County, Florida)

The ordinance also provides for exceptions, such as housing located at the perimeter of a project where only one or two housing types may be allowed to make the development compatible with adjacent uses.

An ordinance can also call for good, cohesive design without spelling out required design details.

> PUD architecture should demonstrate the cohesive planning of the development and present a clearly identifiable design feature throughout. It is not intended that buildings be totally uniform in appearance or that designers and developers be restricted in their creativity. Rather, cohesion and identity can be demonstrated in similar building scale or mass; consistent use of facade materials; similar ground-level detailing, color or signage; consistency in functional systems, such as roadway or pedestrian way surfaces, signage, or landscaping; the framing of outdoor open space and linkages, or a clear conveyance in the importance of various buildings and features on the site. (Somerville, Massachusetts)

Some ordinances include tables of design elements that are either required or optional. Some also require that a qualified design team must prepare the development plan for a PUD.

These ordinances are meant to illustrate the format in which design guidelines can appear, not necessarily the design guidelines a community should adopt. Some of the provisions quoted here are also debatable, such as an anti-monotony requirement. Sameness in design is not necessarily a bad thing.

Compliance with design guidelines in a PUD ordinance should result in the inclusion of detailed design guidelines for each project in the development plan. The development plan for the Hidden Springs development in Ada County, Idaho, is an example. The statement of general architectural principles provides, for example:

> Hidden Springs is not intended to be developed with one prevalent architectural style. Variety in the architecture is encouraged. An emphasis, however, will be placed on indigenous architectural styles, the use of quality materials and complementary relationships between building and site design features. (Ada County, Idaho)

Compliance with design guidelines in a PUD ordinance should result in the inclusion of detailed design guidelines for each project in the development plan.

Design guidelines can also be included in the private covenants, conditions, and restrictions adopted for the development and in development agreements.

PERMITTED USES

The PUD ordinance should indicate what uses are permitted. Cluster housing residential developments are limited to single-family residential use, with limited ancillary uses (see below). How uses are designated for other developments will depend on whether the PUD district is an overlay or a new base district. If it is an overlay district, the ordinance may limit permitted uses to those in the underlying zoning district or may authorize additional uses, either in the ordinance or by special exception. If it is a new base district it will specify the uses permitted.

PUD ordinances typically authorize limited ancillary nonresidential uses for residential developments, such as cluster housing:

> Commercial uses shall include those uses necessary or convenient for the enhancement of the value or utility of the PUD as authorized by the Board of Commissioners in its ordinance approving a PUD. Such uses shall be designed with respect to their nature, development intensity, and location so as to primarily serve the residents of the PUD. Commercial development shall be designed and landscaped in a manner that is compatible with residential

development and that provides for traffic flow or circulation that does not interfere with residential areas inside or outside the PUD. No outside storage of materials or equipment shall be permitted in commercial areas in a PUD. (Carroll County, Georgia)

If a PUD is adopted as a new base district, the legislative body may designate an existing zoning district as the zoning district for the PUD, and its use regulations will apply. If an existing zoning district is not designated, the ordinance can list the permitted uses for the PUD district in a table or textually. This list can be quite extensive, especially if the PUD is mixed-use development. The following provision illustrates a textual statement of uses for a variety of residential building types:

> Residences may be a variety of housing types and ownership types. Single-family detached, attached single-family, cluster homes, two-family homes, town houses, and multifamily residential developments are permitted. (Carroll County, Georgia)

Another alternative is to allow the legislative body to decide what uses are permitted when it approves the PUD district and the development plan. It can permit any uses permitted in any district in the zoning ordinance:

> Permitted uses within a planned commercial or industrial development are those uses permitted by the [legislative body] and specified in the adopting ordinance. The permitted uses may include all uses permitted in all districts. (Palm Beach, Florida)

The legislative body can also be given the authority to approve any use consistent with the comprehensive plan. These uses may or may not be limited to uses already allowed in any district in the zoning ordinance:

> Any use consistent with the comprehensive plan, whether or not permitted in any of the zoning districts contained in this title, may be permitted in a PUD approved under these regulations. The development plan shall show the uses allowed for the PUD, and the legislative body shall specify the allowable uses in the ordinance adopting the PUD district and the final development plan. (Adapted from Roseville, Minnesota, and Clark County, Washington)

Some PUDs, especially master-planned communities, may include uses not shown on the comprehensive plan. In that case, reconsideration and amendment of the comprehensive plan should occur before PUDs are approved.

Some PUDs, especially master-planned communities, may include uses not shown on the comprehensive plan. In that case, reconsideration and amendment of the comprehensive plan should occur before PUDs are approved. The following provision can be helpful:

> If the PUD includes uses not designated in the comprehensive plan, the application shall be referred to the planning commission for further review and shall be tabled until such time as the comprehensive plan is amended to authorize the uses that are designated.

The ordinance should also require the application for the approval of the development plan to list the uses shown on the plan and to indicate whether and how they are permitted in the zoning ordinance. The following provision assumes uses designated for the PUD must be uses permitted in one of the zoning districts in the zoning code:

> The application shall list the uses for which approval is requested in the PUD and shall indicate whether they are permitted uses in the zoning ordinance and the section under which they are permitted. All uses listed in the application must be a permitted or accessory use in the one of the zoning districts contained in the zoning code. (Adapted from Manatee County, Florida)

Some ordinances require a marketing study, either as the basis for approving a commercial PUD or for increasing the amount of commercial development allowed in residential developments. If applied to limit the amount of allowed commercial development, however, this kind of study may be subject to objections that it has been used to limit competition (Mandelker 2003, Sections 5.43–5.48). The following provision is typical:

> The applicant for a commercial or office PUD shall prepare a market feasibility report, which shall analyze:
>
> (1) All existing competing commercial facilities within a [five]-mile radius of the site, and a delineation of estimated market areas for the PUD and projected numbers of users assigned to each respective primary and secondary market area; and
>
> (2) The impact of the proposed nonresidential development on the quality and character of existing and anticipated future residential development within the neighborhood, including traffic impacts. (Lenaxa, Kansas)

MIXED-USE DISTRICTS

The ordinance can use the variety of alternatives described in the permitted uses discussion above to designate uses for mixed-use PUDs, although the ordinance can include specific authority for mixed-use projects. The following provision assigns the designation of allowable uses to the development plan:

> The uses proposed in a Concept Plan for Mixed-Use PUD can been entirely residential, entirely nonresidential, or a mix of residential and nonresidential uses. The location of these proposed uses in the PUD must be shown in the Concept Plan, with a maximum density for each type of residential use and a maximum square footage for each type of nonresidential use. (Apex, North Carolina)

Because a mixed-use PUD may be intended as infill development or for other specific locations, the ordinance may also want to indicate where these developments should be located.

Because a mixed-use PUD may be intended as infill development or for other specific locations, the ordinance may also want to indicate where these developments should be located:

> The Mixed-Use PUD District is authorized to provide for high-density, mixed-use multifamily residential development, generally with a minimum density of [40] dwelling units per acre and secondary office and other commercial uses. These districts should be located in those limited areas where mixed-use development is in accordance with the adopted comprehensive plan, such as areas delineated as Transit Station Areas and Urban and Suburban Centers. Mixed-Use PUD District regulations are designed to promote high standards in design and layout, and to encourage compatibility among uses within the development and their integration with adjacent developments. (Adapted from Fairfax County, Virginia)

The ordinance can also provide site development guidelines:

> Mixed-Use PUDs shall be in complexes with carefully located buildings, parking and service areas, open space, and use mixtures that are scaled and balanced to reduce general traffic congestion and to provide interdependent uses and uses that are compatible with adjacent and surrounding land uses. (Adapted from Manatee County, Florida)

MASTER-PLANNED COMMUNITIES

Master-planned communities need special attention in PUD ordinances because of their size and because they can contain a variety of developments. It is possible that the essential features of a PUD ordinance, such as requirements for traffic and pedestrian circulation systems, can be applied to or adapted for master-planned communities, and the ordinance can provide an expanded set of permitted uses. Nevertheless, some attention must be given to the special characteristics of these developments. Size is one issue, and attention should also be given to design features, such as the mix and location of uses, street and pedestrian connectivity, and internal traffic capture. Master-planned communities create their own environment, so ordinance standards for these communities should be generally stated to give developers design flexibility.

The following example is based on the Fairfax County, Virginia, ordinance, modified from a statement of findings the legislative body must make when approving a master-planned community. It is a generalized set of approval standards that may be used with any other requirements the ordinance may contain. The suggested size of the master-planned community is 750 acres, but a community can decrease or increase the minimum size depending on what it believes is essential for a community of this type. Words in brackets are optional:

> The Master-Planned Community (MPC) District is established to permit the development of planned communities on a minimum of [750] contiguous acres of land under one ownership or control. These planned communities shall be permitted only in accordance with a development plan, which shall constitute a part of the adopted comprehensive plan when approved and shall be subject to review and revision from time to time. The Master-Planned Community District regulations are designed to permit a greater amount of flexibility to a developer of a planned community by removing many of the restrictions of conventional zoning. This flexibility is intended to provide an opportunity and incentive to the developer to achieve excellence in physical, social, and economic planning. The [legislative body] shall not approve a Master-Planned Community District unless it finds the proposed master-planned community satisfies all of the following criteria:
>
> 1. A variety of housing types, [including an adequate amount of affordable housing, and] employment opportunities, and commercial services to achieve a balanced community for families of all ages, sizes, and levels of income.
>
> 2. An orderly and creative arrangement of all land uses with respect to each other and to the entire community.
>
> 3. A planned and integrated comprehensive transportation system [including requirements for street and pedestrian connectivity and internal traffic capture and] providing for a separation of pedestrian and vehicular traffic, to include facilities such as mass transportation, roadways, bicycle or equestrian paths, and pedestrian walkways.
>
> 4. The provision of cultural, educational, medical, and recreational facilities for all segments of the community.
>
> 5. The location of structures to take maximum advantage of the natural and manmade environment.
>
> 6. The provision of adequate and well-designed open space for the use of all residents.
>
> 7. The staging of development in a manner which can be accommodated by the timely provision of public utilities, facilities, and services.
>
> 8. Compliance with all of the requirements of this ordinance. (Adapted from Fairfax County, Virginia)

Howard County, Maryland, has a provision for a New Town district that requires a minimum size of 2,500 acres. Approval requirements are similar to those for other PUDs, though there must be a showing that public facilities are adequate under the adequate public facilities ordinance, and there are minimum and maximum acreage requirements for different uses. The ordinance also states that "each additional phase shall be of such size and at such location or locations as will permit effective and economic development of the portion so zoned as a part of the New Town."

Master-planned communities create their own environment, so ordinance standards for these communities should be generally stated to give developers design flexibility.

AGRICULTURAL AND NONURBAN PUDS

PUDs in agricultural and nonurban areas may also require special treatment. Some of the PUDs discussed above, such as cluster residential housing and the village development concept adopted in Sarasota County, are examples of PUDs for agricultural and nonurban areas. Cluster residential housing can be allowed in agricultural areas as a way of limiting housing development on agricultural land while preserving the remainder of the area for agricultural use. Some critics fault this type of development, however, as they believe it simply provides an entry for incompatible urban development in agricultural areas. Exclusive agricultural zoning, which allows only farm-related development, is viewed as preferable.

The following ordinance, which is adapted from Manatee County, Florida, authorizes freestanding, clustered, residential PUDs at low project densities in agricultural areas. It is a typical cluster housing ordinance with a common open space provision that requires 35 percent of the project to be in common open space. The section reproduced here addresses the site planning requirements that can integrate the PUD with the surrounding agricultural area, prevent any negative impacts on agriculture, and protect the PUD from any adverse influences from adjacent agricultural use:

> The legislative body may approve an Agricultural PUD of clustered housing not to exceed an average project density of [three] dwelling units to the acre. Site planning within the PUD shall provide protection of the development from potentially adverse surrounding influences, such as active agricultural operations. The orientation and clustering of the residential development shall be towards internal streets and pedestrian systems and away from adjacent local or thoroughfare streets and other adjacent land uses. A buffer containing a minimum of 200 feet in width shall be provided along district boundaries. The right-of-way along a project boundary may not be counted towards the 200-foot buffer.
>
> Strong consideration shall be given to the compatibility of the development with any surrounding agricultural operations, and the development plan shall include means to mitigate any potential impact of the development on such operations. Mitigation measures may include, but are not limited to, berms, larger setbacks, or additional screening. The preservation of significant upland vegetation habitats and wetland areas shall be encouraged. The development plan shall include measures to protect and enhance prime agricultural lands, open water bodies, wetlands, and sensitive upland habitats. (Manatee County, Florida)

The Boulder County, Colorado, PUD ordinance authorizes a PUD on agricultural land that allows housing to be clustered in one area of the project, while the remaining area is preserved for agriculture through a conservation easement.

The Boulder County, Colorado, PUD ordinance authorizes a PUD on agricultural land that allows housing to be clustered in one area of the project, while the remaining area is preserved for agriculture through a conservation easement. The following provision includes the major elements of the PUD provision and is adapted from that ordinance. Since this is a residential PUD, the uses authorized in the underlying zoning district apply:

> The [Legislative Body] may approve an Agricultural Residential PUD (ARPUD) in order to preserve agricultural, environmental, or open space resources. The means for preserving these resources shall be a conservation easement held by [name community] on that part of the PUD not developed for residential use. An ARPUD must have a minimum size of [35] acres, and [75] percent of the ARPUD must be covered by one or more of the following areas designated by the comprehensive plan: agricultural lands of state or national significance, designated open space, critical wildlife habitats and corridors, critical plant associations and rare plant sites, natural landmarks and natural areas, wetlands, and archeological site.

Any use, or combination of uses, allowed in the underlying zoning district may be included in an ARPUD. The uses permitted in the ARPUD must be specifically defined and approved as a part of the development plan. The average project density of an ARPUD shall not exceed [three] dwelling units per acre, and the developed area shall not exceed [25] percent of the total project area. The residential housing shall be located on the least productive agricultural land and in such a manner as to have little impact on any environmental or open space resource area, shall be located outside any known hazard area, and shall be clustered in such a manner to make efficient use of land resources and infrastructure. (Adapted from Boulder County, Colorado)

Mitigation requirements, such as those included in the Manatee County ordinance, can also be added. Boulder County also authorizes a Mountain PUD for the preservation of forestry land in mountain areas.

TRANSFER OF DEVELOPMENT RIGHTS

Some PUD ordinances that authorize development in agricultural areas require the preservation of agricultural land in these areas. The measures used to achieve this preservation may include a transfer of development rights (TDR) program that authorizes the transfer from preserved agricultural areas to areas where development is allowed. The agricultural areas are called sending areas, and the areas where development is allowed are called receiving areas. Owners of land in sending areas are assigned a specified number of development rights they can sell to owners of land in receiving areas to compensate for the loss of development rights on preserved land.

A substantial number of communities have adopted programs for the TDR as a way of preserving agricultural areas (Pruetz 2003). These programs apply throughout the community, and if the TDR is considered necessary for PUDs in agricultural areas, the PUD ordinance can make an existing TDR program apply. TDR programs are complex, and reference to an existing program may be the preferred alternative.

Some PUD ordinances contain their own TDR programs. The Sarasota County, Florida, ordinance, for example, contains a TDR program for its village and similar developments. Boulder County, Colorado, authorizes a TDR PUD in which the mechanism for protecting agricultural land is a TDR program contained in that ordinance. This is a detailed program that requires a decision on how much development will be allowed on sending and receiving sites. A TDR occurs only after the conveyance of a conservation easement on the sending site and the approval of a plan for development on the receiving site. Most TDR programs include similar requirements.

AFFORDABLE HOUSING

The provision of affordable housing has become a major issue in many communities, and a number have adopted inclusionary zoning ordinances that require developers to build a certain percentage of the housing in their developments as affordable, below-market-rate housing (Meck, Retzlaff, and Schwab 2003). These ordinances are usually applied at the time of subdivision approval. Affordable housing programs can be complex, and require decisions on what income group will occupy the affordable housing units, how they will be distributed, and controls on resale and rental to keep them in the affordable housing market. They may also authorize density bonuses to offset the additional cost of providing affordable housing, so that the cost of this housing is not passed on to purchasers of housing at market rates.

Some communities have required the provision of affordable housing in PUDs, especially master-planned communities that have thousands of units and can include an affordable housing element as part of their development plan. As with other requirements that can be complex and may be treated in other ordinances, it may be best to reference an existing affordable housing program if a community has one and make it apply to PUDs.

Some communities have included affordable housing requirements in their PUD ordinances, however. The following provision contains the elements that should be included:

(1) The development plan shall include an affordable housing element that provides housing affordable to low-income families. This requirement shall be fulfilled by one of the following:

   (A) A set-aside of no fewer than [20] percent of the units for occupancy by, and at rates affordable to, families earning no more than [65] percent of the median area income, adjusted for family size; or

   (B) A dedication of developable land of equivalent value, or its equivalent in cash.

(2) Affordable housing shall be appropriately designed and integrated into the overall development plan for the PUD [and shall not be limited to one phase of the development if the development is to be built in phases].

(3) The planning commission shall adopt rules stating how eligibility for affordable housing shall be determined and may set priorities for the sale or rental of affordable housing that may give priority to employees of the [local government.]

(4) Affordable housing provided under this section shall be restricted by deed, restrictive covenant, or other legal agreement accepted by the [planning commission] that requires its sale or rental at an affordable price or rent for a period of [25] years from the date the first certificate of occupancy was issued. The [local government] shall have a right of first refusal to buy or rent any affordable housing unit offered for sale or rental during this period. Rental and sales prices may only increase by (a) the increase in the cost of living since the unit was first sold, as determined by the Consumer Price Index, and (b) the fair market value of any improvements to the structure or lot.

(5) The applicant or its successor shall prepare an annual monitoring report on the affordable housing program, which shall include a description of how the affordable housing plan and deed, covenant or other legal restrictions are being enforced on the sale and rental of affordable housing.

(6) A PUD that provides affordable housing as required by this section [shall or may] receive a density bonus of one additional unit of housing for each unit of affordable housing that is provided in the development. (Adapted from San Diego, California, and Sarasota County, Florida)

More detail or different requirements may be substituted on issues such as income eligibility and restrictions on sale and rental. Sarasota County, for example, has detailed income and eligibility standards. A community may also want to limit the density bonus by specifying a designated percentage bonus increase.

DENSITY

Bonuses

Density is an important issue in a PUD ordinance. Density is not a problem if the ordinance provides only for residential developments with no density increase. If a density bonus or increase is contemplated, the legislative body must decide what the density will be, either in the ordinance or when the development plan is approved, unless the ordinance provides specific criteria that guide a decision on density by the planning commission.

The jurisdiction can authorize a density bonus in a number of ways. One of the most common is to authorize one in return for the provision of designated amenities, such as the provision of common open space and good design, which are assumed to be the justification for a density increase. This type of provision is usually enacted for a residential development where the density increase allowed is marginal, though some ordinances allow density increases up to 25 or 30 percent. The Nevada PUD law authorizes density increases of this kind and indicates the project characteristics a legislative body can take into account when authorizing density increases. The following provision is an adaptation of the Nevada statute for inclusion in a PUD ordinance. Language in brackets has been added. As originally written the statute did not limit the density increase:

> The [net *or* gross] density or intensity of land use otherwise allowable on the site under the provisions of a zoning ordinance previously enacted may not be appropriate for a PUD approved under Section [xxx]. The [legislative body] may vary the density or intensity of land use otherwise applicable to the land within the PUD [by not more then [20] percent] when it approves a [concept *or* preliminary plan] for the PUD in consideration of:
>
> (1) The amount, location, and proposed use of common open space.
>
> (2) The location and physical characteristics of the site of the proposed planned development.
>
> (3) The location, design, and type of dwelling units.
>
> (4) The criteria for approval of a tentative map of a subdivision pursuant to [the subdivision statute]. (Adapted from Nevada Revised Statutes, Section 278A.010)

This provision is useful for a cluster housing development that does not have an increase in density and for a PUD approved in an overlay district where the density that applies is the density in the existing zoning. Assuming that net density is the basis for an increase, it would be calculated as explained in Chapter 2 of this PAS Report for a cluster housing development and calculated from the existing zoning for an overlay zone. The density increase would then be applied to that number.

The Nevada statute authorizes density increases based on subjective factors that define the character of a development. As an alternative, an ordinance can assign a designated density increase when the development includes specific design features identified in the ordinance. This type of ordinance provides objective criteria for the increase. The St. Charles County, Missouri, ordinance is an example. It authorizes the planning commission to recommend density bonuses up to a total of 25 percent in return for the inclusion of selected features in the PUD. Some of the features are:

> 2 percent: Provision of pedestrian ways and bicycle paths beyond conventional sidewalk requirements, as required [by ordinance].
>
> 2 percent: Provision of tree and shrub planting, including peripheral and interior screening, fences, the landscaping of parking lots, and the use of existing trees in the plan.
>
> 2 percent: Building site designs and placements which advance the conservation of natural terrain, and minimize future water runoff and erosion problems.
>
> 3 percent: Recreational facilities, not to exceed 1 percent for each: swimming pool, tennis court, community center, or clubhouse building. (St. Charles County, Missouri)

The Lathrop, California, PUD ordinance provides an even more extensive list of features that can authorize a density bonus subject to an overall density bonus cap of 25 percent:

> 1. The planning commission may grant a density bonus up to 12.5 percent if the proposal meets all of the following minimum criteria:

a. Provision of a private internal street system (where possible) designed to avoid traffic congestion and provide for ease of access and circulation by emergency vehicles;

b. Provision of a common recreational open space area equal to 12.5 percent of total site area, excluding required yards;

c. Provision of peripheral visual buffers along property lines adjacent to existing or planned single-family housing areas which are designated for low density or very low density by the general plan;

d. Provision of back-on housing design and placement along arterial streets, where applicable, including a seven-foot-high ornamental block wall along the property line, landscaping between the wall and sidewalk in an area at least six feet in width, and waiver of direct access from the street. The waiver of access shall be recorded in the form approved by the city attorney.

2. The planning commission may grant a density bonus up to 25 percent if the proposal meets all of the applicable criteria described under subsection (D)(1) above, plus at least three of the following additional criteria:

a. The provision of common recreational open space or other open space amenities equal to 25 percent of total net site area, excluding required yards;

b. Pedestrian circulation substantially separated from the internal street system (total separation not required);

c. Provision of a separate area for the parking of recreation vehicles (RVs) at a ratio of one space for every 10 dwelling units;

d. Provision of landscaped corridors of common area as a substitute for individual front yards for single-family detached or attached housing, to be maintained by a homeowners association or other appropriate approach to guaranteed maintenance;

e. Provision of guest parking, in addition to basic requirements for off-street parking as prescribed by [ordinance], equal to one-half space per dwelling unit. Guest parking may be provided as parallel parking, as parking in-set at an angle to the street, or both; provided that such parking is consistent with [ordinance parking standards]. (Lathrop, California)

If a PUD ordinance does not continue the existing density or adopt the density of an underlying zoning district, it must specify the project density for the development.

These ordinances illustrate the use of density bonuses to obtain development features that are optional for the developer but that the community would like included. (Please see the plan for a Lathrop, California, PUD on the CD-ROM accompanying this PAS Report.) Recall that the York Township, Pennsylvania, traditional neighborhood district ordinance authorizes densities bonuses for designs that fit the traditional neighborhood format. Carroll County, Georgia, has a density bonus provision that provides bonuses for the preservation of natural features and archaeological and historic sites, as well as recreational facilities.

Just how the density bonus provision is drawn depends on how much density a community wishes to allow and for what reasons. Not all communities may want to allow density bonuses for all of the development features identified in the Lathrop ordinance, for example, and they may want to limit density bonuses to a lesser amount. Density bonuses may also be most useful for residential projects where design and other factors can allow a marginal density increase. For larger projects, such as master-planned communities, the jurisdiction should assign density limits when the concept plan is approved, and those limits should fit the project's development and design character.

Standards

If a PUD ordinance does not continue the existing density or adopt the density of an underlying zoning district, it must specify the project density for the development. This is usually done either by specifying the number of dwelling units per acre or a lot size for each dwelling unit. Specified density limits can also be adopted and may be a preferable method.

One alternative is to specify in the PUD ordinance the density allowed in a PUD zoning district. This can be done for the entire project or for specified areas in the project. The Fairfax County, Virginia, master-planned community ordinance is an example of the second approach. It specifies high-, medium-, and low-density areas. Here is the high-density provision.

> High: The overall density within the entire area of a master-planned community district that is designated for high density shall not exceed 60 persons per acre of gross residential area. The density in any one high density area shall not exceed 50 dwelling units per acre. (Fairfax County, Virginia)

Another alternative is to omit density limits and, instead, to provide in the ordinance that the legislative body shall decide on the density for the project either when it approves the PUD zoning district or when it approves a concept or preliminary plan following adoption of the zoning district. Because project density is an important decision that can affect the availability of public facilities and other growth issues, compliance with density designations in the comprehensive plan should be required if the local government has an adopted plan. The following ordinance contains factors to guide that decision:

> The allowable density for a PUD shall be within the range established in the comprehensive plan. Factors to be considered in assigning density are: site analysis, topography, drainage ways, views, soils, layout of lots, and site sectional studies. (Sparks, Nevada)

SITE DEVELOPMENT, DIMENSIONAL, AND BULK STANDARDS

Conventional zoning ordinances contain site development standards that regulate lot size, lot frontage and coverage, setbacks, and height. These standards can create an unattractive and rigid form of development that PUD ordinances are intended to prevent. The ordinance should authorize the jurisdiction to decide on development standards as projects are approved. The legislative body can make this decision when it approves the PUD zoning district if it is zoned as a new base district. The concept plan will not include site development standards. These will be in the development plan, which can be approved by the planning commission under standards contained in the ordinance or by the legislative body.

If the PUD district is adopted as an overlay zone, the site development standards in the underlying zoning will apply, but the ordinance can authorize a waiver to provide more flexibility. The following provision authorizes a wavier if the PUD plan is better or at least as good as what would be allowed under the underlying zoning:

> Bulk Incentives: In any PUD, the planning commission may recommend and the [legislative body *or* planning commission] may authorize exceptions to the applicable bulk regulations within the boundaries of a PUD if:
>
> (1) The [legislative body *or* planning commission] finds the exception serves the purpose of promoting an integrated site plan no less beneficial to the residents or occupants of the PUD, as well as the neighboring property, than is allowable under the bulk regulations of the underlying zoning district for buildings developed on separated zoning lots; and
>
> (2) The overall [floor area ratio *or* density] for the PUD will not exceed by more than [20] percent the [density *or* maximum floor area ratio] established for the underlying zoning district.

Manatee County authorizes exceptions to height limits. The ordinance sets a minimum height but authorizes exceptions based on compatibility,

relationship to adjacent properties, roofline and facade design, building materials, open space, and compliance with the policies of the comprehensive plan.

Another alternative keeps fixed standards but provides variety by authorizing different standards for different housing types, such as single-family detached homes, zero lot line homes, alley-loaded homes, and semi-attached townhomes. This can be done textually or in a matrix. The guidelines for housing types in the Cabarrus County, North Carolina, residential subdivision ordinance are an example and can be used in a PUD ordinance. They cover the following site development requirements for each of the home types listed in the first sentence of this paragraph:

- Minimum lot dimensions: Lot area and average lot width
- Minimum site dimensions in feet: Per building, per unit, and width
- Minimum yard dimensions in feet: Front yard, front yard (corner), front yard (single), front yard (total, and rear yard)
- Maximum height
- Maximum lot coverage: Impermeable surface coverage and structural coverage (Cabarrus County, North Carolina)

Fixed standards also can be eliminated, but the ordinance must then authorize the legislative body or planning commission to decide on the site development requirements. The ordinance standards that authorize this decision must provide an opportunity for good design, yet ensure that site development requirements are acceptable and project residents have needed

A community can authorize exceptions to height limits by considering issues like compatibility, relationship to adjacent properties, roofline and facade design, building materials, open space, and compliance with the policies of the comprehensive plan. These townhomes in The Glen near Chicago clearly meet several of these considerations.

privacy. Some of this can be handled through building spacing requirements, which are discussed in the next section. The following provision contains generalized standards for this decision:

Dimensional and Parking Restrictions

The [legislative body *or* planning commission] may approve a development plan that modifies and establishes lot size limits, required facilities, buffers, open space areas, setback requirements, height limits, building size limits, off-street parking regulations, landscaping requirements, and density and intensity limits that differ from those in the underlying zoning ordinance, where these regulations or changes are consistent with and implement the purposes of this chapter and the criteria for approval of a PUD. Dimensional, parking, and use restrictions of the underlying zoning shall not apply to the area within an approved PUD unless expressly retained in the development plan. (Adapted from Traverse City, Michigan)

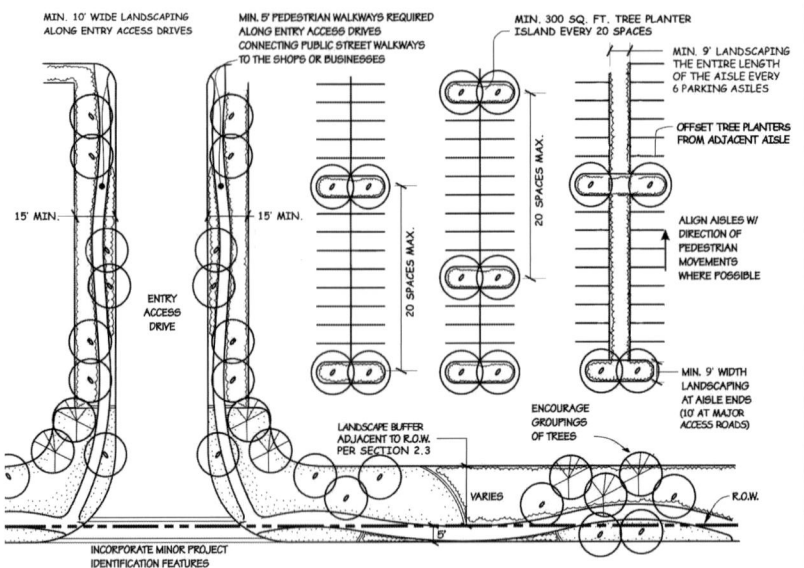

Figure 4-4. Sample Parking Lot and Parking Lot Landscaping Requirements.

Kiley Ranch North Phase 1 Final Development Handbook, p. 3–8.

An ordinance can also provide a comprehensive set of design standards that cover site development features. Standards of this kind can be context-sensitive and provide better guidance for creative design opportunities. The Sparks, Nevada, *Design Standards Manual* is an example. It contains detailed site development guidelines that must be followed. For example:

> On commercial and office sites three acres and larger, a minimum 15 percent of the total primary building frontage shall be located at or near the front setback line. Such siting, together with landscape treatment, reinforces and strengthens the streetscape, and helps to screen off-street parking areas. (Sparks, Nevada)

The manual contains the following building orientation standards for multifamily development:

Building Orientation

a. Buildings shall be generally oriented with varying setbacks to provide visual interest and varying shadow patterns. There shall be variations in the buffers.

b. Buildings shall be oriented in such a way as to create courtyards and open space areas. Clustering of multifamily units shall be consistently planned throughout the development.

c. To provide indoor privacy between living spaces, there should be distance separations, buffering, or changes in the angle of units.

d. Private outdoor space shall be designed with maximum consideration for privacy, such as separations and orientation of the outdoor space.

e. Building orientation shall provide opportunities for public spaces, for recreation, and for general open space. Public spaces shall be located within central areas accessible to the majority of the surrounding units. The open space shall be useable areas and not steep slopes or riparian areas. (Sparks, Nevada)

Building Spacing

Ordinances may need to include requirements for the spacing of buildings if they do not prescribe traditional, fixed-site development standards. Requirements for building spacing are important to prevent overcrowding of the site, to ensure privacy, and to prevent negative impacts on adjacent areas. This again is a problem that can be handled through comprehensive design standards, but some communities have adopted specific requirements. Fairfax County, Virginia, for example, has no site development standards in its master-planned community ordinance except for building spacing, which is set under a negative impact standard:

1. Maximum building height: No Regulation

2. Minimum yard requirements:

    A. The location and arrangement of structures shall not be detrimental to existing or prospective adjacent dwellings or to the existing or prospective development of the neighborhood.

    B. No single-family detached dwelling shall be erected closer than [16] feet to any other single-family dwelling unless a lesser distance is specifically identified on an approved final development plan.

    C. No single-family detached or attached dwelling or accessory structure shall be erected closer than 15 feet to any public street right-of-way line unless shown on an approved final development plan.

3. Maximum floor area ratio: No Regulation

4. Maximum percentage of lot coverage: No Regulation (Fairfax County, Virginia)

Spacing requirements can also be governed by site planning standards that provide a specific criterion linked to planning practice:

> Spacing between principal buildings in the development shall be at least [12] feet and shall be consistent with recognized site planning principles, including, but not necessarily limited to: Natural landscape, topography, usable backyard area for use by residents, and openness normally afforded by intervening streets and alleys. (Adapted from Antioch, Illinois)

Another option is to state a minimum distance. This can especially be an issue for multifamily dwellings in a single-family residential area:

> Multifamily dwellings must be spaced at least [20] feet apart and a distance of at least [50] feet from a single-family dwelling for each [10] feet in height of a multifamily structure with a minimum distance of [50] feet. (Adapted from Carroll County, Georgia)

A fixed-distance provision may be acceptable for small and standardized PUDs but can be arbitrary if PUDs vary in size and character Exceptions can be made available, of course.

A more flexible standard can be more workable, as in this example from the Sparks, Nevada, Design Standards Manual:

> Adjacent residential and nonresidential uses shall be as separated as is necessary to maintain a livable residential environment. This may be achieved with masonry walls, landscaping, berms, building orientation, and activity limitations. (Sparks, Nevada)

Figure 4-5. Sample Bufferyard Landscaping Requirements.

Bufferyards, which have been adopted as requirements in some communities, provide another method for dealing with building spacing.

Perimeter Requirements

Special attention needs to be paid to development and design problems at the perimeter of PUDs, where they may not be compatible with adjacent areas. Perimeter requirements will vary depending on the size of the development and its character. A single-family residential PUD in a single-family residen-

Figure 4-6. Illustration of Perimeter Sign and Landscape Requirements

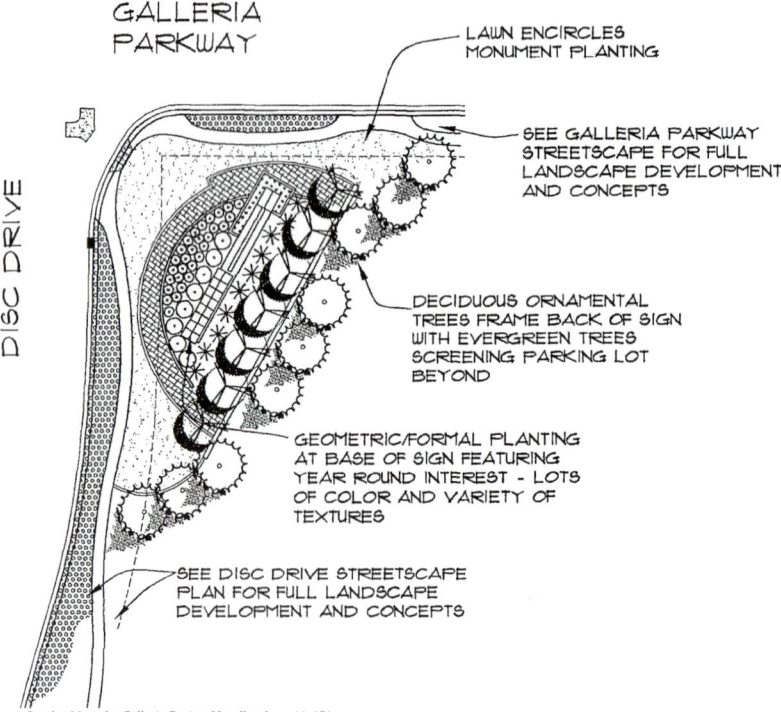

tial area will not have compatibility problems. A mixed-use development in a residential area may have perimeter compatibility problems. Smaller developments will find it more difficult to include protective features at perimeters because enough space may not be available. Larger developments can more easily be designed with adequate perimeter protection. This, again, can be part of a comprehensive design review process.

The following comments from my earlier report are still relevant:

> Perimeter and screening requirements are difficult to draft. For example, if only part of the perimeter is developed with high-rise structures, the appli-

cation of a fixed additional setback applicable to such structures may result in unpleasant irregularities and wasted space. Topographical features will also affect the treatment of boundaries. If the boundary of a project is on a hill, the placing of high-rise buildings near the edge of the hill may improve rather than detract from visual amenities. Nor do high-rise structures create the only problems, as low-rise commercial and industrial buildings may have to be screened from adjoining uses. Size is another factor, as substantial perimeter setbacks may be impracticable in small projects. Another problem is that the planned development is difficult to relate to adjacent land uses if the surrounding area is undeveloped at the time the planned development is constructed. Even more specialized problems arise if the planned development abuts a major highway, or if the land adjoining the planned development is in another zoning jurisdiction. The best approach appears to be a generalized standard.... (Mandelker 1966, 51)

With very large developments, such as master-planned communities, a step-down density strategy can be helpful at perimeters. In this strategy, density is stepped down at the perimeter from the average density for the development:

> Densities and intensities within [200] feet of the perimeter of a development shall be stepped down [20] percent from the average density and intensity of the PUD.

This kind of requirement can also be staggered, with a greater density step-down required next to the perimeter and a smaller density step-down in the next adjacent band of development. Another possibility is to prohibit or limit intensive development next to the perimeter, such as retail and office uses, or to limit the height of buildings in these areas.

The traditional way of treating areas near perimeters is through setbacks that are screened or landscaped and kept free of buildings and structures. The ordinance may state the depth of the perimeter setback:

> A setback area of not less than [25] feet shall be provided and maintained along all exterior boundaries. This shall be kept free of buildings, structures, and parking and shall be maintained in landscaping. (Adapted from Deerfield, Illinois)

This section can also reference landscaping standards, either in the PUD ordinance or elsewhere.

The perimeter setback area can also be required to be the same as the setback in an adjacent area:

> Yards and open spaces adjoining the boundaries of the development shall not be less than the yard requirements of the adjoining village residential district. A landscaped and land-sculptured buffer strip at least [10] feet wide shall be provided along all peripheral lot lines. Larger- than-minimum-width buffer strips may include pedestrian walkways, bike paths, or recreational trails. They are encouraged where such trails could connect the residential area to various community amenities, including, but not necessarily limited to, schools and parks. (Antioch, Illinois)

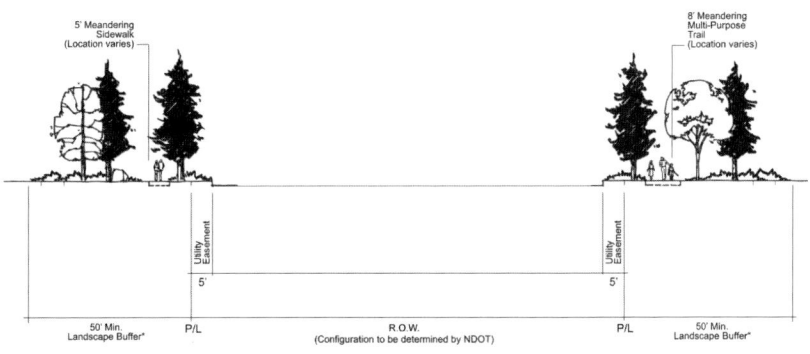

Figure 4-7. Sample Highway Landscaped Buffer.

Kiley Ranch North Phase 1 Final Development Handbook, p. 2–46.

Another alternative is to eliminate fixed setbacks, and provide standards in the ordinance under which the planning commission or legislative body can decide on the depth of a setback area and its treatment as the development plan for each development as it is approved:

> The perimeter of a cluster development shall be buffered from adjacent property not included in the project in a setback area adequate to protect the privacy and amenity of adjacent existing uses. The setback area shall be buffered using one or a combination of the following methods:
>
> (1) Buffer yards and transition areas as specified in [state ordinance]; or
>
> (2) Density transition areas; or
>
> (3) Berm; or
>
> (4) Landscaping or screening as required by [state ordinance].
>
> The [legislative body *or* planning commission] shall determine the depth of the setback area and the buffering methods selected that shall be included in the [PUD district *or* final development plan.] These may vary in different areas and phases of the PUD. (Adapted from Queen Creek, Arizona)

Parking, Loading, Access, Buffering, Screening, Landscaping, Utilities, and Signs

Many or all of the problems related to parking, loading, access, buffering, screening, landscaping, utilities, and signage in site development are usually covered independently in zoning, subdivision, or other ordinances. Cary, North Carolina, for example, has extensive landscaping, buffering, screening and tree protection regulations that apply to PUDs and other developments. Bufferyard requirements that require screening and landscaping are also found in a number of zoning ordinances as a method of making adjacent uses compatible. Currtuck County, North Carolina, is one of numerous examples of zoning ordinances with good bufferyard requirements. Design standards can include screening and buffering requirements, as in the Franklin, Tennessee, design standards. Municipalities have also developed extensive regulations for parking, loading, and signs.

When the zoning ordinance already covers these problems adequately, the PUD ordinance can make existing code requirements apply. The following provision applies broadly to circulation systems and open space as well as other site development requirements:

Figure 4-8. Sample Frontyard Landscaping Requirements.

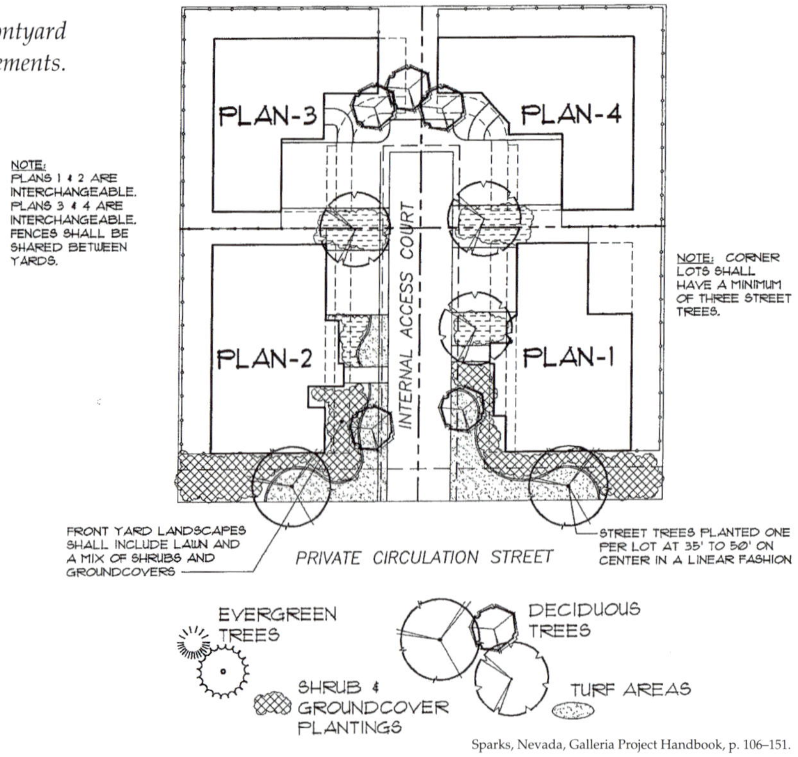

Sparks, Nevada, Galleria Project Handbook, p. 106–151.

The Subdivision and Zoning ordinances and Standards adopted by the Planning Commission shall govern the spatial arrangement of uses and structures on the site and all other elements of site design and improvement, including the design and improvement of pedestrian and vehicular circulation and parking; access; landscaping; the location and improvement of open spaces for light, air, recreation and other purposes; provisions for utilities, facilities and services; signs; and the relationship of the PUD to adjacent areas. (Adapted from Pittsburgh, Pennsylvania)

PUD ordinances may also contain regulations for some or all of these requirements, either to establish an independent set of regulations or to modify regulations included elsewhere. When design plans must be included in the development plan, they can include directives for these project elements. The availability of extensive recommendations and ordinances governing all of these issues suggests communities should consult them if they want to include these requirements in their PUD ordinances.

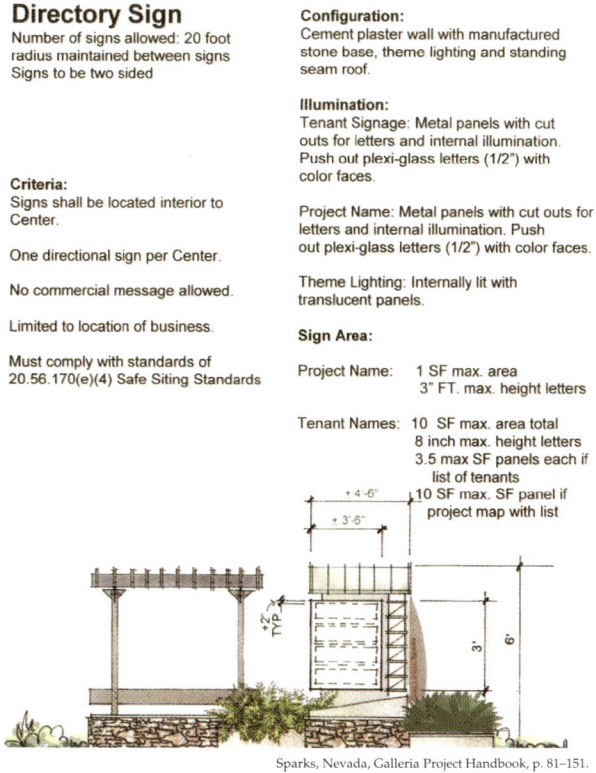

Figure 4-9. Sample Regulations for a Directory Sign.

Sparks, Nevada, Galleria Project Handbook, p. 81–151.

Open and Common Open Space

The provision of open space has always been an important feature of PUDs, and ordinance provisions requiring open space in PUD ordinances are now substantially standardized. Initially the principal concern was to provide common open space in residential developments consisting of activity centers, such as clubhouses, tennis courts, and swimming pools. Common open space is still an important feature of many PUDs, but equal attention is now given to the preservation of natural resource areas where development is not allowed. This is a fairly complex area of PUD regulation. What is acceptable as common open space must be carefully defined and provision made for maintenance and management and the creation of homeowners associations.

Definition, adequacy, development and use. A first priority is to require the set-aside of an adequate amount of open space and common open space and to define each:

(1) A minimum of [25] percent of the [gross *or* net] project area shall be set aside as open and common open space exclusive of street right-of-way. [Fifty] percent of this area shall be set aside as open space.

(2) Common open space is an area or areas within the boundaries of the PUD designed, set aside, and maintained for use by all residents of the PUD, or by residents of a designated portion of the development, that is not dedicated as public lands and does not include open space as defined in paragraph (4).

(3) The location of common open space shall be planned as much as possible as a contiguous area located for the maximum benefit of the residents, preserving, and where possible, enhancing natural features. Buildings, structures, and improvements permitted in the common open space must be appropriate to the uses authorized for the common open space and must conserve and enhance the amenities of the common open space, having regard to its topography and unimproved condition. [Common open space shall include a reasonable amount of active recreation facilities.]

(4) Open space shall consist of primary and secondary open space:

(a) Primary open space: The following are primary open space areas and shall be designated as open space, unless the applicant demonstrates that this provision would constitute an unusual hardship and is contrary to the purposes of this PUD ordinance: The 100-year floodplain; stream buffer areas; slopes above [25] percent in a contiguous area of at least [25,000] feet; wetlands; habitat for federally listed endangered or threatened species; archeological sites, cemeteries and burial grounds; agricultural lands of at least [20] contiguous acres; and existing healthy native forests

(b) Secondary open space. The following are secondary open space areas and shall be included within the required open space to the maximum extent possible: Important historic sites; existing healthy, native forests of at least one contiguous acre; other significant natural features [and scenic viewsheds, such as ridge lines, hedge rows, field borders, meadows, fields, peaks, and rock outcroppings], particularly those that can be seen from public roadways; agricultural lands of at least [five] contiguous acres containing at least [25] percent prime farmland soils; areas that connect the tract to neighboring open space, trails or greenways; soils with severe limitations for development due to drainage problems; landscaped site elements, such as arterial street buffers, district boundary buffers, civic greens, and landscaped medians.

(5) Open space is limited to the following uses: Pedestrian, bike and multipurpose trails; passive recreation areas, including pocket parks; active recreation areas, such as ball fields and playgrounds, not exceeding [50] percent of the required open space and limited in impervious area to [10] percent of the required open space; agriculture, and silviculture or pasture uses.

(6) The development plan shall:

(a) Identify the uses and development allowed in the open and common open space.

(b) Identify any commercial recreational land use anticipated that shall not be part of the required minimum amount of common open space;

(c) Identify any community or institutional recreational facility deemed appropriate by the [planning commission] and made necessary by the magnitude and density of the PUD, which shall be included in the minimum acreage for common open space but which shall not exceed [50] percent of the minimum area required to be in common open space.

(d) Include a schedule that shall coordinate the preservation of open space and the provision of common open space with the construction of the PUD, taking into account the location of the open space and common open space and any phases in the construction of the PUD. (Adapted from Warrenton, Virginia; Cabarrus County, North Carolina; So Mosena and Bangs 1973; Mandelker 1966; and Nevada Revised Statutes, Section 278A.010)

This is a comprehensive provision that requires the inclusion of open and common open space, defines each, and specifies how each is to be used. It also sets priorities for the preservation of open space areas. A community may not want to include all of these open space areas in the ordinance, may have others they want to include, or may want to modify the priorities. Some of the open space listed as secondary, for example, might be given a primary priority.

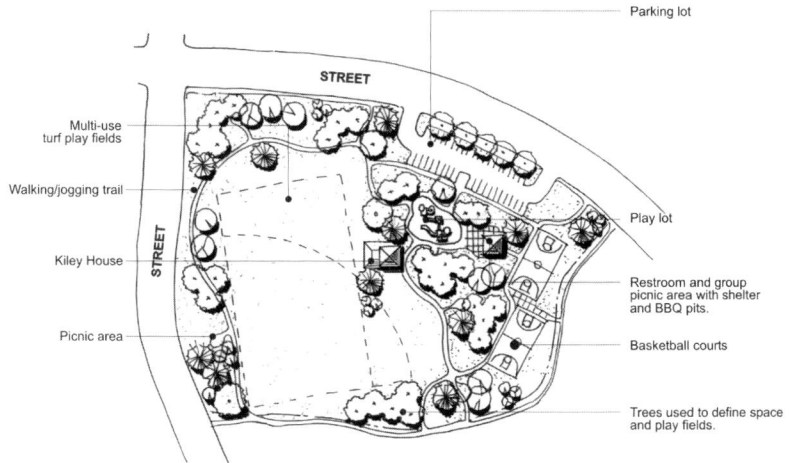

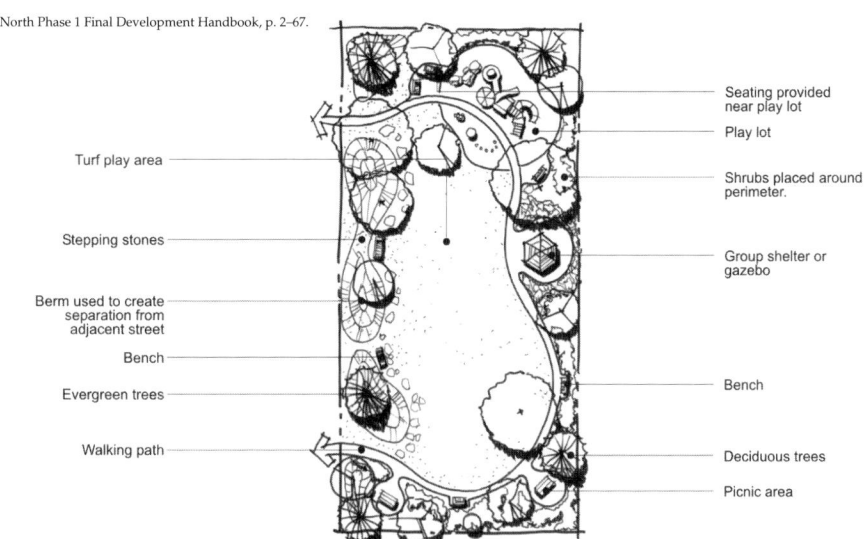

Figure 10. Concept Sketches for a Neighborhood Park (left) and a Vest Pocket Park (bottom).

The standards included in this provision are intentionally open because it is difficult to include more precise criteria without creating too rigid requirements. One exception is the required open space percentages and other quantitative requirements. They are in brackets because the percentages to be selected are a matter for local decision, though many communities require an open space allocation of as much as 40 or 50 percent of the PUD. These percentages may vary depending upon the density, character, and location of the development. Higher-density development may need more open space, and an infill development in an urban area may not need any.

The contiguity requirement in paragraph (3) ensures that common open space will be accessible and usable. It is possible to provide a more specific requirement:

> **Contiguity:** At least [60] percent of the required common open space shall be in a contiguous tract, and the minimum width for any required open space shall be [50] feet. For the purposes of this section, "contiguous" shall include any common open space bisected by a residential street (including a residential collector). (Adapted from Cabarrus County, North Carolina)

Paragraph (5) lists the uses permitted in open space areas. Areas like floodplains, wetlands, and hillsides may be governed by a separate local ordinance, which should be identified. Floodplains and wetlands may be subject to regulation under federal and state law. Paragraph (6) identifies issues the development plan should cover. Subparagraphs (b) and (c) apply primarily to larger developments, such as master-planned communities that may require larger facilities not located in common open space areas. It is essential to list the uses and development allowed in open and common open space, as required by the PUD or any other ordinance or by state or federal law. The development schedule is a phasing requirement intended not to allow density in one phase to exceed the project average if the provision of open space areas is deferred. The phasing requirement discussed above can also be included here.

Ownership and maintenance. The PUD ordinance needs to contain provisions for the ownership and maintenance of open space and common open space:

(1) Open space and common open space shall be protected in perpetuity by one of the following:

   (a) A deed of conveyance of title to [name government entity], which shall state the restrictions governing the use, improvement, maintenance, and preservation of open and common open space as conditions to the deed of conveyance.

   (b) A deed of conveyance to a homeowners association.

   (c) For open space: a permanent conservation or development easement in favor of [name government or private entity], or a permanent restrictive covenant for conservation purposes or prohibiting development in favor of [name government or private entity].

(2) If open or common open space is deeded to a homeowners association, the applicant shall record a declaration of covenants, conditions, and restrictions, which shall include, but not be limited to, all of the following:

   (a) They shall govern the use of the open or common open space and restrict its uses to those specified in this ordinance and in the final development plan;

   (b) They shall run with the land in perpetuity;

   (c) They shall provide for a lien on the open or common open space to secure collections of assessments levied by the homeowners association;

   (d) They shall grant the city the authority to maintain open or common open space, assess the cost of maintenance against the owners of the property jointly and severally, and enforce the recorded covenants, conditions, and restrictions; and

   (e) They shall be filed with the development plan. (Adapted from Franklin, Tennessee, and San Antonio, Texas)

This provision is broad enough to include both open and common open space, but language referring to open space preservation can be deleted if only common open space is to be provided. The purpose of paragraph (1) is to ensure some permanent legal document that will guarantee the protection of open and common open space in perpetuity. The alternatives identified are the usual techniques used for preservation of this type. The additional requirements in paragraph (2) apply if the deed is to a homeowners association. They require the filing of protective covenants, restrictions, and conditions to ensure the continuing integrity of the common open space and authorize their enforcement by the local government. The Nevada PUD law includes a detailed provision authorizing enforcement by the municipality that can be adapted for inclusion in a local ordinance (see sidebar).

The ordinance can also require security for the maintenance of the common open space:

> To secure the maintenance of the common open space, the applicant shall provide a nonrevocable letter of credit, set-aside letter, assignment of funds, certificate of deposit, deposit account, bond, or other readily accessible source of funds. A bond will be accepted only when a bond is required by state statute, or when circumstances make a bond the only reasonable form of assurance, as determined by the Director of Planning, and the bond adequately protects the interests of the City. (Adapted from Belleville, Illinois)

Homeowners associations. A PUD ordinance should include requirements for a homeowners association if it is contemplated that these associations will manage and maintain open and common open space. The homeowners association will be established by a private instrument, which is governed by a statute that provides for the method and type of organization, authority, voting rights, levy of fees, and other requirements. The ordinance should specify the contents of the private instrument that will create the homeowners association so that a permanent association with the required responsibilities and authorities is ensured. Maintenance and management can especially be problems and are major concerns in the provision that follows:

> If common open space is to be deeded to a homeowners association, the applicant, as a condition to the approval of the final development plan, shall provide for and establish the association before any property is sold. The dedicatory instrument of the homeowners association shall comply with, but not be limited to, the following requirements:
>
> (1) The association shall own, manage, and maintain the common open space and facilities, and there shall be a management plan for the use and permanent maintenance of the common areas and facilities in the common open space. It shall also preserve and manage any open space as required in the final development plan.
>
> (2) The association shall be self-perpetuating and adequately funded by regular assessments, special assessments, or both, to accomplish its purposes. The association shall be authorized to adjust assessments in order to meet changing needs.
>
> (3) The association shall not be dissolved, nor shall it dispose of any common open space or facilities, by sale or otherwise, except to an organization conceived and established to own and maintain

---

ENFORCEMENT OF PROVISIONS FOR MAINTENANCE OF COMMON OPEN SPACE, NEVADA REVISED STATUTES, SECTION 278A.18

1. If the association for the common-interest community or another organization which was formed . . . to own and maintain common open space or any successor association or other organization, at any time after the establishment of a PUD, fails to maintain the common open space in a reasonable order and condition in accordance with the plan, the city or county may serve written notice upon that association or other organization or upon the residents of the PUD, setting forth the manner in which the association or other organization has failed to maintain the common open space in reasonable condition. The notice must include a demand that the deficiencies of maintenance be cured within 30 days after the receipt of the notice and must state the date and place of a hearing thereon. The hearing must be within 14 days of the receipt of the notice.

2. At the hearing the city or county may modify the terms of the original notice as to the deficiencies and may give an extension of time within which they must be cured. If the deficiencies set forth in the original notice or in the modification thereof are not cured within the 30-day period, or any extension thereof, the city or county, in order to preserve the taxable values of the properties within the PUD and to prevent the common open space from becoming a public nuisance, may enter upon the common open space and maintain it for one year.

3. Entry and maintenance does not vest in the public any right to use the common open space except when such a right is voluntarily dedicated to the public by the owners.

4. Before the expiration of the period of maintenance set forth in subsection 2, the city or county shall, upon its own initiative or upon the request of the association or other organization previously responsible for the maintenance of the common open space, call a public hearing upon notice to the association or other organization or to the residents of the PUD, to be held by the city or county. At this hearing, the association or other organization or the residents of the PUD may show cause why the maintenance by the city or county need not, at the election of the city or county, continue for a succeeding year.

5. If the city or county determines that the association or other organization is ready and able to maintain the common open space in a reasonable condition, the city or county shall cease its maintenance at the end of the year

6. If the city or county determines the association or other organization is not ready and able to maintain the common open space in a reasonable condition, the city or county may, in its discretion, continue the maintenance of the common open space during the next succeeding year, subject to a similar hearing and determination in each year thereafter.

7. The decision of the city or county in any case referred to in this section constitutes a final administrative decision subject to review.

the common open space and facilities, and the conditions of a transfer shall conform to the approved development plan and be subject to the dedicatory instrument(s).

(4) Association membership shall be mandatory for each property owner and successive owner.

(5) The association shall be responsible for liability insurance and local taxes for the common open space and facilities.

(6) Property owners shall pay their pro rata share of the cost of managing and maintaining the common open space, and assessments levied by the association shall be a lien on their property.

(7) Control shall be transferred to the property owners when the PUD is [75] percent completed. (Adapted from So, Mosena, and Bangs 1973, and San Antonio, Texas)

The basis for levying fees and assessments is not stated in the ordinance, and this decision can be left to the documents that create the homeowners association. Fees assessed per lot are most common, though some fees are assessed on a square-footage basis or as a percentage of property taxes. The time for transfer of control specified in paragraph (6) can be modified depending on when the community and the developer want control to be transferred. Some developers prefer delaying transfer until the project is completed. The San Antonio, Texas, ordinance contains definitions of the terms used in this provision (see sidebar).

Preservation of natural resource areas. A PUD ordinance can require the development plan to include measures for the preservation of natural resource areas in addition, or as an alternative to, requiring their inclusion as open space in a project subject to private protective measures. If this is done, changes will be needed in a number of provisions in the ordinance. Additional language will have to be included in the statement of purpose. The following provision is one example:

Preservation of Natural Resources

Conservation of natural topographical and geological features with emphasis on:

a. Conserving existing surface and subsurface water resources

b. Preserving wetlands, floodplains, hillsides, woodlands, and other significant natural environmental features.

c. Preventing soil erosion.

d. Protecting surface-, ground-water, and other environmental resources, including green spaces, significant habitat, and land with exceptional scenic beauty. (Adapted from Carroll County, Georgia)

Additions will also have to be made in the section specifying the contents of the development plan application, which should be required to show any natural resource areas included in the PUD. The following provision is an example:

The development plan application shall include graphic information showing:

- The location of existing wetlands.
- A delineation of areas affected by mean annual and 100-year floods.
- A delineation of all other proposed preservation or conservation areas. (Pasco County, Florida)

The development plan, in addition, should indicate what measures will be taken to protect these areas:

The development plan shall contain measures for the protection of natural features, water resources, wetlands, and other ecological systems on the site, which may include:

a. Controls on the siting and location of buildings or improvements to ensure the protection of subsurface and surface water resources, protection of conservation preservation and hillside areas as designated on the development plan, and the protection of scenic and environmentally significant natural resources, such as tree stands, rivers, streams, ponds, and lakes.

b. Controls that ensure the protection of natural drainage systems through the limitation of land disturbances for drainage improvements, through the use of on-site stormwater retention, the maintenance of existing vegetation along stream corridors, and the use of innovative drainage designs or concepts.

c. Controls that minimize potential increased flood problems of developed areas within the PUD and surrounding areas.

d. Their designation as common open space areas. (Adapted from Lenaxa, Kansas and Pasco County, Florida)

As an alternative, the ordinance can provide for an evaluation of environmental resources included in the development plan as the basis for deciding on preservation measures. The following is an example:

> Intact and functioning environmental systems, such as waterways and wetland systems, shall be preserved and maintained in the PUD. The areas to be preserved shall be identified on the development plan and shall be evaluated by the [planning commission] on a case-by-case basis to address the individual natural features of each area. Management guidelines for each area shall be determined by applying the "Principles for Evaluating Development Proposals in Native Habitat" in the comprehensive plan. These principles in order of priority are to: 1) protect listed species, 2) create and enhance connectivity, 3) protect native habitat,

---

SAN ANTONIO, TEXAS, PJD ORDINANCE DEFINITION OF TERMS FOR CREATION OF PROPERTY OWNERS ASSOCIATION*

San Antonio, Texas, PUD Ordinance Definition of Terms for Creation of Property Owners Association*

"Property owners association" means an incorporated or unincorporated association that:

A. is designated as the representative of the owners of property in a residential subdivision;

B. has a membership primarily consisting of the owners of property covered by the dedicatory instrument for the residential subdivision; and

C. manages or regulates the residential subdivision for the benefit of the owners of property in the subdivision.

"Dedicatory instrument" means each governing instrument covering the establishment, maintenance, and operation of a residential subdivision. The term includes restrictions or other similar instruments subjecting property to restrictive covenants, bylaws, or similar instruments governing the administration or operation of a property owners association, to properly adopted rules and regulations of the property owners association, and to all lawful amendments to the covenants, bylaws, rules, or regulations.

"Property owners association" means the designated representative of the owners of property in a subdivision and may be referred to as a "homeowners association," "community association," "civic association," "civic club," "association," "committee," or similar term contained in the dedicatory instrument. It shall be an incorporated or unincorporated association that:

A. is designated as the representative of the owners of property in a residential subdivision;

B. has a membership primarily consisting of the owners of property covered by the dedicatory instrument for the residential subdivision; and

C. manages or regulates the residential subdivision for the benefit of the owners of property in the subdivision.

"Regular assessment" means an assessment, a charge, a fee, or dues that each owner of property within a PUD is required to pay to the property owners association on a regular basis and that is designated for use by the property owners association for the benefit of the residential subdivision as provided by the dedicatory instrument.

"Special assessment" means an assessment, a charge, a fee, or dues, other than a regular assessment, that each owner of property within a PUD is required to pay to the property owners association, according to the procedures required by the dedicatory instrument, for:

A. defraying, in whole or part, the cost whether incurred before or after the assessment, of any construction or reconstruction, unexpected repair, or replacement of a capital improvement in common areas owned by the property owners association, including the necessary fixtures and personal property related to the common areas; or

B. maintenance and improvement of common areas owned by the property owners association; or

C. other purposes of the property owners association as stated in its articles or the dedicatory instrument for the residential subdivision.

* This ordinance has been edited from its original format.

and 4) restore native habitat. The relative size and functional value of each feature shall be assessed as a part of the site design process to determine the protection measures required. Based on an assessment of the quality and quantity of on-site natural resources, departures from the above prioritization are allowed. (Adapted from Sarasota County, Florida)

The management guidelines in this comprehensive plan emphasize species protection, but other management guidelines can be adopted. Other natural resource areas, such as floodplains, can also be added.

VESTED RIGHTS

The vested rights problem arises when there is a change in the regulations that apply to the PUD after it has been approved. This may occur if the legislative body decides that change is necessary or if the legislative body changes in composition following an election. Under the majority vested rights rule, a developer has a vested right if the community issues a building permit before the change, and the developer relies on it by making substantial expenditures on the development. In slang terms, it is usually said the developer "has to get sticks and bricks into the ground." Once that occurs, the local government cannot change the land-use regulations that apply (Mandelker 2003, Sections 6.12-6.22). A leading case is *Avco Community Developers, Inc. v. South Coast Regional Comm'n.* (553 P.2d 546 (Cal. 1976)). Under an alternate theory, a developer is protected against regulatory change if the local government is estopped to change the land use regulations that apply. Most courts treat the vested rights and estoppel doctrines as equivalents.

The majority vested rights rule may possibly protect the developer of a small PUD who can expect to receive and can act on building permits in a reasonably short period of time. Difficulties arise for a PUD planned in phases. In phased developments, the developer applies initially only for building permits in the first phase. The developer may be able to secure vested rights in this phase, but cannot claim vested rights in subsequent phases because she has not applied for, much less obtained building permits for each of the subsequent phases. This problem is serious for a large-scale development, such as a master-planned community, which may take years to complete.

A change in the land-use regulations that apply to a PUD after it is approved can have a major impact. It may require the replanning and reapproval of the development and possibly a reduction in density or a change to different uses that may make the development unprofitable. Several alternatives exist for dealing with this problem. One is to rely on a favorable court decision, if there is one, that vests development rights in the approved development plan and all subsequent phases. This is not too helpful, as few cases have recognized vested rights at this stage of a development. Another alternative is a state statute or local ordinance that establishes and protects vested rights. Such statutes and ordinances are discussed below.

A final alternative is a development agreement. The agreement can provide that the regulations under which the development was approved will not be changed for a period of time, though there are exceptions when change is necessary to protect the public from environmental or other damage. Development agreements are discussed in Chapter 3.

To remedy the vesting problem that occurs under the majority judicial rule, some states have adopted statutes that vest rights in "site-specific development plans," (Arizona Revised Statutes, Sections 9-1202, 11-1202; Colorado Revised Statutes, Section 24-68-193; North Carolina General Statutes, Section 153A-344.1; South Carolina Code, Section 6-29-1510; Texas Local Government Code, Section 245.003; see also Florida Statutes, Section 380.06(21)(b), which limits review of subsequent phases of a development to issues identified in DRI master plan development approval) defined as "a plan submitted to a local government by a landowner that describes with reasonable certainty the type and intensity of use for a specific parcel or parcels of property" (North Carolina General Statutes, Section 153A-344.1(b)(5)). The statutes include PUD plans within this definition. Some statutes spell out the contents of a site-specific plan in more detail. For example:

> Unless otherwise expressly provided by the county such a plan shall include the approximate boundaries of the site; significant topographical and other natural features effecting development of the site; the approximate location on the site of the proposed buildings, structures, and other improvements; the approximate dimensions, including height, of the proposed buildings and other structures; and the approximate location of all existing and proposed infrastructure on the site, including water, sewer, roads, and pedestrian walkways. What constitutes a site-specific development plan under this section that would trigger a vested right shall be finally determined by the county pursuant to an ordinance, and the document that triggers such vesting shall be so identified at the time of its approval. (North Carolina General Statutes, Section 153A-344.1(b)(5))

The statutes provide that the local government must review a site-specific development plan under the regulations in force when the plan was submitted. Once the development plan is approved, the vested right is the right to develop pursuant to the approved development plan despite later amendments to the land-use regulations. Rights vest under the statute without a need for additional administrative approval. The vested right runs with the land. One problem with these statutes is that they may require a site plan specific enough for the issuance of a building permit in order to vest rights. Development plans may not be that specific.

Local governments are authorized or required to adopt an ordinance that implements the statute, and the ordinance may supplement the statutory requirements, such as by modifying the definition of a site-specific development plan. A local government may also have the option to select a different time for vesting, but this time must be prior to the issuance of a building permit. Some statutes authorize local governments to require a site-specific development plan for each phase of a development in order to vest rights in that phase. If an ordinance is not adopted, the statute may include a provision that defines the nature of the development approval that vests the right to develop.

The protected vested right terminates after a period of time, usually two or three years, though the Arizona statute allows the local government to decide on the length of time when it approves the PUD (Arizona Revised Statutes, Section 9-1202 (C)(F)). Other statutes authorize local governments to extend the protected period for up to five years. The Texas law does not have a time limit. Time limits in these laws may be too short for master-planned communities that are built over an extended period of time. A vested rights statute may authorize the use of development agreements, however.

The statutes include exceptions to vested rights protection:

- The owner can consent in writing to be subject to new regulations.

- New regulations can be made to apply if natural or man-made hazards on the property are a threat to public health, safety, or welfare.

- The protected development right does not include federal or state laws or generally applicable laws, such as building, plumbing, fire, electrical, or similar codes; or overlay zones that do not affect the type of use or density.

- The vested right does not apply if just compensation is paid for all expenditures made in reliance on the right.

Some communities have adopted provisions in their PUD ordinances, without the benefit of a statute, that confer vested rights. A local government can adopt an ordinance that vests "as of right" as in the state statutes, or it can provide an administrative process in which it reviews and can approve applications for vested rights. This type of ordinance should provide for an application process and criteria under which an application for a vested right will be approved:

> The owner of a PUD for which a final development plan has been approved may submit an application in sufficient detail to the [legislative body] for a Vested Rights Determination to develop the PUD under the regulations contained in the final development plan. The [legislative body] shall make a determination finding vested rights if they are based upon:
>
> (a) common law vesting, equitable estoppel, or contractual rights, if the owner proves by a preponderance of evidence that, acting in good faith reliance upon some act or omission of the [local government], it has made a substantial change in position or has incurred such extensive obligations and expenses that it would be highly inequitable and unjust to destroy the right to develop or to continue the development of the property;
>
> (b) the approved final development plan, or a phase plan approved subsequent to the final development plan, if the owner has in good faith reasonably relied upon the final development or phase plan to its detriment, has provided or made provision for required public improvements, and no approvals or permits have lapsed or been revoked. (Adapted from Carroll County, Georgia)

It is also possible to provide some vested rights protection for an approved concept plan:

> An applicant receiving approval of a concept plan shall be entitled to rely on, and implement by subsequently approved development plans, the type, intensity, and density of land uses set forth in the approved concept plan. (Southlake, Texas)

Here is a checklist for drafting a vested rights provision in a PUD ordinance:

- Will vested rights protection be based on a concept plan, a development plan, a phase plan, or some or all of these?

- Will vested rights protection for an earlier plan protect a later plan?

- How should these plans be defined?

- Should there be a time period for a vested right? Should an extension be allowed?

- Should there be exceptions to vested right protection? If so, what should they be?

- Should there be an administrative determination of vested rights as an alternative to vesting on the basis of a plan? If so, what should the criteria be for authorizing a vested right?

CHAPTER 5

The Law of
Planned Unit Development Regulation

As a new and innovative form of land-use regulation, PUD presents novel legal issues. The cases I have cited in this chapter are representative. Citations to additional cases are provided in the margins. A review of these cases can be helpful in understanding the legal issues.

The legal issues range from the usual questions involving an interpretation of an ordinance (see, e.g., Approval of Request for Amendment to Frawley Planned Unit Development, 638 N.W.2d 552 (S.D. 2002)), which upheld the interpretation that a concept plan can be required) to problems of delegation of power, statutory authority, and judicial review. Not all of the legal questions raised by PUDs have been settled, and some problem areas remain. This chapter outlines the major issues.

DELEGATION OF LEGISLATIVE POWER

An important issue raised by PUD ordinances is whether they violate the separation of powers by delegating legislative powers to administrative agencies. The majority rule is that standards and criteria for decision making by administrative agencies must be specific enough so that a claim of improper legislative delegation cannot be made. When making this decision, courts will look to definitions contained in the ordinance and its statement of purpose as well as the criteria provided for decision making. Generalization is difficult. Courts differ in how strictly they apply the delegation of power doctrine, however, and what may be an acceptable standard in one state may not be in another.

Delegation of power problems are easiest to address when there is no change in use. One court did not find an improper delegation when the PUD was limited to residential uses, and the ordinance spelled out all of the elements of a project (*Yarab v. Boardman Twp. Bd. of Zoning Appeals*, 860 N.E.2d 769 (Ohio App. 2006). Courts have also not found an improper delegation in ordinances that contained typical approval standards, such as standards for compatibility, adequate public facilities, access, and design (*Tri-State Generation and Transmission Co. v. City of Thornton*, 647 P.2d 670 (Colo. 1982), which reviewed typical standards, such as need, compatibility, design, adequate facilities, and compliance with the comprehensive plan; *Prince George's County v. M & B Constr. Corp.*, 297 A.2d 683 (Md. 1972), reviewed typical cluster housing standards; *Zanin v. Iacono*, 487 A.2d 780 (N.J.L. Div. 1984), reviewed adequate utilities, access, and environmental impact standards and rejected a vagueness challenge); *Appeal of Moreland*, 497 P.2d 1287 (Okla. 1972), which reviewed density and use standards). They have struck down ordinances when no standards were provided (*Harnett v. Board of Zoning, Subdivision & Bldg. Appeals*, 350 F. Supp. 1159 (D. St. Croix 1972), finding no standard for internal traffic circulation; and *Beaver Meadows v. Board of County Comm'rs*, 709 P.2d 928 (Colo. 1985), finding no standards for consideration of off-site roads), and when the standards were not mandatory or only a general welfare standard was included with no additional criteria (*City of Miami v. Save Brickell Ave., Inc.*, 426 So. 2d 1100 (Fla. App. 1983), where criteria were listed but held not mandatory; and *Louisville and Jefferson County Planning Comm. v. Schmidt*, 83 S.W.3d 449 (Ky. 2001), which struck down a health, safety, and welfare standard).

A court may also decide that a review standard in a PUD ordinance is unacceptable. In *Soble Constr. Co. v. Zoning Hearing Bd.*(329 A.2d 912 (Pa. Commw. 1974), the ordinance required the developer to "demonstrate that a sufficient market" existed for its PUD. The court invalidated this requirement because it was an improper attempt to zone "for the purpose of limiting competition."

AUTHORITY TO ADOPT A PUD ORDINANCE UNDER THE STANDARD ZONING ENABLING ACT

Although a number of states have adopted legislation that authorizes PUD ordinances, in states that have not, a question remains as to whether a PUD ordinance is authorized by the Standard Zoning Enabling Act, which does not have provision for this kind of regulation. PUD regulations present several statutory authority problems under the Standard Zoning Enabling Act. The Standard Act did not confer the review powers commonly exercised under PUD regulations by zoning agencies, such as the planning commission and board of adjustment. Nor did the Standard Zoning Enabling Act authorize the case-by-case review typical under PUD regulations.

The uniformity requirement in the Standard Zoning Enabling Act presents another problem. The Standard Act and state zoning acts require uniform zoning regulations for each zoning district. Some commentators argue that the uniformity requirement limits zoning districts to the single-use traditional districts of zoning practice. Under this interpretation, the uniformity requirement would prohibit zoning districts with the mixed uses allowed by PUD regulations.

Despite these problems, the Standard Zoning Act has not been a major barrier to the adoption of PUD regulations. The courts have rejected claims that PUD regulations are not authorized by the standard form of zoning legislation. In *Campion v. Board of Alderman* (899 A.2d 542 (Conn. 2006), the Connecticut court held that a PUD adopted by the City of New Haven was authorized by the Standard Zoning Enabling Act. In the court's view, the planned development district was comparable to the creation of any other zone (in particular floating zones), and thus the lack of particular language for planned development was not determinative of the New Haven board's lack of enabling authority. The court had previously upheld floating zones as authorized by the zoning enabling legislation without specific authority. The court responded to the plaintiff's contention that a planned development district lack of specific uses made it different from a floating zone by concluding that the differences are mostly procedural and that the actual outcome in either case, the change of a zone's boundaries by creating a new one, is the same. (See also *Orinda Homeowners Comm. v. Board of Supvrs.*, 90 Cal. Rptr 88 (Cal. App. 1970).)

Chrinko v. South Brunswick Twp. Planning Bd (187 A.2d 221 (N.J.L. Div. 1963) upheld a density transfer PUD ordinance for residential subdivisions that did not authorize density increases:

> Although the state zoning law does not in so many words empower municipalities to provide an option to developers for cluster or density zoning, such an ordinance reasonably advances the legislative purposes of securing open spaces, preventing overcrowding and undue concentration and promoting the general welfare. (at 225)

Chrinko also rejected a uniformity objection to the density transfer ordinance and noted that the ordinance "accomplishes uniformity because the option is open to all developers."

The courts have approved the inclusion of PUD regulations in zoning ordinances (*Dupont Circle Citizens Ass'n v. District of Columbia Zoning Comm'n*, 355 A.2d 550 (D.C. App. 1976), and inclusion in the subdivision control ordinance is another possibility. In *Prince George's County v. M & B Constr. Co.* (297 A.2d 683 (Md. 1972), the court held that the authority to approve a density transfer PUD was properly delegated to the planning commission in the exercise of its subdivision control powers.

The court held the bargaining and negotiation that occurs in the PUD review process is not invalid as contract zoning in *Rutland Envtl. Protection Ass'n v. Kane County* (334 N.E.2d 215 (Ill. App. 1975):

> Since the overall aims of...[PUD] zoning cannot be accomplished without negotiations and because conferences are indeed mandated by the regulatory ordinance, the conduct of the . . . county cannot be read as contributing to contract zoning. (at 219)

PROCEDURES FOR REGULATING PUDS

The courts have considered a variety of zoning procedures local governments can use to regulate PUDs. PUD regulations may require a rezoning to a PUD district by the legislative body, and this may take the form of a floating zone in which the zone is first placed in the text of the ordinance and then approved as applications are presented. Courts have approved this procedure for PUDs (*Town of North Hempstead v. Village of North Hills*, 342 N.E.2d 566 (N.Y. 1975).

A rezoning to a PUD district often precedes the approval of the development plan. This is a two-step process the courts have approved. A municipality may rezone to a PUD district without complying with requirements in the ordinance for development plans (*Barlow v. City of Hastings*, 2006 Mich. App. LEXIS 2421 (Mich. App. 2006)).

Rezoning for a PUD zoning raises questions of compliance with the comprehensive plan, if compliance is required by statute or ordinance. Compliance with the comprehensive plan depends on what policies and objectives the plan contains, and what the PUD ordinance requires concerning compliance with the plan. Courts will uphold PUD rezonings if they find the rezoning has complied with the comprehensive plan (held consistent: *Evans v. Teton County*, 73 P. 3d 84 (Idaho 2003), which resulted in approval of the concept plan and rezoning; *Town of North Hempstead v. Village of North Hills*, 342 N.E.2d 566 (N.Y. 1975); *Cheney v. Village 2 at New Hope, Inc.*, 241 A.2d 81 (Pa. 1968); *Wiggers v. County of Skagit*, 596 P.2d 1345 (Wash. App. 1979), and see also *Friends of Farm to Market v. Valley County*, 46 P.3d 9 (Idaho 2002), regarding use of a conditional use permit). And there are cases where consistency and rezoning were found lacking: *Cathedral Park Condominium Comm. v. District of Columbia Zoning Comm'n*, 743 A.2d 1231 (D.C. App. 2000), which was remanded to determine consistency with comprehensive plan; *Amcon Corp. v. City of Eagan*, 348 N.W.2d 66 (Minn.1984), in which failure to follow plan evidence of arbitrary action was ruled.

Once a rezoning has been adopted by the legislative body, the planning commission may have the authority to approve a development plan for a PUD to determine whether it complies with the criteria contained in the ordinance. *Cheney v. Village 2 at New Hope, Inc.* (241 A.2d 81 (Pa. 1968); also see *Sheridan Planning Comm'n v. Board of Sheridan County Comm'rs*, 924 P.2d 988 (Wyo. 1996) is a leading case. In *Cheney* the legislative body rezoned a large tract of land from low-density residential to a PUD. The planning commission then approved a plan for the PUD and issued building permits. The ordinance rezoning for the PUD specified allowable uses, maximum densities and heights, and a minimum distance between buildings. The state had a zoning act based on the Standard Act, and the court held it authorized the creation of a zoning district with this mixture of uses. The court approved the delegation of authority to the commission to approve PUDs, even though the zoning statute did not specifically authorize this delegation. It held the flexibility needed in the administration of PUD regulations required a delegation to the planning commission as the most appropriate zoning agency to carry out the review process. Notice, however, that the ordinance specifically designated the uses, densities, and site development standards that applied to approved PUDs.

In *Lutz v. City of Longview* (520 P.2d 1374 (Wash. 1974), however, the court invalidated a PUD ordinance that delegated to the planning commission the authority to approve a PUD as a floating zone. The court distinguished *Cheney* because in that case the legislative body rezoned the land for a PUD and the ordinance delegated only the review of project details to the planning commission.

These cases underscore the importance of deciding whether the PUD review process is legislative or adjudicative and quasi-judicial. The legislative body must have the authority to make the legislative zoning decisions concerning the approval of PUDs. This issue also determines which local agency can be delegated the authority to process PUD applications. The planning commission, for example, can decide only questions that are adjudicative or quasi-judicial. Delegation of PUD review authority to the legislative body does not necessarily mean a court will characterize the PUD review process as legislative, however. A court could hold the PUD review process quasi-judicial if the ordinance contains criteria the legislative body applies in the review of PUD applications (Dillon Cos. v. City of Boulder, 515 P2d 627 (Colo. 1973). The referendum power is also implicated here, because referenda may be held only on legislative, not administrative, matters.

Whether the PUD review process is held legislative or quasi-judicial may depend on how extensively the governing body changes the zoning regulations. In *Peachtree Dev. Co. v. Paul* (423 N.E.2d 1087 (Ohio 1981), the court was asked to rule about the legitimacy of the governing body having approved a PUD that significantly departed from the single-family zoning regulations. It included multifamily and commercial uses at higher densities than the zoning regulations allowed. (See also the cases listed in the sidebar.) The court held the PUD approval was a legislative act subject to referendum, and that "the board's action was the functional equivalent of altering the zoning classification of a sizeable section of . . . [the] Township."

PUDs can also be approved as conditional uses or special exceptions by the board of adjustment or governing body. Cases upheld this delegation because they characterized the PUD review process as adjudicative in the ordinances under review (*Mullin v. Planning Bd.*, 456 N.E.2d 780 (Mass. App. 1983);*Chandler v. Kroiss*, 190 N.W.2d 472 (Minn. 1971); *Appeal of Moreland*, 497 P.2d 1287 (Okla. 1972); *State ex rel. Marsalek v. Council of the City of South Euclid*, 2006 Ohio LEXIS 2899 (Ohio 2006); compare *Cetrulo v. City of Park Hills*, 524 S.W.2d 628 (Ky. 1975)). The approval of a residential density transfer development as cluster housing in a subdivision ordinance has also been approved (*Prince George's County v. M & B Constr. Co.*, 297 A.2d 683 (Md. 1972).

An important question is whether the PUD review procedure can be made mandatory. A Florida court invalidated a rezoning for a PUD initiated by a county that included a detailed site plan showing buildings, uses, and densities (*Porpoise Point Pt'ship v. St. John's County*, 532 So. 2d 727 (Fla. App. 1988). The court held that PUD is a voluntary procedure intended to provide development flexibility not available in the usual zoning district and that it cannot be forced on a developer who simply wants land rezoned.

JUDICIAL REVIEW OF DECISIONS APPROVING PUDs

In addition to determining compliance with a comprehensive plan when this is required, courts review decisions to deny or approve rezonings, conditional uses, and other approvals for PUDs to decide whether they are an impermissible spot zoning or whether they comply with approval standards contained in the PUD ordinance. The standard of review adopted by the court is critical in determining whether the decision to approve or deny will be upheld.

Legal issues concerning an interpretation of the ordinance are always questions of law decided by the court. For other issues, the distinction between legislative and quasi-judicial decisions determines the standard of judicial review. As the Utah court explained:

> This court has long recognized that municipal land use decisions should be upheld unless those decisions are arbitrary and capricious or otherwise illegal. Indeed, municipal land use decisions as a whole are generally entitled to a "great deal of deference." However, in specific cases the determination of whether a particular land use decision is arbitrary and capricious has tradi-

---

CASES CONCERNING WHETHER PUD REVIEW PROCESS IS HELD LEGISLATIVE OR QUASI-JUDICIAL

Summit Mall Company, LLC, v. Lemond, 132 S.W.3d 725 (Ark. 2003) (approval of commercial PUD held legislative); *Blakeman v. Planning & Zoning Comm'n*, 846 A.2d 950 (Conn. App. 2004) (approval of PUD is legislative); *State ex rel. Helujon, Ltd. v. Jefferson County*, 964 S.W.2d 531 (Mo. App. 1998) (held legislative); *Todd-Mart, Inc. v. Town Bd. of Webster*, 370 N.Y.S.2d 683 (App. Div. 1975); *State ex rel. Comm. for the Referendum of Ordinance No. 3844-02*, 792 N.E.2d 186 (Ohio 2003) (approval of subsequent development as being in compliance with existing PUD standards is administrative act not subject to referendum); *City of Waukesha v. Town Bd.*, 543 N.W.2d 515 (Wis. App. 1995) (cannot approve PUD through conditional use procedure when districts where PUDs allowed not legislatively designated); *Sheridan Planning Comm'n v. Board of Sheridan County Comm'rs*, 924 P.2d 988 (Wyo. 1996).

> **CASES UPHOLDING OR REJECTING DECISIONS TO DENY OR APPROVE HUD PROJECTS**
>
> **Upholding denial:**
> City of Tuscaloosa v. Bryan, 505 So. 2d 330 (Ala. 1987); Dore v. County of Ventura, 28 Cal. Rptr. 2d 299 (Cal. App. 1994); Ford Leasing Dev. Co. v. Board of County Comm'rs, 528 P.2d 237 (Colo. 1974); Bradley v. Payson City Corp., 70 P.3d 47 (Utah 2003) (city council denial of rezoning request valid under reasonably debatable standard); Whitesell v. Kosciusko Cty. Bd. of Zoning Appeals, 558 N.E.2d 889 (Ind. App. 1990); Croteau v. Planning Bd., 663 N.E.2d 583 (Mass. App. 1996); Coronet Homes, Inc. v. McKenzie, 439 P.2d 219 (Nev. 1968); Fallone Props., L.L.C. v. Bethlehem Township Planning Bd., 849 A.2d 1117 (N.J. App. Div. 2004) (upholding denial for failure to comply with open space requirement; conservation easement not enough); Board of Supvrs. v. West Chestnut Realty Corp., 532 A.2d 942 (Pa. Commw. 1987); Citizens for Mount Vernon v. City of Mount Vernon, 947 P.2d 1208 (Wash. 1997) (rezoning for commercial PUD held spot zoning).
>
> **Reversing denial:**
> Woodhouse v. Board of Comm'rs, 261 S.E.2d 882 (N.C. 1980) (applicant satisfied ordinance criteria); Ohio Valley Orthopaedics & Sports Med., Inc. v. Board of Trustees, 816 N.E.2d 1088 (Ohio App. 2004) (denial of PUD modification improperly based on concerns about unknown tenants and traffic flows); West v. Mills, 380 S.E.2d 917 (Va. 1989); Old Tuckaway Assocs. Ltd. Partnership v. City of Greenfield, 509 N.W.2d 323 (Wis. App. 1993).
>
> **Upholding approval:**
> Moore v. City of Boulder, 484 P.2d 134 (Colo. App. 1971) (held not spot zoning); Evans v. Teton County, 73 P.3d 84 (Idaho 2003) (change in density in PUD complied with zoning ordinance); Davis v. City of Leavenworth, 802 P.2d 494 (Kan. 1991); I, 964 S.W.2d 531 (Mo. App. 1998) (upholding PUD rezoning though county considered economic benefits); Huntzicker v. Washington County, 917 P.2d 1051 (Or. App. 1996) (approval complied with ordinance); Petersen v. City of Clemson, 439 S.E.2d 317 (S.C. App. 1993) (same); Smith v. Georgetown County Council, 355 S.E.2d 864 (S.C. App. 1987) (same); McCallen v. City of Memphis, 786 S.W.2d 633 (Tenn. 1990); Wiggers v. County of Skagit, 596 P.2d 1345 (Wash. App. 1979) (held not spot zoning).
>
> **Reversing or remanding approval:**
> Fort Morgan Civic Ass'n v. Baldwin County Comm'n, 890 So. 2d 139 (Ala. Civ. App. 2003) (rejecting decision that parcels were contiguous and could be approved as one); Cathedral Park Condominium Comm. v. District of Columbia Zoning Comm'n, 743 A.2d 1231 (D.C. App. 2000) (remanding approval for failure to give adequate attention to density and open space problems); Blagden Alley Ass'n v. District of Columbia Zoning Comm'n, 590 A.2d 139 (D.C. App. 1991) (remanding approval); BECA of Alexandria, L.L.P. v. County of Douglas, 607 N.W.2d 459 (Minn. App. 2000) (reversing approval of PUD with severely restrictive conditions); Springville Citizens for a Better Envt. v. City of Springville, 979 P.2d 332 (Utah 1999) (remanding because city violated mandatory provisions of ordinance in its approval); Citizens for Mount Vernon v. City of Mount Vernon, 947 P.2d 1208 (Wash. 1997) (cannot approve PUD that is inconsistent with underlying zoning).

tionally depended on whether the decision involves the exercise of legislative, administrative, or quasi-judicial powers. When a municipality makes a land-use decision as a function of its legislative powers, we have held that such a decision is not arbitrary and capricious so long as the grounds for the decision are "reasonably debatable." When a land-use decision is made as an exercise of administrative or quasi-judicial powers, however, we have held that such decisions are not arbitrary and capricious if they are supported by "substantial evidence." (Bradley v. Payson City Corp., 70 P.3d 47, 51 (Utah 2003, citations omitted).

If the PUD application is reviewed through a conditional use or similar quasi-judicial procedure, the usual judicial review standards. Review is usually on the record by writ of certiorari or something similar. Under the usual standards for judicial review, a court will determine whether the board had jurisdiction, whether the proceedings were fair and regular, and whether the board's decision was unreasonable, oppressive, arbitrary, fraudulent, without evidentiary support, or based on an incorrect theory of law (BECA of Alexandria, L.L.P. v. County of Douglas by Bd. of Comm'rs, 607 N.W.2d 459 (Minn. App. 2000)).

The arbitrary and capricious standard does not mean courts will always uphold local decisions on PUD applications. They review these decisions carefully because PUD ordinances contain specific criteria for PUD approval, and courts must consider whether these criteria have been met by the PUD applicant. There is no discretion to deny when the approval requirements in the ordinance are specific and the applicant has met all of these requirements (C.C. & J. Enters., Inc. v. City of Asheville, 512 S.E.2d 766 (N.C. App. 1999)).

There is more discretion to reject when the ordinance contains generalized health, safety, and general welfare requirements (Dore v. County of Ventura, 28 Cal. Rptr.2d 299 (Cal. App. 1994), which upheld a denial based on safety and incompatibility findings)). Courts apply these principles to uphold or reject decisions to deny or approve PUD projects. (See sidebar for a list of cases on both sides.)

Criteria for approval or denial must be contained in the PUD ordinance, and a court will reverse a denial of a PUD application that is based on criteria the ordinance does not include. In RK Dev. Corp. v. City of Norwalk (242 A.2d 781 (Conn. 1968); see also cases in sidebar), the governing body denied a PUD because of "[t]he safety for the sake of the children up there; the welfare of the community and also the health hazards." The PUD contained specific site development standards for PUD applications but did not contain criteria authorizing denial for any of these reasons. The court held the denial was illegal because the ordinance did not prohibit PUDs for "any reason" given by the governing body. It was not entitled to substitute "pure discretion" for "a discretion controlled by fixed standards." The reasons given by the governing body were vague and uncertain and did not indicate how the applicant failed to comply with the ordinance.

PUD regulations often contain purpose clauses that state the purposes PUDs are intended to serve. An important question is whether these clauses enact substantive requirements that must be met by a PUD application or are simply explanatory statements of purpose. In *Dupont Circle Citizens Ass'n v. District of Columbia Zoning* (426 A.2d 327 (D.C. App. 1981), the court held not. The ordinance contained a purpose clause stating that PUDs must provide an environment and amenities "superior" to what the zoning regulations could provide. This type of purpose clause is sometimes included in PUD ordinances. The court held the purpose clause did not enact a "comparison" test that required the commission to make findings of fact in the adjudicative PUD review procedures showing the purposes of the ordinance had been met. It could support its conclusion that a PUD met the purposes stated in the ordinance with "subsidiary findings of basic facts on material issues" raised by the PUD application. (See also *C.C. & J. Enters., Inc. v. City of Asheville*, 512 S.E.2d 766 (N.C. App. 1999), in which the court said the city could not deny an application that met ordinance standards because of noncompliance with statement of ordinance intent; and *Smith v. Georgetown County Council*, 355 S.E.2d 864 (S.C. App. 1987), in which the zoning ordinance did not require "public interest" finding). These cases underscore the importance of careful drafting of purpose clause language.

AMENDMENTS TO DEVELOPMENT PLANS

Amendments to final development plans are a frequent occurrence for PUDs as markets and objectives change. The courts hold that major changes in the plan cannot be made administratively but require the same review procedure used to approve the PUD initially (*Millbrae Ass'n for Residential Survival v. City of Millbrae*, 69 Cal. Rptr. 251 (1968); *City of New Smyrna Beach v. Andover Dev. Corp.*, 672 So.2d 618 (Fla. App. 1996)). The PUD ordinance can resolve uncertainties in the amendment process by distinguishing between minor and major changes and providing that minor changes can be made administratively. (But see *Bailey v. Zoning Bd. of Adjustment*, 801 A.2d 492 (Pa. 2002) (rule authorizing planning commission to approve "minor modifications" not authorized by ordinance). If the PUD was approved as a special exception, amendments to the plan can be made in the special exception process if the amendment does not authorize a use change that requires a rezoning (*Chandler v. Kroiss*, 190 N.W.2d 472 (Minn. 1971)). A use change requires a rezoning. (*McCarty v. City of Kansas City*, 671 S.W.2d 790 (Mo. App. 1984). A court can review an amendment to a development plan to decide whether it is a reasonable modification of the original plan. (Compare *Gray v. Trustees, Monclova Twp.*, 313 N.E.2d 366 (Ohio 1974), which invalidated a legislative amendment that allowed a clubhouse site to be used for nonresidential purposes, with *Foggy Bottom Ass'n v. District of Columbia Zoning Comm'n*, 639 A.2d 578 (D.C. App. 1994), which upheld a plan amendment by the zoning commission that eliminated a mini-park. See also *Frankland v. City of Lake Oswego*, 517 P.2d 1042 (Or. 1973), which held that a sketch plan bound the developer.

PUD DENIAL CASES OVERTURNED DUE TO LACK OF ORDINANCE CRITERIA FOR DENIAL

DeMaria v. Enfield Planning & Zoning Comm'n, 271 A.2d 105 (Conn. 1970); *Hall v. Korth*, 244 So. 2d 766 (Fla. App. 1971); *LaSalle Nat'l Bank v. County of Lake*, 325 N.E.2d 105 (Ill. App. 1975); *Woodhouse v. Board of Comm'rs*, 261 S.E.2d 882 (N.C. 1980); *Gross Builders v. City of Tallmadge*, 2005 Ohio App. LEXIS 3865 (Ohio App. 2005) (city had no authority to deny certificate based on alleged developer failure to comply with comprehensive plan since it failed to incorporate the plan into its zoning code); *Mullins v. City of Knoxville*, 665 S.W.2d 393 (Tenn. App. 1983).

CHAPTER 6

Planned Unit Development Statutes: A State-By-State Summary

Local governments began incorporating planned unit development provisions into zoning ordinances in the 1950s and 1960s, sometimes before states had adopted enabling legislation expressly permitting the local governments to do so. The rationale of the early drafters of PUD ordinances was that it was simply an extension of the use of the traditional police power to protect the health, safety, and general welfare. Although the courts have sustained the authority to adopt PUD ordinances under the Standard Zoning Enabling Act, a substantial number of statutes have now adopted legislation authorizing the regulation of PUDs. It ranges from brief enabling legislation in some states to detailed legislation that specifies procedures and requirements in others.

The first model PUD law was drafted in 1965 by the late Chicago land-use lawyer Richard Babcock and other attorneys for a joint project of the Urban Land Institute (ULI) and the National Association of Home Builders. The model was proposed as a means to use "recent planning innovations" to better serve the general objectives of the Standard Zoning Enabling Act and to meet new demands for housing. Under the act, local governments were granted authority to enact a PUD ordinance that must:

- refer to the state act,

- include a statement of objectives for PUDs designate a local agency to review PUDs, and

- provide development standards and procedures for their review and approval.

There is no simple formula on what to include in state enabling legislation. A brief legislative delegation of authority to regulate PUDs, as some states have done, is a minimum.

The ULI/Babcock model was enacted almost in its entirety in New Jersey and Pennsylvania. There have been difficulties in implementation because of its detail. Other states that have adopted PUD legislation in varying detail include Arkansas Colorado, Connecticut, Idaho, Illinois, Kentucky, Massachusetts, Mississippi, Montana, Nebraska, Nevada, New York, and Ohio. Connecticut adopted but later repealed PUD legislation, and has adopted a more simplified statute. Enabling provisions in this legislation can also be adapted for inclusion in local ordinances if there is authority to do so, and this PAS Report has provided examples of where this can be done.

This chapter includes summaries of PUD legislation in states that have adopted these laws. The statutory summaries and legislation included here provide ideas on how to draft enabling legislation if this is considered necessary. In addition, APA's *Growing Smart*^{SM} *Legislative Guidebook* contains model legislation, discussed in Chapter 3, that authorizes PUDs as a conditional use and through subdivision. Authorizing PUD through the zoning process is preferable if zoning changes will be needed in PUD approvals.

There is no simple formula on what to include in state enabling legislation. A brief legislative delegation of authority to regulate PUDs, as some states have done, is a minimum. Statutes can also specify procedures local governments should follow in reviewing and approving PUDs. States should probably be careful in specifying what kind of PUDs are allowed, however, because local governments need some flexibility in deciding on the PUDs they want to approve. Legislation can be most helpful when it provides minimal and necessary requirements that local governments are required to adopt in their local ordinances. Michigan reenacted PUD legislation in 2006 that includes provisions on uniformity, phasing, and adequate public facilities. The Nevada statute is more helpful than most in providing a format for PUD regulation that local governments can adopt.

STATE SUMMARIES OF PUD LEGISLATION

ARKANSAS
Arkansas Code Annotated, Section 14-56-416
Zoning ordinances may provide for "large-scale unified development."

COLORADO
Colorado Revised Statutes, Section 24-67-101 et seq.
Colorado's "Planned Unit Development Act of 1992" enables counties and municipalities to authorize PUDs in "order that the public health, safety, integrity, and general welfare may be furthered in an era of increasing urbanization and of growing demand for housing of all types and design. . . ."

Section 24-67-103: Definitions
This section contains definitions of plan, common open space, and planned unit development, which means "an area of land, controlled by one or more landowners, to be developed under unified control or unified plan of development for a number of dwelling units, commercial, educational, recreational, or industrial uses, or any combination of the foregoing, the plan for which does not correspond in lot size, bulk, or type of use, density, lot coverage, open space, or other restriction to the existing land use regulations."

Section 24-67-104: Authorization Procedure
This section provides that "[a]ny county with respect to territory within the unincorporated portion of the county or any municipality with respect to territory within its corporate limits may authorize planned unit developments...." To do so, a county or municipality must enact a resolution or ordinance that refers to this article, outlines objectives of the development, designates a board authorized to review PUD applications, sets forth standards of development consistent with the provisions of this statute, sets forth the procedures applying to the application for, hearing on, and tentative and final approval of PUDs that shall afford procedural due process to interested parties, and requires a finding by the county or municipality that the PUD plan is in general compliance with any master or comprehensive plan for the county or municipality. Authorizing resolutions or ordinances must be enacted and amended in accordance with other statutory procedures.

Section 24-67-105: Requirements for Enabling Legislation
Authorizing local resolutions and ordinances must set forth standards and conditions consistent with the provisions of this section. No PUD may be approved without the written consent of the landowner whose properties are included within the PUD. The local ordinance must set forth the uses permitted and the minimum number of units or acres within a PUD, standards governing density or intensity of land use, and information which must be submitted with the PUD application. The ordinance may establish the sequence of development among the various types of uses and standards for inclusion of common open space. Provisions for inclusion of common open space may require the landowner to provide for and establish an organization for the ownership and maintenance of common open space or require that other adequate arrangements for ownership and maintenance thereof be made. A local government may enforce the maintenance obligation. Design, construction, and other requirements applicable to a PUD may be different from or modifications of the requirements otherwise applicable by reason of any zoning or subdivision regulation, resolution, or ordinance of the county or municipality as long as such requirements substantially comply with the subdivision statutes and appropriate regulations promulgated thereunder. Subdivision regulations applicable to PUDs may differ from those otherwise applicable.

Section 24-67-105.5: Requirements for Enabling Legislation
The county planning commission or governing body may request redesign of all or any portion of a PUD submitted for approval, but any such request must include specific, objective criteria. If the applicant redesigns the PUD in accordance with the request, no further redesign shall be required unless necessary to comply with a duly adopted county resolution, ordinance, or regulation. Any required public hearing on any PUD shall be conducted expeditiously and concluded when all those present and wishing to testify have done so. Public hearings must not continue more than 40 days from the date of commencement unless the applicant consents in writing to a continuation to a specific date. Unless withdrawn by the applicant, any PUD that has been neither approved, conditionally approved, nor denied within a time mutually agreed to by the county and the applicant at the time of filing shall be deemed approved. The county may extend the time period to receive a recommendation from an agency to which the PUD was referred, but the extension must not exceed 30 days, unless the agency has notified the county that it will require additional time to complete its recommendation.

Section 24-67-106: Common Open Areas and Governmental Use
This section specifies that the "provisions of the plan relating to the use of land and the location of common open space shall run in favor of the county or municipality and shall be enforceable at law or in equity by the county or municipality without limitation on any power or regulation otherwise granted by law. All provisions of the plan shall run in favor of the residents,

occupants, and owners of the planned unit development . . . to the extent expressly provided in the plan and in accordance with the terms of the plan" and to that extent the provisions can "be enforced at law or in equity by residents, occupants, or owners." With the exceptions listed below, "those provisions of the plan authorized to be enforced by the county or municipality may be modified, removed, or released by the county or municipality[.]" No "modification, removal, or release of the provisions of the plan by the county or municipality shall affect the rights of the residents, occupants, and owners of the planned unit development to maintain and enforce those provisions at law or in equity[.]" "[N]o substantial modification, removal, or release of the provisions of the plan by the county or municipality shall be permitted except upon a finding by the county or municipality, following a public hearing called and held in accordance with [statutory] . . . provisions . . . that the modification, removal, or release is consistent with the efficient development and preservation of the entire planned unit development, does not affect in a substantially adverse manner either with the enjoyment of land abutting upon or across a street from the planned unit development or the public interest, and is not granted solely to confer a special benefit upon any person."

Colorado is an example of a fairly comprehensive statute.

However, "in the case of any land located within a planned unit development that has been set aside for a governmental use or purpose as specified in the plan, the plan agreement, or related documents, a governmental entity that holds legal title to the land may, with the approval of the county or municipality in which the land is located, as applicable, and following a public hearing called for and held in accordance with [statutory] . . . provisions…[s]ubdivide all or any portion of the land[,] [r]emove or release all or any portion of the land from any limitations on its use or purpose by the governmental entity as specified in the plan, . . . or [s]ell or otherwise dispose of all or any portion of the land." One or any combination of those three actions "shall only be undertaken upon a finding by the county or municipality" following the above-mentioned public hearing, "that all or any portion of the land is not reasonably expected to be necessary for a governmental use or purpose or that the governmental use or purpose will be furthered by disposal of the land." "[T]he future use of all or any portion of the land shall in all other respects be consistent with the efficient development and preservation of the entire [PUD] and with the plan." "Residents and owners of the [PUD] may, to the extent and in the manner expressly authorized by the provisions of the plan, modify, remove, or release their rights to enforce the provisions of the plan, but no such action shall affect the right of the county or municipality to enforce the provisions of the plan."

Section 24-67-107: Applicability
This section provides that "[t]he provisions of this article apply to home rule municipalities unless superseded by charter or ordinance enactment." Municipalities with previously enacted provisions regarding PUDs may continue employing those provisions exclusively. However, municipalities must maintain compliance with the subdivision statutes and regulations adopted thereunder. Municipalities "may provide for concurrent…processing of [PUD] and subdivision applications." "This article shall be liberally construed" to encourage use of PUDs . . . although not to the exclusion of other types of developments.

Section 24-67-108: Model Guidelines
This section provides that the department of local affairs must develop model resolutions and ordinances to serve as guidelines for counties and municipalities in enacting enabling resolutions and ordinances pursuant to this article.

CONNECTICUT
Connecticut General Statutes Annotated, Section 8-2a
This section provides that the "zoning commission of each city, town or borough" may allow cluster development within its zoning regulations.

Section 8-18: Definition of Cluster Development
This section defines "cluster development" to be a building pattern concentrating units on a particular portion of a parcel so that at least one-third of the parcel remains as open space to be used exclusively for recreational, conservation, and agricultural purposes except that nothing herein shall prevent any municipality from requiring more than one-third open space in any particular cluster development.

Sections 8-13b to 8-13l
These sections were repealed in 1985. Connecticut General Statutes Annotated, Section 8-2d is a savings clause providing that any local regulations concerning PUD adopted prior to the repeal shall continue to be valid and any PUD proposed in accordance with those regulations shall continue to be governed by them.

IDAHO

Idaho Code Annotated Section 67-6515
This section allows governing boards to arrange by ordinance for the processing of PUD applications for areas of land in which a variety of residential, commercial, industrial, and other land uses are provided for under single ownership or control. These ordinances may include, but are not limited to, requirements for minimum area, permitted uses, ownership, common open space, utilities, density, arrangements of land uses on a site, and permit processing.

Some states provide limited enabling authority.

ILLINOIS

65 Illinois Compiled Statutes Annotated 5/11-13-1.1
This section allows the corporate authorities of any municipality to provide for special uses, including planned developments. A planned development may "be permitted only after a public hearing before some commission or committee designated by the corporate authorities, with prior notice thereof" given in conformance with applicable statutes. A planned development may be "permitted only upon evidence that such use meets standards established for such classification in the ordinances, and the granting of permission therefore may be subject to conditions reasonably necessary to meet such standards." Any proposed planned development "which fails to receive the approval of the commission or committee designated by the corporate authorities to hold the public hearing shall not be approved by the corporate authorities except by a favorable majority vote of all alderman, commissioners or trustees of the municipality then holding office." "[T]he corporate authorities may by ordinance increase the vote requirement to two-thirds of all aldermen, commissioners or trustees of the municipality then holding office."

KENTUCKY

Kentucky Revised Statutes Annotated, Section100.203(1)(e)
This section allows cities or counties to regulate "[d]istricts of special interest to the proper development of the community, including, but not limited to, exclusive use districts, historical districts, planned business districts, planned industrial districts, renewal, rehabilitation, and conservation districts" as well as "planned neighborhood and group housing districts."

MASSACHUSETTS

Massachusetts General Laws Annotated, Chapter 40A, Section 9
This section provides that zoning ordinances must provide for special permits allowing specific types of uses in specified districts, including cluster developments and PUDs as defined in the section. These ordinances must also provide that special permits shall lapse within a specified time period not greater than two years. Applications for these permits must be filed with the municipal clerk and the permit-granting authority. The granting authority must give notice and hold a public hearing upon the application within 65 days of its filing, and a decision must follow within 90 days of the hearing. Should the granting authority fail to provide a decision the application is deemed approved if statutory notice requirements are met.

MICHIGAN

Michigan Compiled Laws, Sections 125.3501, 125.3503, 125.3603
Michigan adopted a PUD law in 2006 for local units of government that reenacted existing legislation. The law defines a PUD as "cluster zoning, planned development, community unit plan, and planned residential development and other terminology denoting zoning requirements designed to accomplish the objectives of the zoning ordinance through a land development project review process based on the application of site planning criteria to achieve integration of the proposed land development project with the characteristics of the project area." The law then provides that "[t]he legislative body may establish planned unit development requirements in a zoning ordinance that permit flexibility

in the regulation of land development, encourage innovation in land use and variety in design, layout, and type of structures constructed, achieve economy and efficiency in the use of land, natural resources, energy, and the provision of public services and utilities, encourage useful open space, and provide better housing, employment, and shopping opportunities particularly suited to the needs of the residents of this state."

All land-use regulations within a PUD shall be determined by the land-use regulations included in the zoning ordinance. A local government may approve a PUD with noncontiguous open space if requested by a landowner. "The PUD regulations need not be uniform with regard to each type of land use if equitable procedures recognizing due process principles and avoiding arbitrary decisions are followed in making regulatory decisions." Local PUD regulations shall specify the body or official responsible for reviewing and approving PUDs, eligibility conditions, review participants, requirements and standards for review, and procedures for application, review, and approval. Standards included in the ordinance shall be consistent with its purpose and the health, safety, and welfare of the community and ensure compatibility with adjacent land uses, the natural environment and "the capacities of public services and facilities affected by the land use." PUD requirements may reference other land development statutes and ordinances.

At least one public hearing must be held, and the ordinance may provide for a preapplication conference before submission of a PUD request and preliminary site plans before the public hearing. A decision shall be made a reasonable time after the public hearing. A request for approval of a PUD will be approved if it is in compliance with the standards stated in and conditions imposed under the zoning ordinance and any other laws. "Final approval may be granted on each phase of a multiphased planned unit development if each phase contains the necessary components to insure protection of natural resources and the health, safety, and welfare of the users of the planned unit development and the residents of the surrounding area."

Conditions may be imposed "to insure that public services and facilities affected by a proposed land use or activity will be capable of accommodating increased service and facility loads caused by the land use or activity, to protect the natural environment and conserve natural resources and energy, to insure compatibility with adjacent uses of land, and to promote the use of land in a socially and economically desirable manner." They must be recorded in the record of the approved action and remain unchanged except by mutual consent.

The PUD regulations may provide either for amendment of the zoning ordinance by the legislative body or approval by a designated body or official. "Final approval may be granted on each phase of a multiphased planned unit development if each phase contains the necessary components to insure protection of natural resources and the health, safety, and welfare of the users of the planned unit development and the residents of the surrounding area." See also Section 125.3501, requiring site plan review for PUDs, and Section 125.3603, providing that an appeal may be taken to the zoning board of appeals only if provided in the zoning ordinance.

MISSISSIPPI

Mississippi Code Annotated, Section 19-5-10

This act authorizes any county's board of supervisors to enter into development agreements with "developers of a master planned community in order to authorize…the master planned community . . . to administer, manage, and enforce the land use restriction and covenants, land use regulations, subdivision regulations, building codes and regulations, and any other limitations and restrictions on land and buildings provided in the master plan for the master planned community." Real estate and property owners within the master planned community will not be "subject to the county ordinances and regulations pertaining to buildings, subdivisions, zoning, the county's comprehensive plan, and any other county ordinances and regulations pertaining thereto" so long as the board of supervisors reviews the "master plan for the master planned community" and finds that the provisions for regulating the subjects listed above are "comparable to, or greater than, similar provisions in the ordinances and regulations of the county." "The term of such a development agreement" must be lesser or equal to the greater of 30 years or "the number of years allowed in the county's subdivision ordinance for terms of

Michigan revised its PUD statute in 2006.

subdivision covenants." The development agreement must include "a boundary survey made by a registered land surveyor" which will "be recorded in the land records of the chancery clerk of the county" and "serve as the description of property within the master planned community which shall not be subject to the county's zoning map."

"The term 'master planned community' means a development by one or more developers of real estate consisting of residential, commercial, educational, health care, open space and recreational components that is developed pursuant to a long range, multi-phase master plan providing comprehensive land use planning and stages of implementation and development." "The real estate described in the master plan must consist of at least 3,500 acres. The master plan may require that not less than 50 percent of the total dwelling units planned for such acreage must be . . . dwelling units within a certified retirement community certified by the Mississippi Department of Economic and Community Development" or "dwelling units where at least one occupant" is 62 years of age[,] . . . [r]eceives pension income reported on his or her most recent federal income tax return filed prior to occupancy[,] or declares himself to be retired." The real estate "must be subjected to a set of land use restrictions imposed by deed restriction or restrictive covenant recorded by the developer in the land records of the chancery clerk of the county as land is developed and sold in phases to users." These restrictions shall provide for "[i]nternal community self-governance by the owners of the property[,] [t]he establishment of one or more legal persons endowed with the powers, rights and duties to administer, manage, own and maintain common areas, establish community activities and enforce the land use restrictions on the common areas and private property[,] and [t]he establishment of assessments and lien rights to fund amenities, services and maintenance of common areas." Finally, the real estate "must be within the territorial boundaries of one or more public utility districts established by the county for the provision of water and sewer facilities and water and sewer services."

The master plan "shall be subject to modification from time to time by the original owner or owners of the real estate described in the initial master plan, its affiliates, successors or assigns, to meet changing economic and market conditions." "[H]owever, any such modifications in the master plan which materially change the regulations, restrictions, covenants and limitations pertaining to buildings, subdivisions and land use regulations approved in the development agreement, or which significantly change the overall plan concept, shall be subject to, and shall not take effect until, approved by the board of supervisors of the county."

MONTANA

Montana Code Annotated, Section 76-3-504(2): Authorizing Language
This section authorizes subdivision regulations that promote cluster development.

Section 76-3-509: Cluster Development Regulation Requirements
This section provides that "[i]f the governing body has adopted a growth policy that meets [statutory] requirements . . . , the governing body may adopt regulations to promote cluster development and preserve open space under this section." Such regulations must "establish a maximum size for each parcel in a cluster development[,] . . . establish a maximum number of parcels in a cluster development[,] and establish requirements, including a minimum size for the area to be preserved, for preservation of open space as a condition of approval of a cluster development subdivision under regulations adopted pursuant to this section. The regulations must require that open space be preserved through an irrevocable conservation easement, granted in perpetuity, as provided [by statute]...prohibiting further division of the parcel."

Such regulations may "establish a shorter timeframe for review of proposed cluster developments[,] establish procedures and requirements that provide an incentive for cluster development subdivisions that are consistent with the provisions of this chapter[,]authorize the review of a division of land that involves more than one existing parcel as one subdivision proposal for the purposes of creating a cluster development" and "authorize the creation of one clustered parcel for each existing parcel that is reviewed as provided [by statute]." Such regulations may also establish exemptions from designated environmental review and park dedication requirements.

The Montana law authorizes cluster development approved as a subdivision.

The Nevada law provides a comprehensive template for local regulation, including local procedures.

NEBRASKA

Nebraska Revised Statutes, Section 19-4401

This section provides that "[e]very metropolitan-, primary-, and first-class city shall have the power to include within its zoning ordinance provisions authorizing and regulating planned unit developments within such city or within the zoning jurisdiction of such city, except such cities shall not have authority to impose such power over organized cities or villages within the zoning jurisdiction of such cities. As used in this section, planned unit development shall include any development of a parcel of land or an aggregation of contiguous parcels of land to be developed as a single project which proposes density transfers, density increases, and mixing of land uses, or any combination thereof, based upon the application of site planning criteria. The purpose of such ordinance shall be to permit flexibility in the regulation of land development, to encourage innovation in land use and variety in design, layout, and type of structures constructed, to achieve economy and efficiency in the use of land, natural resources, energy, and the provision of public services and utilities, to encourage the preservation and provision of useful open space, and to provide improved housing, employment, or shopping opportunities particularly suited to the needs of an area."

Such authorizing and regulating ordinances must establish criteria for the review of proposed developments to ensure that the proposed use is compatible with adjacent uses of land and the capacities of public services and utilities affected by the development, and to ensure that approval of such development conforms to the comprehensive plan and is consistent with public health, safety, and general welfare of the city. "Within a planned unit development, regulations relating to the use of land, including permitted uses, lot sizes, setbacks, height limits, required facilities, buffers, open spaces, roadway and parking design, and land-use density shall be determined in accordance with the planned unit development regulations specified in the zoning ordinance. The planned unit development regulations need not be uniform with regard to each type of land use." The approval procedure for proposed PUDs under the PUD ordinance must be "generally similar to the procedures established for the approval of zone changes. In approving any planned unit development, a city may . . . impose reasonable conditions as deemed necessary to ensure that a planned unit development shall be compatible with adjacent uses of land, will not overburden public services and facilities, and will not be detrimental to the public health, safety, and welfare. Such conditions or agreements may provide for dedications of land for public purposes."

NEVADA

Nevada Revised Statutes Annotated, Chapter 278A, Section 278A.010: Short Title

"This chapter may be cited as the Planned Unit Development Law."

Section 278A.020: Legislative Declaration

"The legislature finds that the provisions of this chapter are necessary to further the public health, safety, morals and general welfare in an era of increasing urbanization and of growing demand for housing of all types and design; to provide for necessary commercial and industrial facilities conveniently located to that housing; to encourage a more efficient use of land, public services or private services in lieu thereof; to reflect changes in the technology of land development so that resulting economies may be made available to those who need homes; to insure that increased flexibility of substantive regulations over land development authorized in this chapter be administered in such a way as to encourage the disposition of proposals for land development without undue delay, and are created for the use of cities and counties in the adoption of the necessary ordinances."

[Nevada Revised Statutes Annotated, Chapter 278A, Section 278A.030–278A.060 provide definitions useful for PUD legislation and regulations, including Section 278A.040, which defines "common open space"; Section 278A.050, which defines "landowner"; and Section 278A.060, which defines "plan" and "provisions of the plan."]

Section 278A.065: "Planned Unit Development" defined

"1. 'Planned unit development' means an area of land controlled by a landowner, which is to be developed as a single entity for one or more planned unit residential developments, one or more public, quasi-public, commercial or industrial areas, or both. 2. Unless otherwise stated, 'planned unit development' includes the term 'planned unit residential development.'"

2. Unless otherwise stated, 'planned unit development' includes the term 'planned unit residential development.'"

Section 278A.070: "Planned unit residential development" defined
"'Planned unit residential development' means an area of land controlled by a landowner, which is to be developed as a single entity for a number of dwelling units, the plan for which does not correspond in lot size, bulk or type of dwelling, density, lot coverage and required open space to the regulations established in any one residential district created, from time to time, under the provisions of any zoning ordinance enacted pursuant to law."

Section 278A.080: Exercise of Powers by City or County
"The powers granted under the provisions of this chapter may be exercised by any city or county which enacts an ordinance conforming to the provisions of this chapter."

General Provisions

Section 278A.090: Specification of Standards and Conditions
"Each ordinance enacted pursuant to the provisions of this chapter must set forth the standards and conditions by which a proposed planned unit development is evaluated."

Section 278A.100: Specification of Uses
"An ordinance enacted pursuant to the provisions of this chapter must set forth the uses permitted in a PUD."

Section 278A.110: Specification of Standards for Density and Intensity of Land Use
This section provides that municipal PUD ordinances establish standards for density or intensity of land use which recognize that density or intensity of use allowable under the otherwise applicable zoning ordinance may not be appropriate in a PUD. Standards may be varied in consideration of common open space, the "location and physical characteristics" of the PUD site, the "location, design and type of dwelling units[,]" and the "criteria for approval of a tentative map of a subdivision pursuant to [statute]." This section also allows departures from the density or intensity of use established for the PUD in individual sections of a PUD proposed to be developed over a period of years.

Section 278A.120: Common Open Space: Amount and Location
This section provides that the PUD ordinance should provide that any common open space be "set aside for the use and benefit of the residents or owners of the development" and "include provisions by which the amount and location of any common open space is determined and its improvement and maintenance secured."

Section 278A.130: Common Open Space: Dedication of Land; Development to be Organized as Common-Interest Community
This section requires that PUD ordinances provide "that the city or county may accept the dedication of land or any interest therein for public use and maintenance," but that such ordinances cannot require that land be "dedicated or made available to public use" as "a condition of the approval of a [PUD]." If land is set aside for common open space, the PUD must be "organized as a common-interest community in one of the forms permitted by statute."

Section 278A.170: Common Open Space: Procedures for Enforcing Payment of Assessment
This section makes "procedures for enforcing payment of an assessment for the maintenance of common open space provided" by statute "available to organizations for the ownership and maintenance of common open space "entitled to receive payments from owners of property for such maintenance...."

Section 278A.180: Common Open Space: Maintenance by City or County upon Failure of Association or Other Organization to Maintain; Notice; Hearing; Period of Maintenance
This section establishes a procedure in the event "the association for the common-interest community or another organization" formed "to own and maintain common open space . . . fails to maintain the common open space in a reasonable order and condition in accordance with the plan. . . ." In that case, "the city or county may serve written notice upon that association or other organization or

upon the residents of the [PUD], setting forth the manner in which the association or other organization has failed to maintain the common open space in reasonable condition." The notice must state the "date and place of a hearing" on the matter. The section provides a procedure by which the city or county "may enter upon the common open space and maintain it" and continue to do so until "the association or other organization or the residents of the [PUD] . . . show cause why the maintenance by the city or county need not" continue.

Section 278A.190: Common Open Space: Assessment of Costs of Maintenance by City or County; Lien
This section states that the "total cost of the maintenance undertaken by the city or county" must be "assessed ratably against the properties within the [PUD] that have a right of enjoyment to the common open space" and that the city or county must file a notice of lien on those properties in the appropriate recorder's office "at the time of entering upon the common open space to maintain it. . . ."

Section 278A.210: Public Facilities
This section states that the "authority granted a city or county by law to establish standards for" public facilities "applies to such improvements within a [PUD], but the "standards applicable to a [PUD] may be different from or modifications of the standards or requirements otherwise required of subdivisions which are authorized under an ordinance."

Section 278A.220: Evaluation of Design, Bulk and Location of Buildings; Unreasonable Restrictions Prohibited
This section provides that ordinances enacted pursuant to this chapter "set forth the standards and criteria by which the design, bulk and location of buildings is evaluated." Any standards for any feature of a PUD must be set forth in a manner that provides sufficient criteria for the evaluation of specific PUD proposals and does not "unreasonably restrict the ability of the landowner to relate the plan to the particular site and to the particular demand for housing existing at the time of development."

Minimum Standards of Design

Section 278A.230: Adoption by Ordinance
This section allows PUD ordinances to "contain the minimum design standards set forth in Nevada Revised Statutes Annotated, Sections 278A.240 to 278A.360.

Sections 278A.240 to 278A.360
These sections contain minimum design standards to govern types of units, minimum site area, drainage, fire hydrants, fire lanes, exterior lighting, maintenance and use of jointly owned areas, parking, setback, sanitary sewerage, and construction, design, names, numbers and signs for streets within a PUD.

Section 278A.370: Utilities
This section provides that the "installation and type of utilities shall comply with the local building code or be prescribed by ordinance."

Enforcement and Modification of Provisions of Approved Plan
See Pennsylvania Statutes Annotated, Title 53, Section 10706 (below).

Procedures for Authorization of Planned Development

Section 278A.430: Applicability and Purposes of Nevada Revised Statutes, Sections 278A.440 to 278A.490, inclusive
"In order to provide an expeditious method for processing a plan for a [PUD] under the terms of an ordinance enacted pursuant to the powers granted under this chapter, and to avoid the delay and uncertainty which would arise if it were necessary to secure approval by a municipality of local procedures of a plat or subdivision or resubdivision, as well as approval of a change in the zoning regulations otherwise applicable to the property, it is hereby declared to be in the public interest that all procedures with respect to the approval or disapproval or a [PUD] and its continuing administration be consistent with the provisions set out in NRS 278A.440 to 278A.590, inclusive."

Sections 278A.440 through 278A.470
See Pennsylvania Statutes Annotated, Title 53, Section 10707 (below).

Section 278A.480: Public Hearing; Notice; Time Limited for Concluding Hearing; Extension of Time
Pennsylvania Statutes Annotated, Title 53, Section 10708 (below).

Sections 278.490 through 278A.510
Pennsylvania Statutes Annotated, Title 53, Section 10709 (below).

Section 278A.520: Status of Plan After Tentative Approval; Revocation of Tentative Approval
See Pennsylvania Statutes Annotated, Title 53, Section 10710 (below).

Proceedings for Final Approval

Sections 278A.530 through 278A.590
See Pennsylvania Statutes Annotated, Title 53, Section 10711 (below).

NEW JERSEY

New Jersey Statutes Annotated, Sections 40:55D-45 to 40:55D-45.8
The New Jersey statutes contain enabling legislation for municipally authorized PUDs. The statute provides that every ordinance pursuant to this article providing for PUDs must require the municipal planning board to adopt five findings of fact and conclusions before approving PUDs:

Departures from zoning regulations must conform to zoning ordinance standards.

Common open space amounts, locations, and purposes must be adequate and maintenance of such space must be provided for.

The development proposal must accommodate public services, transportation, light and air, recreation, and visual enjoyment.

The proposal must not be likely to have an unreasonably adverse impact on the area in which it will be developed.

Proposals contemplating construction over a period of years must protect the interests of the public and of the residents, occupants, and owners of the proposed development in the total completion of the development.

Proposed developments must include a general development plan for the planning board's review. These plans contain the permitted number of dwelling units, the amount of nonresidential floor space, the residential density, and the nonresidential floor area ratio for the development. The time period during which the general development plan will be in effect must be determined in light of the plan's specifications, prevailing economic conditions, the timing schedule to be followed, the developer's capability and likelihood of completing the proposed development in a timely fashion, and any conditions attached to the plan's approval.

General development plans may include several additional elements. These include, but are not limited to, a general land-use plan, a circulation plan, an open space plan, a utility plan, a storm water management plan, an environmental inventory, a community facility, a housing plan, a local service plan, a prospective fiscal report, a proposed timing schedule, and a municipal development agreement between the municipality and the developer.

Any developer of a parcel of land greater than 100 acres in size may submit a general development plan for a PUD for the planning board's review. The planning board must grant or deny general development plan approval within 95 days of the plan's submission or approval will be deemed granted. Once a general development plan has been approved, it may be amended or revised only upon application by the developer and approval by the planning board. Approval must be obtained for modification of the proposed timing schedule; the planning board must review proposed modifications in light of the factors delineated in the act. The developer must also get the approval of the planning board if it wishes to make any variation in the location of land uses within the PUD, or increase the density of residential development or the floor area ratio of nonresidential development in any section of the PUD subsequent to approval of the general plan. Certain minor changes in the development plan do not require the planning board's approval.

The developer must notify the local government administrative officer by certified mail upon the completion of each phase of the development. Should the developer fail to complete any phase of the development within eight months of the date provided for in an approved plan, or if at any time the municipality has cause to believe that the developer is not fulfilling his obligations pursuant to the approved plan, the municipality must notify the developer by certified mail and conduct a hearing to determine whether the developer is in violation of the approved plan. The municipality may then terminate the approval of

New Jersey and Pennsylvania adopted the ULI model law in full.

the general development plan if it finds good cause to do so. Likewise, the municipality has cause to terminate general development plan approval if the developer fails to apply for preliminary approval of the PUD within five years of the date upon which the general development plan was approved. Approval of a general development plan terminates with the completion of the development.

NEW YORK

New York Town Law, Section 261-C, and New York Village Law, Section 7-703-A, and New York General City Law, Section 81-F
These laws provide that these local governments may utilize zoning legislation to implement procedures and requirements for PUDs in furtherance of the town comprehensive plan and zoning provisions.

New York Town Law, Section 278
[Similar authorization is contained in New York General City Law, Section 37, and New York Village Law, Section 7-738]

The New York law also authorizes the approval of cluster development as a subdivision.

This section authorizes the approval of cluster development during the subdivision review process. Cluster development is defined as "a subdivision plat or plats, approved pursuant to this article, in which the applicable zoning ordinance or local law is modified to provide an alternative permitted method for the layout, configuration and design of lots, buildings and structures, roads, utility lines and other infrastructure, parks, and landscaping in order to preserve the natural and scenic qualities of open lands."

The law states that "[t]he purpose of a cluster development shall be to enable and encourage flexibility of design and development of land in such a manner as to preserve the natural and scenic qualities of open lands." The planning board may approve a cluster development after a public hearing if the development will benefit the town and meet any criteria contained in a local cluster housing ordinance. The board may attach conditions on the ownership, maintenance, and use of open space in order to insure the preservation of the natural and scenic qualities of such land. "A cluster development shall result in a permitted number of building lots or dwelling units which shall in no case exceed the number which could be permitted, in the planning board's judgment, if the land were subdivided into lots conforming to the minimum lot size and density requirements of the zoning ordinance or local law applicable to the district or districts in which such land is situated and conforming to all other applicable requirements."

The plat is to be recorded and may include "areas within which structures may be located, the height and spacing of buildings, open spaces and their landscaping, off-street open and enclosed parking spaces, streets, driveways and any other features required by the planning board. In the case of a residential plat or plats, the dwelling units permitted may be, at the discretion of the planning board, in detached, semi-detached, attached, or multi-story structures."

OHIO

Ohio Revised Code Annotated, Section 303.022 (counties) and Section 510.021 (townships)
These sections contain enabling legislation for PUDs. They may be established or modified through zoning resolutions or amendments. PUD regulations must "apply to property only at the election of the property owner" and "include standards to be used . . . in determining whether to approve or disapprove any proposed development" within the PUD. Zoning regulations, subdivision regulations, and platting regulations "may vary" within a PUD "in order to accommodate unified development and to promote the public health, safety, and morals, and the other purposes of this section." There are four different ways in which PUD may be established. One is through the adoption of a conditional use. The other three are as follows:

Subsection (A)
The county or township may adopt PUD regulations which "establish standards that will apply to property that becomes part of a [PUD.]" Property owners electing to have PUD regulations apply to their property must "apply to have the zoning map amended pursuant to" the statute that authorizes a rezone of their property as a PUD, which will no longer be subject to any previously applicable zoning regulations. Once property has been rezoned, "subsequent development" must comply with regulations adopted for the PUD by the

county or township. "[A]ny approval or disapproval of subsequent use or development of property in a [PUD] as being in compliance with regulations established as authorized by this division shall not be considered to be an amendment or supplement" to a county zoning ordinance but may be appealed under the administrative procedures act.

Subsection (B)
The county or township may adopt regulations for individual PUDs. Upon application for PUD status, the board of county commissioners may grant that status and adopt "regulations as part of that same procedure that will apply only to that [PUD]." A PUD must comply with these regulations and not any other regulations, compliance to be determined by the county or township. "[A]ny approval or disapproval of subsequent use or development of property in a [PUD] as being in compliance with regulations established as authorized by this division shall not be considered to be an amendment or supplement" to a county zoning ordinance but may be appealed under the administrative procedures act.

Subsection (C)
The county or township may adopt PUD regulations and amend the zoning map to rezone the property as a PUD. Any "other zoning regulations and zoning district that exist at the time a [PUD] district is established . . . continue to apply within the [PUD] district unless the board or the county zoning commission approves an application of an owner of property within the district to subject the owner's property to [PUD] regulations under this division." Applications must include a "development plan that complies with the [PUD] regulations." Whether the application and plan comply with these regulations is determined by the county or township. This determination is appealable under the administrative procedures act. (See Meck and Pearlman 2006, Section 11.25).

See also Ohio Revised Code, Chapter 349, which authorizes the establishment of a New Community Organization

PENNSYLVANIA

Purdon's Pennsylvania Statutes and Consolidated Statutes Annotated, Title 53, Sections 10701–10713

Section 10701: Purposes
This section sets out the purposes of Pennsylvania's PUD statute. In drafting the statute the legislature intended to encourage flexible land use to meet growing demand for housing with varieties of dwelling type. The legislature also intended to foster the conservation of common open space. The statutes were also drafted to provide for the timely implementation of PUDs and the objective evaluation of proposed development plans.

Section 10702: Grant of Power
This section grants the governing body of every municipality the power to enact, amend, and repeal provisions within a zoning ordinance fixing standards and conditions for planned residential development" (PRD). The governing body of a municipality may approve, modify, or disapprove any PRD plan or delegate those powers to the planning agency. PRD provisions must specify which body will administer them, set forth PRD regulations and specify procedures for PRD applications as well as hearings for both tentative and final approval of PRD plans.

Section 10702.1: Transferable Development Rights
This section enables municipalities to incorporate provisions for transferable development rights in PRD ordinances.

Section 10703: Applicability of Comprehensive Plan and Statement of Community Development Objectives
This section provides that PRD regulations shall be "based on and interpreted in relation to the statement of community development objectives of the zoning ordinance and may be related to either the comprehensive plan for the development of the municipality prepared under the provisions of this act or a statement of legislative findings." Each PRD application must also be "based on and interpreted in relation to the statement of community development objectives, and may be related to the comprehensive plan, or shall be based on and interpreted in relation to the statement of legislative findings."

Section 10704: Jurisdiction of County Planning Agencies
This section provides that counties adopting PRD provisions must send every municipality within the county a certified copy of such provisions and any

subsequent amendments. County authority to adopt PRD provisions may "not supersede any local planned residential development, zoning or subdivision and land development ordinance" adopted by a municipality within that county. However, any application for tentative approval of a PRD plan submitted to a municipality must be forwarded to the county planning agency for a recommendation.

Section 10705: Standards and Conditions for Planned Residential Development

This section provides that PRD regulations shall specify standards, conditions, and regulations to be used in evaluating proposed PRDs and sets requirements for PRD regulations. They specify the manner in which PRD provisions must regulate permissible uses, timing of development, density of land use, intensity of land use, common open space and its maintenance, building standards and provision of water. It also outlines the procedure to be followed by the municipality should the "organization established to own and maintain common open space . . . fail to maintain the common open space in reasonable order and condition in accordance with the development plan."

Section 10706: Enforcement and Modification of Provisions of the Plan

This section provides that "the enforcement and modification of the provisions of the development plan as finally approved...be subject to" several requirements. The development plan's provisions relating to the use, bulk and location of buildings, common open space, and intensity of use or density of residential units must run in favor of the municipality. Express provisions of the development plan must run in favor of the PRD residents. It also details the circumstances under which the municipality may modify, remove, or release its right to enforce development plan provisions as well as the circumstances under which the PRD residents may modify, remove, or release their rights to enforce development plan provisions.

Section 10707: Application for Tentative Approval of Planned Residential Development

This section provides that all procedures for "the approval or disapproval of a development plan for a [PRD] and the continuing administration thereof...be consistent with" several provisions. The section details the required contents of a PRD application for tentative approval, including a form consistent with municipal PRD provisions enacted pursuant to the statute, technical information, and a statement explaining why a PRD is in the public interest and consistent with the municipality's comprehensive development plan. It also provides that the "application for tentative and final approval of a development plan for a [PRD] prescribed in this article shall be in lieu of all other procedures or approvals. . . ."

Section 10708: Public Hearings

This section requires that "a public hearing pursuant to public notice on said application shall be held by the governing body or the planning agency, if designated, in the manner prescribed [by statute] within 60 days after the filing of an application for tentative approval" of a PRD. "The governing body or the planning agency may continue the hearing from time to time, and where applicable, may refer the matter back to the planning agency for a report, provided, however, that . . . the public hearing or hearings shall be concluded within 60 days after the date of the first public hearing." It also authorizes the municipality to offer mediation to aid completion of proceedings authorized by the statute.

Section 10709: The Findings

This section provides that the governing body or planning agency "within 60 days following the conclusion of the public hearing provided for in this article or within 180 days after the date of filing of the application, whichever occurs first, shall, by official written communication, to the landowner," either grant tentative approval, grant tentative approval subject to specified conditions, or deny tentative approval to the development plan. The grant or denial must include "findings of fact related to the specific proposal" and reasons for the grant or denial. A grant of tentative approval may include "the time within which an application for final approval of the development plan" or part thereof "shall be filed."

Section 10710: Status of Plan After Tentative Approval

This section provides that a grant of tentative approval shall "be deemed an amendment to the zoning map, effective upon final approval, and shall be noted on the zoning map." Tentative approval does not "qualify a plat of the [PRD] for recording nor authorize development or the issuance of any building permits [but may not be] impaired by action of the municipality pending [application for final approval], provided applications are filed . . . within the periods of time specified in the official written communication granting tentative approval." Should the landowner elect to abandon the development plan after tentative approval is granted or fail to apply for final approval within the required time period, tentative approval will be deemed revoked.

Section 10711: Application for Final Approval
This section provides that the application for final approval of a development plan shall "be made to the official of the municipality designated by the ordinance and within the time or times specified by the official written communication granting tentative approval." It outlines the required contents of the application for final approval, procedures for its review, the landowner's remedies if the plan is rejected, and the effect of the landowner's abandonment of the plan after final approval.

Section 10712: Repealed

Section 10712.1: Jurisdiction
This section gives district justices initial jurisdiction over enforcement proceedings.

Section 10712.2: Enforcement Remedies
This section provides that anyone found liable to a municipality in civil court for violating PRD provisions must pay a judgment of not more than $500 plus court costs and attorney's fees. Each day a violation persists will constitute a separate violation unless the district justice determining that there has been violation determines the violation was committed in good faith, in which case the violating party will have five days to remedy the violation, after which each additional day the violation persists will constitute a separate violation.

Section 10713: Compliance by Municipalities
"Municipalities with [PRD] ordinances shall have five years from the effective date of this amendatory act to comply with the provisions of this article."

VIRGINIA

Virginia Code Annotated, Section 15.2-2286.1
This section applies to any county or city that had a population growth rate of 10 percent or more since the next-to-latest decennial census but excludes any county or city with a density of more than 2,000 people per square mile. It authorizes standards, conditions, and criteria for clustering of single-family dwellings and open space preservation in zoning or subdivision ordinances that apply to at least 40 percent of the unimproved land in residential and agricultural zoning districts. The governing body may include provisions to ensure quality development, preservation of open space, and compliance with the comprehensive plan and land-use ordinances. Density calculations shall be be based on the criteria contained in applicable land-use ordinances.

Development of cluster housing is permitted by right under the subdivision ordinance, and approval shall be by administrative staff without a public hearing. A special exception or special or conditional use shall not be required. Ordinances may also provide for cluster housing at a greater density calculation than that permitted by the applicable land-use ordinance, either by right or with approval as a special exception, special or conditional use permit, or rezoning.

The Virginia law is a cluster development law that emphasizes the preservation of open space.

Partially Annotated List of References

Alexandrakis, Emmanuel, and Brian J.L. Berry. 1994. "Housing Prices in Master-Planned Communities: Are There Premiums? The Evidence for Collin County, Texas 1980-1991." *Urban Geography* 15, no. 1: 9-24.

Premiums are paid in times of upswings but are eroded down to cost of providing planned amenity packages at time of downswings.

Arendt, Randall G. 2004. *Crossroads, Hamlet, Village, Town*. Revised edition. Planning Advisory Report No. 523/524. Chicago, Ill. American Planning Association.

Discussion of conservation principles in urban planning.

_____. 1996. *Conservation Design for Subdivisions*. Washington, D.C. Island Press.

This is the seminal work on natural resource preservation in subdivision design.

Babcock, Richard F. 1965. *Legal Aspects of Planned Unit Residential Development*. Washington, D.C.: The Urban Land Institute.

Babcock, Richard F., and David N. McBride. 1965. "The Model State Statute." *University of Pennsylvania Law Review* 114, no. 1: 140–70.

Contains the text of a model statute for planned residential development. Also published by the Urban Land Institute in 1965 in *Legal Aspects of Planned Unit Development. Technical Bulletin* No. 52.

Burger, Mark T., and D. Paskowitz. 1997. "Better Retail for Master-Planned Communities." *Urban Land* 56, no. 5: 15–16.

Describes an integrated, retail/entertainment center in Mission Valejo, California.

Callies, David L., Daniel J. Curtin, and Julie A. Tappendorf. 2003. *Bargaining for Development*. Washington. D.C. The Environmental Law Institute.

A handbook on the use of development agreements in land-use regulation.

CNU (Congress for the New Urbanism). 2004. *Codifying New Urbanism*. Planning Advisory Report No. 526. Chicago, Ill. American Planning Association.

Curtin, Daniel J., and Cecily T. Talbert. 2006. *California Land Use and Planning Law*. 26th ed. Point Arena, Calif: Solano Press.

Delogu, Orlando, Samuel B. Merrill, and Phillip. R. Saucier. 2004. "Some Model Amendments to Maine (and Other States') Land Use Control Legislation." *Maine Law Review* 56, no. 2: 323-364.

Contains model legislation for planned unit infill development.

Eugene, Oregon, Department of Planning and Development. n.d. *Planned Unit Development: General Information* (on file with author).

Ewing, Reid. 2006. "Fatal and Non-Fatal Injuries." In *Understanding the Relationship Between Public Health and the Built Environment*. Washington. D.C.: United States Green Building Council, chapter 3.

Discusses links between roadway and network design, traffic calming, and other aspects of transportation with incidents of injuries.

_____. 2000a. "Future of Land Development." In *Metropolitan Development Patterns*. Cambridge, Mass.: Lincoln Institute of Land Policy, 66–71.

Discusses the emergence of hybrid forms of development incorporating new urbanist and traditional designs.

_____. 2000b. "There's a Hybrid in Your Future: Tomorrow's Development Will Look Like Today's Only More So." *Planning* 66, no. 11: 18–21.

This is a slightly different version of the paper published in 2000 by the Lincoln Institute.

Ewing, Reid. 1996. *Best Development Practices.* Chicago, Ill.: American Planning Association.

Details project development practices for land use, transportation, housing and other issues with recommendations now followed in planned unit developments and sometimes local ordinances.

_____. 1991. *Developing Successful New Communities.* Washington. D.C.: The Urban Land Institute.

Includes chapters on the land planning and the development process.

Ewing, Reid, and Robert Hodder. 1998. *Best Development Practices: A Primer for Smart Growth.* Washington. D.C.: International City/County Management Association and U.S. Environmental Protection Agency.

This is a summary of Ewing's 1996 book with projects outside Florida added.

Forrest, Clyde W. 1995. "Planned Unit Development and Takings Post Dolan." *Northern Illinois Law Review* 15, no. 3: 571–85.

Discusses planned unit development in Illinois.

Fries, James H., and Stefan V. Reyniak. 1996. "Putting Takings Back Into the Fifth Amendment: Land Use Planning After *Dolan v. City of Tigard.*" *Columbia Journal of Environmental Law,* no. 1: 103–82.

Discusses five planned unit development ordinances from Rhode Island, and whether their common open space provisions are an unconstitutional exaction.

Fulton, William, and Paul Shigley. 2005. *Guide to California Land Planning.* 3d ed. Point Arena, Calif.: The Solano Press.

Franklin, Tennessee. 2004. *Land Use Plan.*

Gause, Jo Ellen. ed. 2002. *Great Planned Communities.* Washington. D.C.: The Urban Land Institute.

Descriptions of planned communities in the United States and abroad.

Georgia Department of Community Affairs. 2004. *Model Code for Alternatives to Conventional Zoning.* Atlanta, Ga.: Georgia Department of Community Affairs. www.dca.state.ga.us/development/PlanningQualityGrowth/programs/modelcode.asp

The code contains a model planned unit development ordinance, available at: www.dca.state.ga.us/development/PlanningQualityGrowth/programs/downloads/Model_Code_2004/pdfs/3_8.pdf

Goldston, Eli, and James H. Scheuer. 1959. "Zoning of Planned Unit Developments." *Harvard Law Review* 73, no. 2: 241–65.

Handy, Susan, Robert G. Paterson, and Kent Butler. 2003. *Planning for Street Connectivity: Getting from Here to There.* Planning Advisory Report No. 515. Chicago, Ill. American Planning Association.

Contains discussion of the benefits of street connectivity, advice about how to determine a connectivity index, and excerpts from several ordinances.

Heidt, Jim. 2004. *Greenfield Development Without Sprawl: The Role of Planned Communities.* Washington, D.C.: The Urban Land Institute.

Discusses benefits of planned communities.

Hinshaw. Mark L. 1995. *Urban Design.* Planning Advisory Report No. 454. Chicago, Ill. American Planning Association.

Jeer, Sanjay, Megan Lewis, Stuart Meck, Jon Witten, and Michelle Zimet. 1997. *Nonpoint Source Pollution: A Handbook for Local Governments*, Planning Advisory Report No. 476. Chicago, Ill. American Planning Association.

Contains sample model ordinance for cluster development.

Kane, Rene C. 2003. "Prairie Flower." *Landscape Architecture* 93, no. 10: 122–31, 156–59.

The Prairie Crossing project, discussed in this PAS Report, has an important conservation element.

Kellenberg, Steven. 2003. "Green Communities." *Urban Land* 62, no. 5: 53–59.

Explains the considerations that go into a green development.

Kendig, Lane. 2004. *Too Big, Boring, or Ugly: Planning and Design Tools to Combat Monotony, the Too-Big House, and Teardowns.* Planning Advisory Report No. 528. Chicago, Ill. American Planning Association.

This report offers planning and design tools to tame the too-big house, shake free of monotonous development, and negotiate the political minefield of teardowns.

Krasnowiecki, Jan Z. 1965. "Planned Unit Development: A Challenge to Established Theory and Practice of Land Use Control." *University of Pennsylvania Law Review* 114, no. 1: 47–97.

Lang, Robert E., and D. Dhavale. 2005. "America's Megapolitan Areas." *Land Lines* 17, No. 3: 1–4.

Describes several areas that are linking major cities, such as Tucson and Phoenix, Arizona.

Lincoln Institute of Land Policy, Sonoran Institute. 2005. *Growing Smarter on the Edge.* Boston, Mass. and Phoenix, Ariz.: Lincoln Institute of Land Policy and Sonoran Institute.

Case studies of planned communities in the western U.S. See the CD-ROM accompanying this PAS Report for the publication's executive summary.

Lockwood, Charles. 2005. "Mountain House." *Urban Land* 62, no. 5: 90–95.

This project includes ecological and jobs-housing balance elements.

Lucas, Wayne, John Rehenkamp. 1994. "Using PUDs to Increase Your Options." *Land Development* 7, no. 2: 12–16.

Mandelker, Daniel R. 2003a. *Land Use Law*. 5th ed. Newark, N.J.: LexisNexis.

_____. 2003b. "Model Legislation for Land Use Decisions." *The Urban Lawyer* 35, no. 4: 635.

Discusses Chapter 10 of APA's Growing Smart Legislative Guidebook that provides model procedures for quasi-judicial land-use decisions. A copy of the chapter is contained on the CD-ROM accompanying this PAS Report.

_____. 1966a. *Controlling Planned Unit Development.* Chicago, Ill. American Society of Planning Officials.

_____. 1966b. "Reflections on the American System of Planning Controls: A Response to Professor Krasnowiecki." *University of Pennsylvania Law Review* 114, no. 1: 98–105.

Martin, John T. 1996. "Building Community." *Urban Land* 55, no. 3: 28–31, 55–56.

Describes the essentials of master-planned communities and what town centers and neighborhoods should contain.

Meck, Stuart. 2006. "Practice Unity." *Zoning Practice*. June 2006.

A discussion of uniform development codes and why we need them.

_____. 2002. *Growing Smart Legislative Guidebook.* Chicago, Ill. American Planning Association.

The Guidebook contains extensive discussion and model statutes for land use regulation.

Meck, Stuart, and Kenneth Pearlman. 2006. *Ohio Planning and Zoning Law*. St. Paul, Minn.: West Publishing.

Meck, Stuart, Rebecca Retzlaff, and Jim Schwab. 2003. *Regional Approaches to Affordable Housing*. Planning Advisory Report No. 513/514. Chicago, Ill. American Planning Association.

Meck, Stuart, Marya Morris, Kirk Bishop, and Eric Damian Kelly. 2006. *Model Smart Land Development Regulations.* Interim PAS Report. Chicago, Ill. American Planning Association.

Contains a model cluster development ordinance. The full PAS Report, updated, expanded, and revised, will be released in fall 2007.

Melby, Karen. 2005. "Quality Control." *Planning* 71, No. 10: 29-31.

Discusses the planned unit development program in Sparks, Nevada, that includes a detailed urban design requirement. A copy of this article is contained on the CD-ROM that accompanies this PAS Report.

McCrummen, Stephane. "Redefining Property Values." *The Washington Post*, April 16, 2006, at A01.

Discusses surveys developers make to tailor master-planned communities to residents' values and tastes.

Middleton, D. Scott. 1997. "Celebration, Florida: Breaking New Ground." *Urban Land* 56, no. 2: 32–36, 54.

_____. 1997. "Woodlands: Designed With Nature." *Urban Land* 56, no. 6: 26-30.

This development is in the Houston area, a master-planned community designed to take natural features into account.

Mitchell, Tucker. 2002. "Going Whole Hog for New Urbanism." *Planning* 68, no. 2: 29–31.

Discusses difficulties in achieving good design with a new Urbanist ordinance.

Moore, Collen Grogan, and Cheryl Siskin. 1984. *PUDs in Practice*. Washington. D.C. The Urban Land Institute.

Discussion of problem and issues in planned unit development, including ordinances and process; focus on factors that have contributed to the success of planned unit developments.

Moudon, Anne Vernez. ed. 1990. *Master-Planned Communities: Shaping Exurbs in the 1990s.* Seattle, Wash.: College of Architecture and Urban Planning, University of Washington

Report of a conference discussed issues in master-planned communities with case examples nationally and in the Seattle area.

Nolon, John R. 2001. "Planned Unit Development." In *Well Grounded: Using Local Land Use Authority to Achieve Smart Growth.* Washington, D.C. The Environmental Law Institute, 226–32.

A primer on planned unit development issues.

Page, Walter G., and Jacques N. Gordon. 2001. "Financing Master Planned Developments: A Form of Real Estate Venture Capital." *Real Estate Finance Journal* 17, No. 2: 29–35.

Discusses financing and risk taking, including entitlements.

Porter, Douglas R., and Matthew R. Cuddy. 2006. *Project Rating/Recognition Programs for Supporting Smart Growth Forms of Development.* Planning Advisory Report No. 538. Chicago, Ill.: American Planning Association.

Pruetz, Rick. 2003. *Beyond Takings and Givings*. Burbank, Calif.: Arje Press.

A review of transfer of development rights programs nationwide.

Priest, Donald E. 2002. *Planned Communities and the Smart Growth Movement.* Washington. D.C. The Urban Land Institute. (on file with author)

Discusses limitations on infill development and the advantages of master-planned communities.

Schmitz, Adrienne. ed. 2003. *The Shape of New Suburbia: Trends in Residential Development.* Washington. D.C. The Urban Land Institute.

Chapters by several authors on development issues and case studies of successful developments.

Schmitz, Adrienne, and Jason Scully. 2006. *Creating Walkable Places.* Washington. D.C.: The Urban Land Institute.

Schmitz, Adrienne, and Lloyd W. Bookout. ed. 1998. *Trends and Innovations in Master-Planned Communities.* Washington. D.C.: The Urban Land Institute.

Chapters by several authors on development issues and three case studies.

Sheridan, Mike. 2002. "MF in MPCs." *Multifamily Trends* 5, no. 3: 26–29, 49–51.

Good discussion of design issues for multifamily housing, shows complexities of design standards.

Shreeve, Elizabeth. 1995. "Mountain House New Town." *Urban Land* 54, no. 9: 53–57

A development near San Francisco and was specifically designed to provide a jobs-housing balance.

Smith, Mark. 1998. "Civano: Lessons for a Region." *Urban Land* 57, no. 7: 56–59, 88–89.

This Tucson sustainable community has jobs-housing balance and affordable housing requirements.

So, Frank S., David R. Mosena, and Frank S. Bangs, Jr. 1973. *Planned Unit Development Ordinances.* Chicago, Ill. American Society of Planning Officials.

This is an update of the 1966 APA report with ordinance drafting suggestions.

Stromberg, Meghan. 2001. "Prospecting for Design Gold." *Professional Builder* 66, no. 6: 71–75.

Discusses eclectic design styles.

Tomioka, Seishoro, and Ellen Miller Tomioka. 1984. *Planned Unit Developments: Design and Regional Impact.* New York. John Wiley & Sons.

Includes a discussion of the then Palm Beach County planned unit development process, a national survey, and some basic suggestions for ordinances.

Treasure Island Regional Planning Council. 2006. *Towns, Villages and the Countryside: A New Pattern of Settlement for North St. Lucie County.* St. Lucie County, Florida, Draft Comprehensive Plan Amendment.

A new urbanist approach to development.

Turque, Bill. 2006. "Developer's Neglect is Costly for Fairfax." *The Washington Post*, June 25, 2006, at Al.

Discusses substantial number of defaults by developers in Fairfax County, Virginia, in providing agreed-to infrastructure in new developments and need for county general funds to provide these facilities.

ULI (Urban Land Instititute). 1999. *Sarasota County, Florida: An Advisory Services Panel Report.* Washington. D.C.: ULI.

A panel report on the county with a smart growth element that includes the village policy proposal later adopted.

Urban Design Associates. 2004. *The Architectural Pattern Book.* New York: W.W. Norton & Company.

Warren, Melissa M. 2002. "Master Planning Las Vegas Style." *Urban Land* 62, no. 9: 95–99.

Discusses the Summerlin master-planned community.

Warrick, Brook, and Toni Alexander. 1997. "Looking for Hometown America." *Urban Land* 56, no. 2: 27–31, 51, 53.

Discusses neotraditional development and other issues that are changing master-planned communities.

Weitz, Jerry. 2003a. *Jobs-Housing Balance,* Planning Advisory Report No. 516. Chicago, Ill. American Planning Association.

———. 2003b. "Wither the Planned Unit Development?" *Practicing Planner* 1, no. 1. www.planning.org/practicingplanner/member/03spring/pud1.htm

White, Mark. 1996. *Adequate Public Facilities Ordinances and Transportation Management,* Planning Advisory Report No. 465. Chicago, Ill. American Planning Association.

Zenner, Patrick R. 1998. *Planned Unit Development in the Southeast—An Analysis of Its Success.* A Thesis Presented for the Master of Science Degree. Knoxville, Tenn.: University of Tennessee.

Study based on survey of projects and ordinances in several local governments.

RECENT PLANNING ADVISORY SERVICE REPORTS

Making Great Communities Happen

The American Planning Association provides leadership in the development of vital communities by advocating excellence in community planning, promoting education and citizen empowerment, and providing the tools and support necessary to effect positive change.

495/496. Everything You Always Wanted To Know About Regulating Sex Businesses. Eric Damian Kelly and Connie Cooper. December 2000. 168pp.

497/498. Parks, Recreation, and Open Spaces: An Agenda for the 21st Century. Alexander Garvin. December 2000. 72pp.

499. Regulating Home-Based Businesses in the Twenty-First Century. Charles Wunder. December 2000. 37pp.

500/501. Lights, Camera, Community Video. Cabot Orton, Keith Spiegel, and Eddie Gale. April 2001. 76pp.

502. Parks and Economic Development. John L. Crompton. November 2001. 74pp.

503/504. Saving Face: How Corporate Franchise Design Can Respect Community Identity (revised edition). Ronald Lee Fleming. February 2002. 118pp.

505. Telecom Hotels: A Planners Guide. Jennifer Evans-Crowley. March 2002. 31pp.

506/507. Old Cities/Green Cities: Communities Transform Unmanaged Land. J. Blaine Bonham, Jr., Gerri Spilka, and Darl Rastorfer. March 2002. 123pp.

508. Performance Guarantees for Government Permit Granting Authorities. Wayne Feiden and Raymond Burby. July 2002. 80pp.

509. Street Vending: A Survey of Ideas and Lessons for Planners. Jennifer Ball. August 2002. 44pp.

510/511. Parking Standards. Edited by Michael Davidson and Fay Dolnick. November 2002. 181pp.

512. Smart Growth Audits. Jerry Weitz and Leora Susan Waldner. November 2002. 56pp.

513/514. Regional Approaches to Affordable Housing. Stuart Meck, Rebecca Retzlaff, and James Schwab. February 2003. 271pp.

515. Planning for Street Connectivity: Getting from Here to There. Susan Handy, Robert G. Paterson, and Kent Butler. May 2003. 95pp.

516. Jobs-Housing Balance. Jerry Weitz. November 2003. 41pp.

517. Community Indicators. Rhonda Phillips. December 2003. 46pp.

518/519. Ecological Riverfront Design. Betsy Otto, Kathleen McCormick, and Michael Leccese. March 2004. 177pp.

520. Urban Containment in the United States. Arthur C. Nelson and Casey J. Dawkins. March 2004. 130pp.

521/522. A Planners Dictionary. Edited by Michael Davidson and Fay Dolnick. April 2004. 460pp.

523/524. Crossroads, Hamlet, Village, Town (revised edition). Randall Arendt. April 2004. 142pp.

525. E-Government. Jennifer Evans–Cowley and Maria Manta Conroy. May 2004. 41pp.

526. Codifying New Urbanism. Congress for the New Urbanism. May 2004. 97pp.

527. Street Graphics and the Law. Daniel Mandelker with Andrew Bertucci and William Ewald. August 2004. 133pp.

528. Too Big, Boring, or Ugly: Planning and Design Tools to Combat Monotony, the Too-big House, and Teardowns. Lane Kendig. December 2004. 103pp.

529/530. Planning for Wildfires. James Schwab and Stuart Meck. February 2005. 126pp.

531. Planning for the Unexpected: Land-Use Development and Risk. Laurie Johnson, Laura Dwelley Samant, and Suzanne Frew. February 2005. 59pp.

532. Parking Cash Out. Donald C. Shoup. March 2005. 119pp.

533/534. Landslide Hazards and Planning. James C. Schwab, Paula L. Gori, and Sanjay Jeer, Project Editors. September 2005. 209pp.

535. The Four Supreme Court Land-Use Decisions of 2005: Separating Fact from Fiction. August 2005. 193pp.

536. Placemaking on a Budget: Improving Small Towns, Neighborhoods, and Downtowns Without Spending a Lot of Money. December 2005. 133pp.

537. Meeting the Big Box Challenge: Planning, Design, and Regulatory Strategies. Jennifer Evans–Crowley. March 2006. 69pp.

538. Project Rating/Recognition Programs for Supporting Smart Growth Forms of Development. Douglas R. Porter and Matthew R. Cuddy. May 2006. 51pp.

539/540. Integrating Planning and Public Health: Tools and Strategies To Create Healthy Places. Marya Morris, General Editor. August 2006. 144pp.

541. An Economic Development Toolbox: Strategies and Methods. Terry Moore, Stuart Meck, and James Ebenhoh. October 2006. 80pp.

542. Planning Issues for On-site and Decentralized Wastewater Treatment. Wayne M. Feiden and Eric S. Winkler. November 2006. 61pp.

543/544. Planning Active Communities. Marya Morris, General Editor. December 2006. 116pp.

545. Planned Unit Developments. Daniel R. Mandelker. March 2007. 140pp.

For price information, please go to APA's PlanningBooks.com or call 312-786-6344.
You will find a complete subject and chronological index to the PAS Report series at www.planning.org/pas.